Information Security and Optimization

Information Security and Optimization

Edited by
Rohit Tanwar
Tanupriya Choudhury
Mazdak Zamani
Sunil Gupta

CRC Press
Taylor & Francis Group
Boca Raton London New York

CRC Press is an imprint of the
Taylor & Francis Group, an **informa** business

A CHAPMAN & HALL BOOK

First edition published 2020
by CRC Press
6000 Broken Sound Parkway NW, Suite 300, Boca Raton, FL 33487–2742

and by CRC Press
2 Park Square, Milton Park, Abingdon, Oxon, OX14 4RN

Library of Congress Cataloging-in-Publication Data

Names: Tanwar, Rohit, editor. | Choudhury, Tanupriya, editor. | Zamani, Mazdak, editor. | Gupta, Sunil, 1979- editor.
Title: Information security and optimization / edited by Rohit Tanwar, Tanupriya Choudhury, Mazdak Zamani, Sunil Gupta.
Description: First edition. | Boca Raton : C&H\CRC Press, 2021. | Includes bibliographical references and index.
Identifiers: LCCN 2020027798 (print) | LCCN 2020027799 (ebook) | ISBN 9780367493455 (hardback) | ISBN 9781003045854 (ebook)
Subjects: LCSH: Information technology--Security measures. | Computer security. | Data encryption (Computer science) | Mathematical optimization.
Classification: LCC QA76.9.A25 I54163 2021 (print) | LCC QA76.9.A25 (ebook) | DDC 005.8--dc23
LC record available at https://lccn.loc.gov/2020027798
LC ebook record available at https://lccn.loc.gov/2020027799

ISBN: 978-0-367-49345-5 (hbk)
ISBN: 978-1-003-04585-4 (ebk)

Typeset in Palatino
by SPi Global, India

Contents

3. Identity Theft and Prevention   25
Atefeh Tajpour and Mazdak Zamani

4. Organization Security Policies and Their After Effects   43
Premkumar Chithaluru and Ravi Prakash

5. Cyber-Attacks and Their Impact on Real Life: What Are Real-Life Cyber-Attacks, How Do They Affect Real Life and What Should We Do About Them? 61

Premkumar Chithaluru, Rohit Tanwar, and Sunil Kumar

11. Cyber Security in Cloud Platforms   **159**
Shiv Dutta Mishra, Bhupesh Kumar Dewangan, and Tanupriya Choudhury

The Editors

Dr. Rohit Tanwar received his bachelor's degree in Computer Science and Engineering (CSE) from Kurukshetra University, Kurukshetra, India, and master's degree in CSE from YMCA University of Science and Technology, Faridabad, India. He received his PhD from Kurukshetra University in 2019.

He has more than 10 years of experience in teaching. Currently, he is working as an Assistant Professor in the Department of CSE at University of Petroleum and Energy Studies (UPES) Dehradun. His areas of interest include Network Security, Optimization Techniques, Human Computing, Soft Computing, Cloud Computing, and Data Mining. He has more than twenty publications to his credit in different reputed journals and conferences. He has been associated with many conferences throughout India as Technical Program Committee (TPC) member and session chair.

Dr. Tanwar is an editor of two forthcoming books with CRC Press and Scrivener Publishing (Wiley) respectively. He is a special issues editor in the EAI endorsed journal on *Transactions on Pervasive Health and Technology* (Scopus Indexed). He is associated with the *International Journal of Communication Systems* (SCIE) (WILEY), and *International Journal of Information Security and Privacy* (IJISP) (Scopus, ESCI), IGI Global as an active reviewer. He is supervising two PhD research scholars in the fields of security and optimization.

He is a lifetime member of the Indian Engineering Teachers Association (IETA), India, and other renowned technical societies. He currently holds the post of Joint Secretary, Faridabad Chapter of INDO–UK Confederation of Science Technology and Research, London. He is a certified Microsoft Technology Associate for Introduction to Programming using Python.

Dr. Tanupriya Choudhury received his bachelor's degree in CSE from West Bengal University of Technology, Kolkata, India, and master's degree in CSE from Dr. M.G.R. University, Chennai, India.

He received his PhD in the year 2016. He has 10 years of experience in teaching as well as in research. He is currently working as an Associate Professor in the Department of CSE at UPES Dehradun.

He received a Global Outreach Education Award for Excellence as Best Young Researcher in GOECA 2018. His areas of interest include Human Computing, Soft Computing, Cloud Computing, and Data Mining. He has filed 14 patents to date and has received 16 copyrights from MHRD for his own software. He has been associated with many conferences in India and abroad. He has authored more than 85 research papers to date. He has delivered invited talks and guest lectures at Jamia Millia Islamia University, Maharaja Agersen College of Delhi University, and Duy Tan University Vietnam amongst others.

He has been associated with many conferences throughout India as a TPC member and session chair. He is a lifetime member of IETA, member of IEEE, and member of IET (UK) and other renowned technical societies. He is associated with various corporations and he is Technical Adviser of DeetyaSoft Pvt. Ltd. Noida, IVRGURU, and Mydigital360. He currently holds the post of Secretary in IETA and also holds the position of Advisor in the INDO–UK Confederation of Science, Technology and Research Ltd., London, UK, and International Association of Professional and Fellow Engineers, Delaware, USA.

Mazdak Zamani received his PhD in Computer Science from Universiti Teknologi Malaysia in 2011. He was a recipient of a Research Student Grant from 2008 to 2010.

He has been an active contributor to his field of research for more than nine years by teaching and designing several courses, serving as leader and researcher for several grants, supervising PhD and master's students, and serving as chair for a research track, as an external and internal examiner for PhD and master's thesis assessments. He has also served as a coordinator for Research and Development, and participated in industrial collaboration, Memoranda of Understanding with other universities, and Letters of Intent with government sections.

Dr. Zamani has published more than 100 journal papers, conference proceeding papers, book chapters, and books on topics related to his area of interest, including Cybersecurity, Multimedia Security, Network Security, and Information Technology. He also has been very active as chair and technical committee/program committee member in more than 100 international conferences. He has acted as reviewer and editor for more than 50 international journals.

Dr. Sunil Gupta has more than 19 years of experience in teaching, research, and industry in the field of Computer Science and Engineering. Prior to joining UPES as a Professor, he has worked with BML Munjal University, Delhi Technical Campus, IP University, Northern India Engineering College, IP University, IIMT, Baddi University of Emerging Science, IFTM University and Physical Laboratory.

He is an active member of the IEEE Society, the Computer Society of India, Computer Science Teachers Association, International Association of Engineers, International Association of Computer Science and Information Technology, and Internet Society (ISOC).

He has conducted various workshops, conferences and FDP. He guides various students in research and project work. He is an authored 69 research papers, 6 patents, and 2 textbooks, *Cryptography and Network Security* and *Wireless Sensor Networks*. His academic interests include Security, Cloud Computing, Big Data, Sensor, Wireless Networks, and Healthcare. He has successfully completed various research and consultancy projects with government and private organizations such as the Department of Science and Technology, Xcrino Business Solutions.

He is a reviewer for international journals, including *Journal of Supercomputing*, published by Springer Netherlands, *International Journal of Wireless Networks*, published by Springer, *International Journal Computer and Electrical Engineering*, Singapore, and a member of the Scientific Committee and Editorial Review Board on Engineering and Physical Sciences for the World Academy of Science, Engineering and Technology.

Contributors

R. Anandan
Department of Computer Science and
Engineering
Vels Institute of Science, Technology &
Advanced Studies (VISTAS)
Chennai, Tamil Nadu, India

A.K. Awasthi
Department of Mathematics
Lovely Professional University
Phagwara, Punjab, India

Rajdeep Chakraborty
Department of Computer Science and
Engineering
Netaji Subhash Engineering College
Kolkata, West Bengal, India

Rahul Chauhan
Graphic Era Hill University
Dehradun, Uttarakhand, India

Gunjan Chhabra
Department of Systemics
University of Petroleum & Energy
Studies (UPES)
Dehradun, Uttarakhand, India

Premkumar Chithaluru
School of Computer Science
University of Petroleum & Energy
Studies (UPES)
Dehradun, Uttarakhand, India

Shailee L. Choudhary
Department of Business Analytics & Data
Science
New Delhi Institute of Management
Delhi, India

Shiv Dutta Mishra
Department of Computer Science and
Engineering
Bhilai Institute of Technology
Durg, Chhattisgarh, India

R.C. Joshi
Graphic Era Hill University
Dehradun, Uttarakhand, India

Keshav Kaushik
School of Computer Science
University of Petroleum & Energy
Studies (UPES)
Dehradun, Uttarakhand, India

Sunil Kumar
School of Computer Science
University of Petroleum & Energy
Studies (UPES)
Dehradun, Uttarakhand, India

Bhupesh Kumar Dewangan
Department of Informatics
University of Petroleum & Energy
Studies (UPES)
Dehradun, Uttarakhand, India

Phani Kumar Gajula
Innominds Pvt. Ltd., India

Jyotsna Kumar Mandal
Department of Computer Science and
Engineering
University of Kalyani
Nadia, West Bengal, India

Rakesh Kumar Saini
School of Computing
DIT University
Dehradun, Uttarakhand, India

Preeti Mishra
Graphic Era Hill University
Dehradun, Uttarakhand, India

Samir Pawaskar
Government Agency, Qatar

Ravi Prakash
School of Computer Science
University of Petroleum & Energy
    Studies (UPES)
Dehradun, Uttarakhand, India

K.N.D. Saile
St. Martin's Engineering College
Secunderabad, Telangana, India

Varun Sapra
Department of Systemics
University of Petroleum & Energy
    Studies (UPES)
Dehradun, Uttarakhand, India

Manish Kumar Sharma
Institute of Engineering and Technology
Chitkara University
Chandigarh, Punjab, India

Anupam Singh
School of Computer Science
University of Petroleum & Energy
    Studies (UPES)
Dehradun, Uttarakhand, India

Kulvinder Singh
Department of Computer Science and
    Engineering
University Institute of Engineering &
    Technology, Kurukshetra University
Kurukshetra, Haryana, India

Ninni Singh
Department of Informatics
University of Petroleum & Energy
    Studies (UPES)
Dehradun, Uttarakhand, India

S. Sridevi
Department of Computer Science and
    Engineering
Vels Institute of Science, Technology &
    Advanced Studies (VISTAS)
Chennai, Tamil Nadu, India

Atefeh Tajpour
University of Shahid Rajaee Teacher
    Training
Tehran, Iran

Amit Verma
School of Computer Science
University of Petroleum & Energy
    Studies (UPES)
Dehradun, Uttarakhand, India

Mazdak Zamani
Felician University
Rutherford, New Jersey

1

Information Security Policy and Standards

Samir Pawaskar

Government Agency in Qatar

1.1 Brief Introduction

The Information Security Policy is the core statement from the business owners/management that conveys the intent and the desire of the organization. It effectively sets the tone for how information security will align and assimilate within the business. The subject of information security policies and standards is a critical domain and forms the cornerstone of any effective Information Security Management System's implementation within a corporate organization. It is also one of the most overlooked areas in every organization.

Organizations believe that writing information security policies and standards is a cut and paste job that can be done by an information security intern using GOOGLE as a ready and useful tool. This chapter helps in understanding the challenges in writing effective policies and addresses how organizations should tackle the subject.

1.2 Definitions

During the course of our work, we come across various terms and definitions that leave us wondering at times what they mean. Can they be used interchangeably? Is a policy the same as a standard? Or wait, is policy a framework? Confused?

In this section, let us try to unravel what all this different *nomenclature* means and how the terms relate to each other. For the sake of simplicity, this section will use references from the British Dictionary and Wikipedia to come up with an acceptable definition.

Legislation:
   British Dictionary: A law or a set of laws.
   Wikipedia: Legislation (or "statutory law") is a law which has been promulgated (or "enacted") by a legislature or other governing body or the process of making it.

Regulation:
   British Dictionary: An official rule that controls how something is done.
   Wikipedia: In government, typically regulation means stipulations of the delegated legislation which is drafted by subject-matter experts to enforce primary legislation.

Executive Order:
   British Dictionary: In the United States, an official instruction given by the president or by a state's governor.
   Wikipedia: In the United States, an executive order is a directive issued by the president of the United States that manages operations of the federal government.

Policy:
   British Dictionary: A set of ideas or a plan for action followed by a business, a government, a political party, or a group of people.
   Wikipedia: A policy is a deliberate system of principles to guide decisions and achieve rational outcomes. A policy is a statement of intent and is implemented as a procedure or protocol.

Standard:
   British Dictionary: An official rule, unit of measurement, or way of operating that is used in a particular area of manufacturing or services.
   Wikipedia: Techniques generally set forth in published materials that attempt to protect the cyber environment of a user or organization[1].
   An established norm or requirement about a technical system[2].

Guidelines:
   British Dictionary: Information intended to advise people on how something should be done or what something should be.
   Wikipedia: A guideline is a statement by which to determine a course of action. A guideline aims to streamline particular processes according to a set routine or sound practice.

Strategy:
   British Dictionary: A detailed plan for achieving success in situations such as war, politics, business, industry, and so on, or the skill of planning for such situations.
   Wikipedia: A high-level plan to achieve one or more goals under conditions of uncertainty (Henry Mintzberg, 1978).

Framework:
   British Dictionary: A system of rules, ideas, or beliefs that are used to plan or decide something.
   Wikipedia: A document that lays out a set of procedures or goals, which might be used in negotiation or decision-making to guide a more detailed set of policies, or to guide ongoing maintenance of an organization's policies[3].

Manual:
   Both British Dictionary and Wikipedia: A book that gives you practical instructions on how to do something or how to use something[4]. A policy manual is generally referred to as a collection of policies in an organization.

---

[1] Refers to Cyber Security Standards.
[2] Refers to Technical Standards.
[3] Refers to Policy Framework.
[4] Refers to general manual and not specifically in the context of policy manual.

1.3 Structure of Policy[5] Documents

Before we discuss the policy structure, let us quickly understand the national context. To build a context, let us use a fictitious organization, named S3 Inc. This particular organization is based in a country called Utopia and has recently hired Mr. ISM as the Head of Information Security.

The organization works in the financial sector and is regulated by a sector regulator.

Typically, any country would have laws that may have an impact on the organization and the business it does. Some legislation may be sector-specific and some general, for example, cybercrime law, information technology related law, etc. The country may also issue specific national policies, standards, or guidelines in line with this legislation.

Further, the sector that an organization operates in may be regulated and have its own sector-specific regulations. For example, sectors like Telecommunications, Internet Services, Finance, and Insurance are usually regulated sectors around the world. In this case, the sector regulators may enforce specific regulations or standards on organizations that operate within the industry. Finally, if an organization is part of a conglomerate or multinational empire, it may have its own policies and standards at a group/conglomerate or parent company level.

As the Head of Information Security, Mr. ISM will have to take into consideration all the relevant legislation, policies and standards (at all levels) that are in play to ensure that his internal policies and procedures are in sync and consistent when he starts drafting organization-specific policies, procedures, and guidelines.

In the following sections, the concepts will be discussed from an organization's perspective, but it is important to take a step back and understand the national context.

In terms of priority and hierarchy, the national legislation would be at the top, since non-compliance with a law could possibly be a crime or punishable offense, followed by the national policies and standards (if they are enforced). At the next level are the sectoral regulations (non-compliance with these regulations could possibly be a punishable offense or incur possible fines), followed by sectoral policies and standards (if enforced). These will be followed by policies and standards defined at the company's group level, at the parent company level, or at a conglomerate level (see Figure 1.1 to understand a typical corporate policy structure (JS OP DE BEECK, 2009)).

FIGURE 1.1
Policy structure.

---

[5] Policy here refers to all documents such as policy, standard, guidelines etc.

From Mr. ISM's perspective, all of these would qualify as legislation (in a nutshell) and need to be considered while drafting the organization's corporate policies and procedures. Within the corporate structure, the policy would be at the top, followed by procedures based on standards and best practices, and supported by guidelines and work instructions (WI).

So how does it work? Typically the policy sets the tone at the highest level, indicates the direction an organization would like to move in, and the objectives it wants to achieve. Once the policy is agreed, an organization would align its business processes with the corporate policy. The processes would be documented through process maps (visual workflows/information flows) and procedures. The procedures would specify in detail how the process would work. The organization may further develop guidelines or WI (at a micro level) to further clarify how the process would work at a micro level. This may especially happen for large or complex processes.

Let us try to understand this with our example.

Utopia has announced an update to its Information Technology Act (2010). As per the new amendments, it has identified Government, Finance, Transport, and Energy as critical sectors for the state of Utopia. Critical organizations operating within these sectors would need to have a formal Information Security Management System (ISMS) in place. The sector regulators for each of these sectors would draw up the criteria for identifying critical organizations within their sectors.

The Utopian Central Bank had issued the Utopian Financial Sector Information Security Standard in 2016. Further, in line with the new amendments to the information technology (IT) law, the Utopian Central Bank has issued a directive amending its licensing regulations that regulate the banking and non-banking financial institutions in Utopia.

The directive, among other things, states that any banking or non-banking financial institutions making an annual business turnover of over 100 million Utopian Dollars for the last two consecutive years would be classified as a Critical Sector Organization. All such organizations will have to implement an ISMS as mandated by the new Information Technology Act. In light of these changes, the management of S3 Inc. met and decided to abide by the new laws and regulations. They hired Mr. ISM as the Head of Information Security and tasked him with implementing the ISMS as required by the new laws and regulations.

Mr. ISM has started the work in earnest and has done a GAP analysis within the organization. One of the first things to be done is creating an Information Security Policy and the policy manual for the organization.

Before writing the Information Security Policy and the policy manual for the organization, Mr. ISM needs to understand the regulatory environment, the IT Law, any other relevant legislation that may be binding upon S3 Inc., its business, any relevant or binding regulations imposed by the sector regulator as part of their licensing, and any standards or policies from the parent/group company. Having understood the legal context, Mr. ISM needs to understand the business of S3 Inc. and its objectives (vision and mission), as this is critical for building an effective policy and procedures.

The most important document will be the Corporate Information Security Policy (CISP), which will set the tone for the information security program within S3 Inc. It will also establish the high-level objectives, program ownership, and accountabilities within S3 Inc. Further, a policy manual will be developed to support the CISP and the information security program. The policy manual will include sub-policies and procedures that will define in detail the various processes developed to support the information security program. For complex or technical processes, it may be helpful to issue additional guidelines to explain and clarify the process to the end-user. In some cases, the complex process may be broken down into tasks, and appropriate WI may be issued to execute these tasks.

1.4 Governance (Understanding the Ownership, Responsibilities, and Accountabilities)

Policy, by definition, is a set of action items; governance, by definition, is the manner or action of governing. Within a corporate environment, the business owners define the objectives and policies as a means to execute and achieve these objectives. It is imperative that a governance framework is in place to ensure effective implementation and execution of policies.

What this effectively means is that the policy should be issued and authorized by the right person and at the right level within the organization. A RACI matrix should be defined, effectively identifying the ownership, responsibilities, and accountabilities for the implementation of policies. As an example, imagine the IT Director issuing an HR Policy asking all employees to start work early. The policy will not be successful because the employees will challenge the authority of the IT Director to issue an HR Policy.

Similarly, can you imagine an information security analyst issuing a policy regulating Internet usage within the organization? Will employees adhere to it? No, because the issuer does not have the required authority.

In the context of information security, the CISP should always be signed off by the CEO or the head of the organization. It indicates clear authority, management support, and commitment from the top.

1.5 Writing Effective Policies (Characteristics and Attributes of an Effective Policy Document)

What is the secret ingredient to make a policy effective? Well, honestly, there is none (see Figure 1.2 to understand how policies work).

However, there are three aspects of a policy life cycle that need to be understood to make it effective. They are strategic, tactical, and operational aspects. Let us understand the strategic aspect of policy.

Foremost, the policy owner/author must be clear on the objective that needs to be achieved with the policy document. Does the intended objective align with the business goals, vision, and mission of the organization? Does the policy contradict an existing policy document or existing legislation? It is important that the policy owner/author understands and considers regulatory and business requirements while drafting the policy. Further, the policy owner/author must assess the operational impacts of the policy. Will the changes be huge? Will they create disruption? Is the disruption justified?

What would be the financial impact of this policy? Here the policy owner/author needs to assess both the costs and the returns. The cost here refers to the financial investment required to implement the policy (e.g., cost of policy development, associated awareness costs, cost in terms of creating/amending processes, cost of systems, if any, that may be

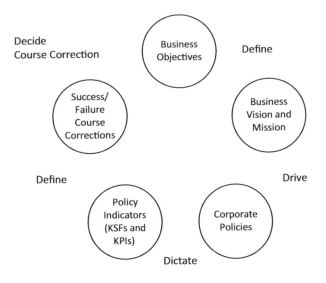
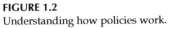

FIGURE 1.2
Understanding how policies work.

required to implement the policy, etc.). Returns here refer to the financial gain the organization would make or save due to this new policy (e.g., possible fines that you would avoid, gains due to process optimization, enhanced sales due to better customer confidence, etc.).

The policy owner/author must also understand and review the collateral damage that could be caused due to the policy. For example, imagine an organization that decided to end its "Work from Home" initiative to mitigate the risks associated with remote access and the costs associated with mitigating those risks. This policy would have an impact on the female workforce (especially young mothers) who may be using the work from home option; similarly this may also impact workforce who may be living far from the office, as this will entail spending long hours commuting to work. There is a possibility that such employees may leave the organization. Some of the other things that need to be considered include the organization's work environment and culture. So briefly, these cover the strategic aspects of a policy life cycle. This aspect should be dealt with as part of the policy needs assessment. Now, let us delve into the tactical aspect.

This involves the actual drafting of the policy document. It is imperative that the policy owner/author effectively translates the organization's strategic considerations into the policy document. The key importance is to ensure that the document is clear, concise, and commonsensical.

Some effective "dos and don'ts" while writing a policy are:

1. The language should be simple. Avoid using legal language.
2. The sentences should be short.
3. Keep the document focused. Do not try to cover everything under the sky in a single document.
4. Do not create ambiguity in the document as it may confuse the readers.
5. The policy documents should be concise, not more than a few pages. Standards, procedures, and guidelines may be detailed and long as necessary (see Figure 1.3 for

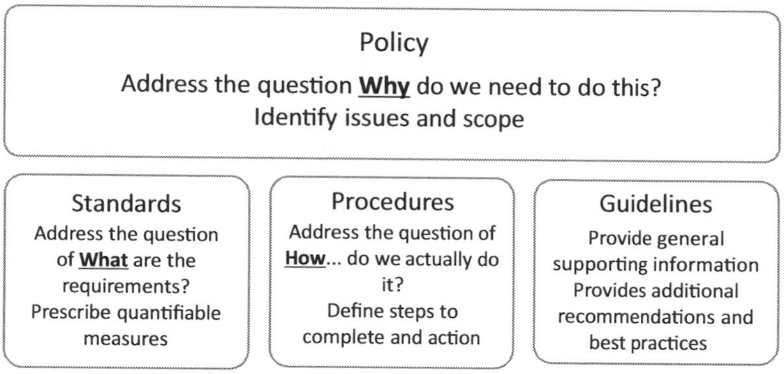

FIGURE 1.3
Understand the contents of various policy documents.

additional clarity on what is expected in each of the documents (Policy vs Standard vs Control vs Procedure, 2020)).

6. Clearly identify the objective of the policy, define the scope and audience for the document, articulate the clauses in lucid language, define the KPIs to monitor and evaluate the policy, define how the policy will be implemented (roles and responsibilities), and analyze the enforcement of the plan (how will it be enforced and the consequences for not abiding by or breaching the policy [e.g., fines, suspension, termination, etc.]).

Last, let us consider the operational aspects of the policy.

Once the policy is drafted, the most important step is to get the document empowered. This is achieved by ensuring that the document is signed off by the head of the organization, or the highest authority accountable for the particular policy.

Imagine a scenario where there is an organization X whose CISP is signed by the CIO and another organization Y whose CISP is signed by the CEO. It goes without saying that the CISP signed by the CEO would have greater acceptance than that signed by the CIO. It will also demonstrate management support at the highest level. Once this is achieved, the policy owner/author needs to work on creating awareness and acceptance of the policy. A communication plan needs to be developed to ensure that the message reaches the intended audience. This can be done through awareness sessions, emails, posters, one to one meetings, and so on. It is necessary that buy-in for the policy is achieved across the organization; only then will the policy be effectively adopted within the organization.

Along with the awareness, the policy owner/author must work on the effective implementation of the policy. Depending on the policy, this may entail new or amended processes, awareness/training of employees, and technology (hardware/software/infrastructure) to implement and achieve the desired objectives.

Lastly, the policy owner/author needs to put in place an effective mechanism to monitor the policy. The identified KPIs should be monitored over a period to verify if the policy is achieving the desired outcomes. There is also a need to monitor any harmful collateral effects that were not envisaged in the beginning. The feedback from this activity will go back into the review cycle and will determine if the policy needs to be tweaked or amended (see Figure 1.2 to understand how policies work).

1.6 Policy Life Cycle (Policy from Cradle to Grave)

Let us now look into the policy life cycle and understand how it works. Broadly, there are five stages in a policy's life cycle, as shown in Figure 1.4.

1.6.1 Development

The development stage of policy consists of multiple sub-steps. Contrary to what many might think, this stage is much more than writing a policy document itself. The most important thing here is not writing the policy itself, but doing a needs assessment.

1.6.1.1 Needs Assessment

It is important to answer the question, "Why do we need this policy?" There could be various reasons for that, for example, the business vision, mission, or objectives have changed; the business has decided to get into a new line of business; there is a change or new direction from the regulators; the business needs to optimize the current processes or operations; or there is a regulatory requirement. The answer to this question will help you understand the objectives of the policy.

1.6.1.2 Policy Drafting

Having clearly understood the objectives and the needs of the business, the next step is to draft the policy document. Depending on the document (whether it is a policy, procedure, and guidelines), you will choose a drafting language. Policy documents are crisp and to the point (generally a two- to three-page document). Standards and procedures are more detailed documents and delve into additional details (technical, operational aspects) to ensure compliance with a policy. These are essentially best practices for achieving specific

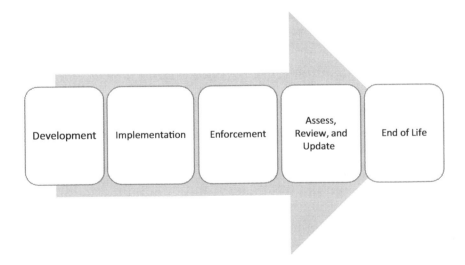

FIGURE 1.4
Policy life cycle.

tasks needed to accomplish a policy objective. Guidelines are detailed documents that will provide comprehensive help to the users on how to implement, operate, or execute a particular task. It may provide guidance on the usage of tools that will facilitate the implementation, operation, or execution of a particular task. This may be a step-by-step approach as well. In some cases, the complex process may be broken down into specific tasks, and the users may be provided with WI on how to execute the specific tasks.

1.6.1.3 Stakeholder Review

Once the document draft is ready, the stakeholders should review the document to ensure its efficacy. Stakeholders may provide feedback on the writing style (typos, grammar, language, tone, etc.), policy clauses (whether the policy makes sense to their business, whether there are operational limitations, auditability challenges, etc.), or any other feedback as deemed applicable. It is essential that any feedback received be addressed in a professional manner. The policy owner/author should either accept the feedback or rationalize it with the stakeholders. This would entail either making the stakeholder understand the policy owner's/author's stance or coming to an agreement by making some modifications to the existing clauses.

1.6.1.4 Identify Key Success Factors and Key Performance Indicators

Before the policy is approved, it is equally important to identify and agree with the management on the key success factors of the policy. The key success factors will be measured or tracked by key performance indicators. Using these indicators, the policy owner/author and the management can, in a rational way, measure the success or failure of policy implementation.

1.6.1.5 Policy Approval

This is the last step in this phase of the policy life cycle and involves getting the policy document vetted and signed off at the appropriate level within the organization hierarchy. Once signed off, the document is ready to be published.

1.6.2 Implementation

Once the policy document is published, the policy owner/author should ensure the implementation of the policy. This involves a number of steps.

1.6.2.1 Communication and Awareness

Communication and awareness is a key step in making a policy implementation successful. The policy owner/author should begin by drafting a comprehensive communication and awareness plan for the policy. The plan should assess the objectives that need to be achieved by the policy, understand the audience and the business it affects, and lastly, the time frames (if any) for the policy objective to be achieved.

The plan should, among other things, draw a timeline for its activities, identify the media to be used, agree on the tone of the message, and the message to be delivered. It should further devise a mechanism to record or assess the effectiveness of the message delivered.

Creating awareness is key to policy implementation, because unless a policy is communicated and people are made aware of the policy and the potential change it may introduce in their daily life or the way they conduct business, and how it will benefit them and/or the business, there may be a natural resistance, as humans instinctively resist change.

1.6.2.2 Create/Update Processes

The next step in implementation is to make changes in your business processes to incorporate the essence of the new policy. This may necessitate creating new processes or updating existing processes to be in compliance with the new policy and be aligned to achieve the desired objectives.

For example, now that S3 Inc. has decided to implement an ISMS, one of the first things Mr. ISM has done is to create an Information Security Steering Committee. This effectively is a new process, wherein all enterprise information security risks will have to be validated by this committee; all new projects, any new line of business that is started, or any new service/product that is launched will have to be validated by the committee. At the same time, it may impact certain existing processes. For example, going forward, any changes, updates, patches, and/or product updates applied by the information technology team will have to be assessed for cyber risks and be vetted by the change management committee or change advisory board.

1.6.2.3 Provide Tools Where Possible

Technology can be a good friend. The policy owner/author should look at all available opportunities to automate the implementation of the policies and use technology effectively to deploy and monitor the performance of the policies. Users should be provided with tools that can help them adopt and implement the policy.

For example, the new security policy mandates users to report security incidents to the security team. In order to help the users comply with the policy, the policy owner/author could create an online form on the intranet or a ready-made email template that users can use to submit incidents to a dedicated mailbox. This will help users in providing all relevant information needed by the security team, as well as ensuring that records collected by the security team are uniform and leave no space for ambiguities.

1.6.3 Enforcement

This is to make sure that the policy is being followed by the intended audience, which could be the internal employees, outsourced staff, vendors, etc. There are two key steps within this phase: monitoring compliance, and influencing the user's behavior using the carrot-and-stick approach.

1.6.3.1 Monitoring Compliance

During the development phase, there was a discussion about identifying success factors and key performance indicators to evaluate the success of the policy. Similarly, during the implementation phase, there was a discussion about creating/amending processes as well as using technology to ensure compliance with the policy.

In the enforcement phase, the policy owner/author needs to follow up through the use of technology and/or records created as part of the updated processes to ensure that the new policy is being complied with.

For example, the new access policy says that vendors should be escorted and be supervised in the data center. The policy owner/author may verify this by checking the access logbook of the data center, or the access control records of data center; these may be cross verified with CCTV logs.

1.6.3.2 *Influencing User's Behavior (The Carrot-and-Stick Approach)*

Humans, by nature, resist change, and it requires a certain amount of conditioning of the human mind before they accept it. This conditioning in part can be achieved through communication and awareness, where the policy owner/author talks about the benefits of the policy and how it could help both the individuals and the organization. The policy owner/author can also subtly convey the message that non-compliance with the policy could lead to monetary losses (fines for individuals or organizations) and/or punishments (loss of jobs or jail sentences).

The human mind also has a rebel streak, and it is important that the message communicated is reinforced from time to time. For example, if the policy subjects observe or believe that non-compliance with the policy does not really lead to any personal fines or punishments or accountabilities, compliance will deteriorate over a period of time. Hence, it is necessary that the human conditioning is maintained over the period of the policy life cycle. It is usually a dual approach, where good actions are rewarded (carrot), and bad actions are punished through disciplinary actions (sticks).

During the initial period, especially in the case of new policies, it may be better to devise a rewards program that effectively motivates the subjects to adhere and comply with the policies. Over a period of time, this could become part of the overall employee appraisal program, which should evaluate an individual's compliance with policies.

1.6.4 Assess, Review, and Update

This is an important phase in the life cycle of any policy. A policy is not "God's word" and is not cast in iron either. The dynamics around the policy can change, and at times, may change rapidly. It is imperative that the policy owner/author has a grip on the policy and is able to steer it, amend it, and keep it relevant in the changing dynamics. Some of the factors that may impact the relevance of the policy include a change in business objectives, change in management, or change in the regulatory regime. The policy owner/author will have to ensure that the policy is adapted to stay in alignment with these changes. This may not be a fairly regular scenario, but one that involves ensuring that within the established context, the policy is delivering as expected.

Let us consider some scenarios and review them in the context we are discussing now.

1. One example is a Remote Access Policy and how it impacts employees who live far away and young mothers. This is an example of the collateral impacts of the policy; the policy owner/author should review the benefits accrued to the organization vis-à-vis this policy and the loss of its staff.
2. Another example is about the data center access, where there are indications that IT staff are not adhering to the "escort vendors" policy because the CCTV footage does not tally with your access control records. This is a pure breach, and the policy owner/author should do a root cause analysis for this behavior. Maybe the IT staff are under pressure, and they cannot spare time to act as escorts to the vendor. This could point to operational challenges in the work environment.

3. Yet another example could be the rise in the number of security incidents reported. This could point to the success of a policy asking employees to report security incidents and does not necessarily mean that the security position of the organization has deteriorated. Every metric needs to be carefully evaluated. A number going high or going low is an indication of neither policy success nor policy failure. So, within the same example, typically the number of incidents would increase in the initial days as users start reporting suspicious activities as incidents. Over a period of time, however, this will plateau as users will improve their skills and ability to identify suspicious activities. In the long run, maybe, as overall organization maturity improves, the technology improves, and the information security team improves its skills, eventually the reported incidents may decrease.

The policy owner/author should ensure that they identify the right metrics for evaluating the success of the policies and also evaluate if there are any collateral impacts that the policy introduces. Based on this feedback, the policy should be tuned from time to time to ensure that the desired objective is achieved.

1.6.5 End of Life

For various reasons, the organization may reach a point when a particular policy may no longer be needed. The reason could either be a change in business objectives, change in management, or change in the regulatory regime, as well as changes in technologies or changes in business processes.

Once the policy owner/author, in agreement with the management, reaches the conclusion that a policy is no longer needed, it is best advised that such a policy is formally revoked through proper notification. The policy owner/author should assess and advise the management, the policy subjects, and the stakeholders on any legal and regulatory requirements related to records pertaining to the old policy.

The policy subjects and the stakeholders should receive suitable communications advising them on the date when the policy ceases to be in force, if the policy will be superseded by any other policy, advice on maintaining documentation and records related to the old policy, and any other information that may be necessary.

References

Henry Mintzberg (May 1978). "Patterns in Strategy Formation," Url: https://web.archive.org/web/20131019210812/https://faculty.fuqua.duke.edu/~charlesw/LongStrat2010/papers/class%2010/Patterns%20of%20Strategy%20Formulation.pdf (Accessed on April 26, 2020)

JS OP DE BEECK. (2009). "Regulations, Policies, Standards, Procedures and Guidelines," Url: https://www.vulpoint.com/regulations-policies-standarts-procedures-and-guidelines/ (Accessed on April 26, 2020).

Policy vs Standard vs Control vs Procedure. (2020). Url: https://www.complianceforge.com/word-crimes/policy-vs-standard-vs-control-vs-procedure (Accessed on April 26, 2020).

2

Vulnerability Management

K.N.D. Saile[1] and Phani Kumar Gajula[2]

[1] *St. Martin's Engineering College, Secunderabad, India*

[2] *Innominds Pvt Ltd, India*

2.1 Introduction

Cybersecurity is defined as the protection of privacy, integrity, and accessibility of data in cyberspace by ISO/IEC 27032 (International Organization for Standardization / the International Electrotechnical Commission) (https://www.iso27001security.com/html/27032. html 2020a). It is a set of practices and tools that are designed to protect confidential information from unauthorized users' access. This unauthorized access can take place through different forms over the network. As a significant amount of data is stored in the systems of the organizations, in sectors like the military, finance, corporate, and medical areas, it is very important to safeguard the data. Vulnerability is the term used in cybersecurity, which refers to a flaw in the system that may lead to an open attack. It is also referred to as a glitch, which a system might encounter and which results in a threat. Bugs in software development are one of the main reasons for a vulnerability to occur, which leads to many kinds of information exploitation. These vulnerabilities are hidden objects, which cannot be traced very easily. But when encountered, vulnerabilities create great exploitation.

In this chapter, we will discuss vulnerabilities, the reasons for vulnerabilities, and vulnerability management. We will also discuss the tools used for vulnerability management and a case study.

2.2 Background

In recent times, with the increase in technology, a huge number of vulnerabilities also came into existence. Zhang et al. (2011a) reported that software vulnerabilities are a major cause of security problems. The National Vulnerability Database (NVD) maintains a huge database of all the vulnerabilities from its inception in 1997. More than 43,000 vulnerabilities have been identified. This database would help in predicting the vulnerabilities. However, the rising vulnerability statistics demands multidimensional threat detection techniques (Tripathi and Singh 2011).

Ali et al. (2012) reported that the Common Vulnerability Scoring System (CVSS) scores each vulnerability found and provides a detailed description of those security vulnerabilities. Peter Mell et al. (2007) discussed that the CVSS provides an open framework for identifying the characteristics and impacts of software vulnerabilities. Zhang et al. (2011b) stated that Information Technology Laboratory (ITL)bulletin reports and the CVSS can take necessary actions to improve the security of their systems.

Hyunchul Joh (IEEE 2012) reported that vulnerability that has been discovered but is unpatched represents a security risk to a system. The CVSS metrics can be used to evaluate the impact of the breach. According to Gonda et al. (2018), attack graphs are one of the best tools for analyzing vulnerability. Assessing the potential risk associated with network assets exposed to attack by vulnerabilities can be done by fuzzy rules for the vulnerability. Dondo (2008) prescribes that most organizations use traditional vulnerability management techniques, but there is a necessity to scan the remote devices attached.

Automation always shows greater advancement than the traditional manual techniques (Williams and Nicollet 2020). Edwards, Chandra Estelle (2020) reported that this helps to prioritize the critical risks. The impact of potential risks is also to be identified. To gain effective security, the remedial action should also be incorporated into all the security controls. As Njogu et al. (2013) state, making the patch available to the network is one of the best solutions provided. Nanda and Ghugar (2017) reported that to deal with the latest vulnerabilities, a sophisticated vulnerability management technique should be incorporated by organizations. The discussions on vulnerability management and how it can be enhanced to provide a great security mechanism are always ongoing in research.

2.3 Vulnerability

Vulnerability is defined in the ISO 27002 standard as "A weakness of an asset or group of assets that can be exploited by one or more threats" (ISO/IEC 2020). A failure or flaw in a program that produces undesired or incorrect results is named as a bug. The bugs, when exploited by heinous actors, turn out to be vulnerabilities. The vulnerabilities range from a system crash to confidential data leakage over a network. These kinds of vulnerabilities that compromise the security mechanisms of a system are called security vulnerabilities.

The following are a few security vulnerabilities that are identified as unforgivable vulnerabilities based on their frequency within Common Vulnerabilities Exposures (CVE) (Christey 2007).

1. Cross-site scripting
2. SQL injection attacks
3. Man in the middle attacks
4. Phishing attacks
5. Buffer overflows
6. Missing authorizations
7. Path traversals
8. Untrusted inputs
9. Downloading codes without integrity checking
10. Missing data encryption.

2.4 Areas of Risk

With growing technology, every business has started communicating with its clients over the network. The exchange of information should be done with high-level security encryptions ensuring proper data security. Viruses and worms often intervene in the network connections, leading to information thefts and disrupting the network connections. Every business that uses the network, be it small scale, large scale, a multinational corporation, or a government organization, is often at risk of vulnerabilities.

The solution to all these vulnerabilities is to have a good vulnerability management mechanism to be followed within the organizations.

2.5 Why Is Software Vulnerable?

In a nutshell, software is vulnerable due to inevitable human errors. Software from the '90s did not have security measures for heap flows and format string errors. Nowadays, though, the vendors are capable of understanding and handling bugs heavy expenditure, have become a major criterion for system maintenance.

Another reason for vulnerabilities is poor code review and testing strategies. An example of this would be testing in an environment which has anti-virus or systems with highly secured encryptions. However, in reality, when an application is deployed to the end-user, it may be within a less secure system, due to which the data is lost or other different kinds of threats occur. Hence, the testing should be done on systems with the basic configurations of the end-user.

Security applications such as firewalls and anti-virus need to be properly configured. Any flaw in the installation process leads to failure in the security mechanism. The usage of a virtual private network (VPN) is also another major constraint on vulnerabilities occurring. Compromising the security mechanisms for other uses is also a breach of vulnerabilities. Many vulnerabilities are easy to detect and fix. The vendors release new patches for the software that helps to fix the threats. A good vulnerability management system helps organizations to reduce the risk of threats (Qualys 2008).

2.6 Vulnerability Management

The main objective of vulnerability management is to detect and remediate vulnerabilities in a timely fashion (Qualys 2008). Vulnerability management is defined as managing the occurrence of attacks by the process of identifying, evaluating, treating, and reporting on vulnerabilities in systems. As shown in Figure 2.1, vulnerability management can be categorized into four phases (ISO 2020b).

- Identifying/discovering vulnerabilities.
- Assessing vulnerabilities.
- Reporting.
- Remediating and Verifying.

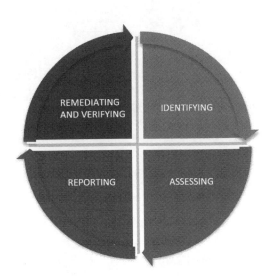

FIGURE 2.1
Vulnerability management cycle.

2.6.1 Discovering Vulnerabilities

This is the first phase of vulnerability management where the initial discovery of threats is done. This can be further divided into two parts.

2.6.1.1 Identifying the Types of Attacks

Based on the type of attack on the system, we can identify the type of vulnerability. For example, if there is frequent leakage of data it can be considered a "man in the middle" attack, which relates to IP spoofing attack. Another example is that if there is a frequent change in the database of the organization, we can identify it as an SQL injection attack. If the user's credentials are compromised, we can consider it to be a phishing attack. Table 2.1 illustrates the different attacks and the type of vulnerability. Table 2.1 also gives a few examples of what kind of attack may be possible based on the area of the system that is affected. With the growing technologies, many vulnerabilities are possible and are gradually increasing day by day.

TABLE 2.1

Types of Attacks

S. No	Types of Attacks	How Does the Attack Affect the System?
1	Man in the middle attack	Data leakage over the network
2	SQL injection attack	Frequent change in the organization's database
3	Phishing attack	The users' data is compromised
4	Cross-site request forgery	Data theft by clicking on similar kind of URL
5	Path traversal or directory traversal	Data in the folder and directory are compromised

2.6.1.2 Inventory of Assets

Maintaining a detailed list of all the assets is a critical step. Assets include both the unauthorized and authorized hardware as well as software assets. After gathering the full list of vulnerabilities, the organization's hardware assets inventory, such as the ports, networks, systems, network Maps, LANs, and router details, are identified as shown in Figure 2.2.

The software assets include the type of software used, its versions, patches, packages, the type of databases used and its hierarchical architecture, etc. It is always best practice to keep a team of two or three to gather all these details and maintain an inventory so that it could be helpful for future phases of vulnerability management. Whenever a new asset is incorporated, it should be maintained in the inventory list.

Figure 2.2 includes laptops, personal computers, mobile devices, servers, routers, switches, hubs, I/O devices, etc. Each of them is identified as a node and these will undergo rigorous penetration testing to check which part of the network is the root cause of the vulnerabilities.

2.6.2 Assessing Vulnerabilities

Once all the vulnerabilities and assets are known, the next phase is to efficiently assess the vulnerabilities. This phase is also known as vulnerability analysis (VA), which defines, identifies, and classifies the security vulnerabilities in a network. The key component of this assessment is to find the rating of the loss incurred by the threat/vulnerability. Based on the rating values, the vulnerabilities are prioritized.

Types of vulnerability assessment:

- In *active assessment*, with the help of any network scanner, the network is scanned to find the hosts and vulnerabilities.
- *Passive assessment* finds the active systems, hosts, and services. The network traffic is sniffed and this process is called passive assessment.
- In *host-based assessment*, the configuration check is done.

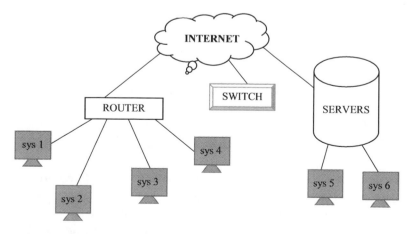

FIGURE 2.2
Hardware assets.

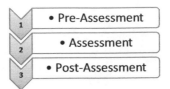

FIGURE 2.3
Assessment levels.

- *Internal assessment* finds out the vulnerabilities in the internal infrastructure of the network.
- *External assessment* assesses the network from a hacker's point of view and finds out what could be exploited.
- *Application assessment* tests the web infrastructure to find any outdated data.
- *Wireless network assessment* determines the track of all the wireless connectivity over the network.

As shown in Figure 2.3, vulnerability assessment is performed at three different levels: 1. pre-assessment level, 2. assessment level, and 3. post-assessment phase.

At the first level, i.e., in the pre-assessment level stage of the assessment, the procedure for planning and ranking the assets is done. At the second level, the network architecture, threat environment, physical assets analysis, policies, and procedures are observed. Finally, at the post-assessment level, the priorities are made and an action plan is jotted down for conducting the next phases. In this analysis phase, the list of areas where the penetration testing is to be done is identified, like the nodes in the network map to trace the vulnerabilities.

What should be scanned?

The answer to this is all the network devices that are connected to the organization's internal and external networks (Qualys 2008).

- Operating systems
- Web servers
- Servers
- Firewalls
- Databases
- Load balancing servers
- Switches and hubs
- Access points

Classifying and ranking the risks

- *Crucial:* The exploitation of the vulnerability is done without any human action.
- *Influential:* The exploitation of the vulnerability could result in data loss and influence the integrity, confidentiality, and availability of the user's data.
- *Medium:* The exploitation is serious, but the intensity is reduced by user action.
- *Low:* The impact of exploitation is minimal or negligible.

2.6.3 Reporting

In this phase, a report is generated for the organization's executives by prioritizing the vulnerabilities that are to be handled to stop the occurrence of threats. This report also consists of the plan of action to be taken to overcome the losses. The security teams monitor closely the steps involved to remediate these issues. The vulnerability summary report (VSR) is made by the claimant by finding the vulnerabilities that are identified. They may also write a detailed note on how the vulnerability was traced out and finally show some process to rectify those vulnerabilities.

2.6.4 Remediating and Verifying

Treating the vulnerabilities can be done in three ways either by remediating, mitigating, or by ignoring or accepting.

Remediating: Remedial action is taken for their prioritized vulnerabilities by fixing the threat completely or by patching the software.

Mitigating involves the organization choosing an alternative method to overcome that vulnerability.

Ignoring/accepting allows the low-risk threats to happen and no action is taken to fix the bug.

Acceptance of a bug may always incur a loss. Hence, most organizations remediate the vulnerabilities with patches to overcome the major havocs in the network.

The verification phase involves checking whether the remedial action is implemented effectively and efficiently. It also provides transparency in organizations' accountability.

With the growing technologies, the vulnerabilities have become more significant in overcoming the security of the organizational data. Hence, regular scrutiny with the help of various organizational tools and vulnerability management techniques is always to be undertaken by the organization's IT team.

2.7 Participants in Vulnerability Management

Usually, there are four participants identified in vulnerability management (Carnegie Mellon University Software Engineering Institute 2016)

1. **The claimant**: A person who researches and identifies the vulnerability in the organization.
2. **The vendor:** The person or organization who has developed the product and is responsible for maintaining the product.
3. **The adjudicator**: The person who mediates disputes between the claimant and the vendor.
4. **The supervisor:** The person who checks the vulnerability from the vendor's side in addition to the claimant.

When a vulnerability is investigated and confirmed, a remedy must be made by the team to rectify the vulnerabilities with required measures.

2.8 Vulnerability Analysis Tools

The following are the types of vulnerability analysis (VA) tools identified (Qualys 2008).

1. **Host-based VA tools:** These tools find and identify the operating system running on a particular host computer and test the system for any deficiencies. These search for common applications and services of the system.

2. **Application layer VA tools:** These tools check for the deficiencies in web servers and the databases.

3. **Scope assessment tools:** These tools check for the application and operating system deficiencies.

4. **Depth assessment tools:** These tools find the unidentified vulnerabilities in a system. These check the depth by inducing a software code that checks the security vulnerabilities by giving random input. These kinds of programs are called fuzzers or fault injectors.

5. **Active tools:** Active tools perform vulnerability checks over the network that consumes the system's resources.

6. **Passive tools:** These tools observe systems data and perform data processing in a separate machine.

Tools may be classified based on the data examined or the location of the vulnerability identified. New vulnerabilities are born every day and new tools are needed to handle those vulnerabilities. The following is the list of tools currently available:

1. Cycorp CycSecure Scanner
2. ISS Network Scanner
3. Saint Vulnerability Scanner
4. Symantec NetRecan Scanner
5. SPIKE Proxy
6. Foundstone's Scanline
7. Cerebus Internal Scanner
8. Shadow Security Scanner

Many more tools are available.
Some of the free scanners available are listed below:

1. Nmap
2. Nessus
3. Whisker
4. Enum
5. Firewalk

With a diverse variety of vulnerabilities, there is much need for research activities in identifying the vulnerabilities and taking the necessary actions in vulnerability management.

The vulnerability management solution you select needs to allow your security team to think like a hacker because it uses the scanning technology to identify and fix vulnerabilities inside and outside the firewall.

2.9 Best Practices for Vulnerability Management

The following are a few best practices that need to be incorporated in the organization to improve vulnerability management (Qualys 2008).

- **Discover network assets:** Discovering the network assets helps to determine the areas that are more susceptible to attacks. Network mapping detects all network devices, which helps to discover widespread network assets.
- **Classify the assets:** Most of the networks in organizations have between 10 and 20 different categories of network assets.
- **Run scans:** Run accurate scans on the assets based on the ranking that is given in the vulnerability pre-assessment phase. This gives you full visibility on the level of risk associated with your assets. Efficient scanning helps to find out the vulnerabilities easily and perform further tasks intelligently. Prioritizing the scans play a major role.
- **Technical reports:** The reports need to be generated by the technical team with all the instructions to be followed to remediate the vulnerabilities. A proper instructed document/report helps in better identification and remediation of the vulnerability.
- **Management reports:** After the technical team has given the instruction report that is to be followed to remediate the vulnerability, the management report is generated to identify the vulnerability trends and mitigate the areas that cause these vulnerabilities. The management report is given by the senior management of the organization.
- **Prioritize patching:** Patches are the codes that are generated to resolve any problem. The patches are generated to fix the bugs with critical importance first, and later moving on to the ones with lower priority.
- **Tracking remediation progress:** Once the vulnerability is identified, it is called a trouble ticket. Once a ticket is generated, the vulnerability management system starts to resolve the issues and keeps track of all the remediation process step by step. The best practice is to keep track of the different patches that are released by the product-based organization at regular intervals and update the system to avoid the vulnerabilities.

Now, with the help of a case study, let us see how an organization can follow vulnerability management techniques during a breach (Thomas 2019).

2.10 A Case Study in Vulnerability Management: Equifax

Equifax is a global organization and is the largest consumer reporting agency. On September 8, 2017, the organization released a note stating that it was attacked by a major cyber-attack compromising all the data of the users and also that the credit card numbers were leaked.

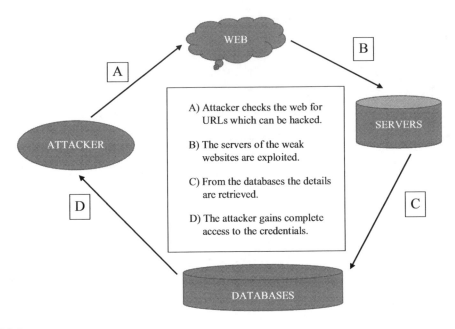

A) Attacker checks the web for URLs which can be hacked.

B) The servers of the weak websites are exploited.

C) From the databases the details are retrieved.

D) The attacker gains complete access to the credentials.

FIGURE 2.4
Attackers' exploitation.

Figure 2.4 shows how attackers exploited Equifax. The organization maintains many of the United States population's personal and financial data. The data stored by Equifax contains personal credit history, which includes account numbers, addresses, credit card statements, etc. When someone wants to borrow money, the lender first checks the borrower's financial history with Equifax and then lends money.

2.10.1 Identifying/Discovering the Vulnerability

Equifax uses Apache Struts as its application framework for one of its web applications. The attackers found a breach in the network and exploited the web application, leading to a security vulnerability CVE-2017-5639. This vulnerability takes over the exception handling issues when the user tries to upload files. They took over the servers and exploited around 143 million records. This led to the loss of confidential information.

2.10.2 Assessment of the Vulnerability

To resolve this problem, assessment was performed by the organization's internal security team. The team first identified the cause of the vulnerability. It performed different types of scans on the system, and after performing the rigorous vulnerability scans they identified two breakdowns. One was a failure to patch, and the other was a failure to identify the application as vulnerable. The patch update that was to be made that week had been missed and that led to a failure in an application. The solution to these two issues was provided by the technical team report followed by the management report.

The assets were identified, which included the software that is used in the organization network nodes, servers, and other peripherals connected via a network. The notifications that were sent from the vendors were analyzed. The internal security staff self-guided research on all possibilities to identify the vulnerability.

2.10.3 Reporting the Vulnerability

A report consisting of the major area where the breach had occurred was generated by the people assigned for the task. In this case study, the vulnerability allowed attackers from a remote location to execute arbitrary commands that can be created remotely using a crafted Content-Disposition, Content-Type, or Content-Length HTTP header with a Content-Type header containing the characters #cmd=string.

2.10.4 Remediating and Verifying

The remedy for the vulnerability was finally given, by installing the missed patch with the security enhancements in the application, and the issue was tracked for its progress. It is observed that the security team conducted a scan to see if the vulnerability existed in the system (Marinos and Clements 2018).It is also observed that the scan did not detect the vulnerability Apache Struts CVE-2017-5638. Finally the organization came out of the breach. From then on, the security mechanisms were enhanced and also the vulnerability management process was performed at frequent intervals to avoid major havocs.

Thus, with the help of this case study, we can say that the security of an organization depends upon incorporation of proper vulnerability management mechanisms to maintain cybersecurity.

References

Ali, Assad, Pavol Zavarsky, Dale Lindskog, and Ron Ruhl. 2012. "A New CVSS-Based Tool to Mitigate the Effects of Software Vulnerabilities." *International Journal for Information Security Research* 2(3): 178–182.

Carnegie Mellon University Software Engineering Institute. 2016. "CRR Supplemental Resource Guide Vulnerability Management Version 1.1." 4. https://www.us-cert.gov/sites/default/files/c3vp/crr_resources_guides/CRR_Resource_Guide-VM.pdf., accessed on Feb 24, 2020.

Christey, S. 2007. "Unforgivable Vulnerabilities." *Black Hat Briefings*.

Dondo, Maxwell G. 2008. "A Vulnerability Prioritization System Using a Fuzzy Risk Analysis Approach." *IFIP International Federation for Information Processing* 278: 525–539.

Edwards, Chandra Estelle, 2020. "Finding Trust in Relational Vulnerability: Interpersonal and Intrapersonal Influences on the Intimacy Process" (Doctoral dissertation). Retrieved from ProQuest database. (Accession No.1552969396).

Gonda, Tom et al. 2018. "Analysis of Attack Graph Representations for Ranking Vulnerability Fixes." *EPiC Series in Computing* 55(September): 215–228.

IEEE. 2012. "Defining and Assessing Quantitative Security Risk Measures Using Vulnerability Lifecycle and CVSS Metrics" 2012 (1). d:%5Cdaten%5CPromotion%5CLiteraturver waltung%5CPromotion-EconomicsOfITSec (Citavi 4)%5CCitaviFiles%5C12Defining andAssessingQuantitativeSecRiskMeasuresUsingVulnerabilityLifecycle&CVSSMetrics.pdf.

ISO. 2020a. "ISO/IEC 27032:2012—Information technology — Security techniques — Guidelines for cybersecurity. https://www.Iso27001security.com/html/27032.html, accessed on March 23, 2020.

ISO. 2020b. "Vulnerability Management and Scanning." https://www.Rapid7.com/Fundamentals/ Vulnerability-Management-and-Scanning/Le, accessed on March 22, 2020. .

ISO/IEC. 2020. "Information Technology – Security Techniques – Code of Practice for Information Security Management," ISO/IEC 27002. https://www.iso.org/committee/45306/x/catalogue/, accessed on March 24, 2020

Marinos, Nick, and Michael Clements. 2018. "Actions Taken by Equifax and Federal Agencies in Response to the 2017 Breach." *United States Government Accountability Office* (August): 40. https://www.hsdl.org/?abstract&did=815269.

Nanda, Sameer and Umashankar Ghugar. 2017. "Approach to an Efficient Vulnerability Management Program." *International Journal of Innovative Research in Computer and Communication Engineering* 5(6):11241–11244.

Njogu, H. W., L. Jiawei, J. N. Kiere. January 2013. "Comprehensive Vulnerability Based Alert Management Approach for Large Networks." *Future Generation Computer System* 29(1), 2013: 27–45.

Peter, Mell, Karen Scarfone, and Sasha Romanosky. A. 2007. Forum of Incident Response and Security Teams (FIRST) *Complete Guide to the Common Vulnerability Scoring System Version 2.0.*

Qualys. 2008. "Vulnerability Assessment for Dummies," 66.

Thomas, Jason. 2019. "A Case Study Analysis of the Equifax Data Breach 1 A Case Study Analysis of the Equifax Data Breach." (December). https://www.researchgate.net/publication/337916068.

Tripathi, Anshu and Umesh Kumar Singh Singh. 2011. "Analyzing Trends in Vulnerability Classes across CVSS Metrics." *International Journal of Computer Applications* 36(3): 38–44.

Williams, A. and Nicollet, M 2020. "Improve IT Security With Vulnerability Management Title."

Zhang, Su, Doina Caragea, and Xinming Ou. 2011a. "An Empirical Study on Using the National Vulnerability Database to Predict Software Vulnerabilities An Empirical Study on Using the National Vulnerability Database to Predict Software Vulnerabilities." (August).

Zhang, Su, Xinming Ou, Anoop Singhal, and John Homer. 2011b. "An Empirical Study of a Vulnerability Metric Aggregation Method." *The Defense Technical Information Center, DTIC Online, USA.* http://oai.dtic.mil/oai/oai?verb=getRecord&metadata Prefix=html&identifier= ADA557504.

3

Identity Theft and Prevention

Atefeh Tajpour[1] and Mazdak Zamani[2]

[1] *University of Shahid Rajaee Teacher Training, Tehran, Iran*

[2] *Felician University, Rutherford, New Jersey*

3.1 Introduction

Identity theft is a cybercrime growing rapidly throughout the world. The year 2011 has been labeled "The year of data breaches", when more than 232.4 million identities were exposed. It is noticeable that there was a 62% increase in the number of breaches. Furthermore, over 552 million identities were exposed via breaches in 2013 (Symantec, 2014). The substantial increase in the use of online banking and the widespread availability of online shopping opportunities, which need online customers to provide sensitive confidential personal and financial information, are critical factors that have contributed to this alarming escalation in the number of stolen identities. An urgent need is for consumers engaging in online commerce to be aware of the risks they are taking in possibly exposing themselves to cybercrime and the need to take preventive measures to minimize these risks (Holt and Turner, 2012). Moreover, as revealed by YenYuen and Yeow (2009), among security concerns for Malaysians, identity theft is one of the three most aggravating causes of concern, which is almost the same for developed countries such as Australia. From the number of lodged police reports on identity theft cases in Malaysia, there is a clear upward trend. Such a situation adds greater urgency to the necessity of informing Malaysians about this crime, as current public awareness of cybercrime is very low and preventive actions are little practiced, hence this alarming escalation in the number of stolen identities (Hazelah et al., 2011). Microsoft Corporation's security intelligence report on Malaysia (May 12th, 2011) refers to "cyber-criminals using more accessible attack methods including social engineering tactics and leveraging exploits created by the most skilled criminals to take a small amount of money from a large number of people" (Adam et al., 2011). Also, Cyber Security Malaysia is involved with educating the public about the dangers of identity theft, which is a global problem, not confined only to the developed countries. However, some countries like Malaysia are being viewed as high risk for travelers who make credit card transactions (Albrecht et al., 2011). Furthermore, according to the president of the Crime Prevention Awareness Board (LKPJ), cyber cheating has become extremely extensive with the Board having received 300 complaints with financial losses exceeding RM1 million in the first six months of 2013. Data from the Police Commercial CID show that in 2012 a total of RM1.6 billion was lost due to cybercrime in Malaysia compared to RM1 billion the previous year (Bernama, 2013). Mohamed (2013) reported that in Malaysia, cybercrime first attracted the general attention of the public following the hacking of the Malaysian Parliament and University Technology Mara websites in 2002. Because of the lack of knowledge, students could not mitigate identity theft victimization (Seda, 2014). Although the costs and spread of this crime are considered in some research, it is necessary for them to be considered empirically. First, identity theft is widely complex, ranging from simple methods such as bag or purse snatching to high tech methods such as sniffing. There is research on procedures used in identity theft, whereas experimental evaluation of online and offline influential factors regarding identity theft victimization is necessary (Holt and Turner, 2012). Second, in the Malaysian context, the increase in identity theft cases has been observed to go in tandem with the number of police reports (Hazelah et al., 2011) and it is expected that students have greater knowledge about the risks of identity theft (Seda, 2014).

This research seeks to address these four gaps. First, this study employs theoretical integration, which is an intriguing and controversial issue in contemporary criminology (Thornberry, 1989). Messner and Krohn (1989) have proposed a new comprehensive model for combating identity theft in respect of consumer behavior. Second, the new model helps to understand the factors that influence identity theft, including a large number (92 factors) of risk and protective behaviors. Third, despite the existence of earlier studies as determined in the literature, this current research simultaneously covers offline as well as online identity theft victimization, and also considers many more predictors compared to those considered in past studies. Fourth, contrary to previous studies, this research considers four types of identity theft as dependent variables to explore explanations for identity theft. From a practical perspective, this research provides suggestions to policy makers to educate and motivate e-commerce customers to follow the recommended protective measures.

3.2 Literature Review

Numerous studies have been conducted with the aim of combating identity theft. In a quantitative study by (Milne et al., 2004), online behaviors that decrease or raise the online identity theft risk were examined among US customers. The exploratory research of Milne (Milne, 2005), recommended by the Federal Trade Commission (FTC), included 13 identity theft preventive acts. This research assessed the influence of consumer education by calculating the degree to which consumers keep themselves safe from identity theft. Also, Wang et al. (2006) proposed a contextual framework for representing the roles of holder and issuer as well as of checker and protector of identity regarding combating identity theft. This framework cannot offer any particular solutions, but it can assist to direct online users' attempts and thinking. Moreover, regarding unavoidable technology improvements, Norberg et al. (2007) proposed a theoretical framework to explain the division between privacy attitudes and behaviors. According to this framework, risk can have a considerable effect on the behavioral intentions of individuals for preparing personal information, although trust can be affected considerably by the actual behavior of individuals. There should be an understanding that individuals' sense of personal privacy will decline continuously unless they try to truly perceive whom they offer personal information to, and what permissions they grant. Regarding the importance of credit transactions, a model depicting identity theft as an equilibrium phenomenon was proposed by Kahn and Roberds (2008). Different kinds of identity theft take place in equilibrium. The identity theft equilibrium incidence indicates the balance between willingness to prevent invasive or costly individual monitoring and the desire to control transactions fraud. The mathematical equilibrium recommends increasing the complexity of identification tools for consumers. On the other hand, Winterdyk and Thompson (2008), by employing a survey, calculated the awareness and perception of self-reports about identity theft and diversity of fraudulent behaviors. The results indicate that students are better informed about identity theft, but are a little more at risk than non-students. According to the results, some educational strategies and policy implications regarding identity theft protection in Canada are proposed. Also, a model based on the theory of protection motivation is represented by Milne et al. (2009). This theory indicates that the motivation of consumers for protection is dependent on the self-efficacy and perceived possibility of the threat, along with the extremity of the threats (Tanner Jr et al., 1991). The model explores the variables that guide consumers in their maladaptive or adaptive reactions in the face of security and privacy threats. Moreover, this study explores parameters that guide consumers to perform risky and protective online behaviors. In this model, identity theft is taken into account as a perceived threat and the likelihood of identity theft is considered as a perceived likelihood of online threat. The study by Higgins et al. (2010) illustrates self-protective behaviors that are employed by college student for combating identity theft. The CCT analysis method in Milne's study is criticized in this research and recommends rash model analysis. The interpretation has some policy implications. The scholar claims that policy makers must try to inform both organizations and student customers concerning information security issues. Shah and Okeke (2011) examined and synthesized previous studies in relation to internal identity theft (employees), the way it is really performed, techniques employed for stealing personal information of customers, and the procedure that businesses can use for mitigating this problem. They recommend a role-based framework that contains all levels of employees to prevent internal identity theft in relation to crime in the organization. Regarding the importance of safeguarding, a conceptual framework was proposed by Pannah (2011) that recommends self-data protection as well as what should be done after an occurrence of identity theft. This framework investigates the effect of exposure to cyber threats, participating in vulnerable internet activities, and proactively safeguarding personal data on the frequency and severity of identity theft. Another model that examines consumer behavior regarding identity fraud and theft is offered by Archer (2011). This study investigates the attitudes and precursors that are associated with behaviors of customers that are employed to discover identity theft. The study considers the relationship between experience of identity theft victimization and level of concern about being a victim of this crime. The study loosely follows the theory of reasoned action (TRA), which posits that beliefs influence views that affect intentions, which, in turn, lead to behaviors. Furthermore, the study of Lewis (2011b), which examined the way consumers describe identity theft prevention, discovered the attributes of consumers that deter identity theft, and explored the way that identity theft threatens to impact consumer exchanges. In this study, the sample is drawn from undergraduate students concerned with identity theft from online universities in the US. Data were collected by employing a questionnaire that included both open and closed (demographic) questions and that was administered through the internet. The objective of this qualitative phenomenological research was to focus on the identity theft problem by examining what consumers do to deter identity theft and express their attitudes. The researcher attempted to identify the behaviors and demographics of individuals engaged in identity theft prevention.

Besides this, Holt and Turner (2012) examined how protective factors impact the respondents' resistance against online identity theft at a Southeastern university. The study outcomes demonstrated initial understanding of how protective factors impacted online identity theft. Moreover, this research examined how resiliency models fit cybercrime victimization. This study examined the relationship between online risky activities and protective behavior and risk of victimization. Data collection among university students and staff was done by a self-report survey. From another perspective, Reyns (2013) employed routine action theory in order to depict where the victims and perpetrators were yet to come close physically and assessed the relationship between identity fraud and the online routine activity of 5,985 respondents from 2008 to 2009 in a British Crime Survey. The respondents were those who engaged in internet banking and online purchasing. The study assessed the correlation of merely limited sorts of online routine activity and identity theft by making use of logistic regression. Another limitation of the study was the lack of low self-control measures which could be complementary in identity fraud victimization on the individual and country levels. Moreover, Seda (2014) highlighted the influence of university students' awareness regarding identity theft and their preventive actions. A number of selection interviews were used from the onset of the primary data collection at Flinders Business School. By using face-to-face interviews, it was concluded that students did not have enough knowledge of the use of suitable measures that could reduce or raise the danger of identity theft. Another review connected with Holtfreter et al. (2015) stated that the self-control/risky lifestyle viewpoint seems to produce a direct perception of the reason why everyone is victimized through numerous methods. According to this particular review approach, a large portion of legal victimization affects the groups with low self-control and high risk lifestyles. Using survey information obtained through phone interviews with respondents aged 60 or thereabouts, the analysis examined whether the theoretical platform somewhat described risky rural purchasing and also identity theft victimization involving elderly Web users. The particular findings reveal which elderly Web users can easily minimize his or her chances of victimization by taking certain safety measures. Due to the limitation, the results reveal hardly any concern with the dynamics involved in identity theft victimization of elderly people away from the US. This kind of analysis seems to be restricted to just one type of online risky behavior. Eventually, Reyns and Henson (2015) attempted to look at the relationship between victims' online routine actions and also online identity theft victimization by employing a country-wide sample in a Canadian general social survey carried out from February to November 2009. As a shortcoming, this research cannot satisfy the readers that such low independent variability and low control variability states the dependent variable. Based on Nagelkerke R2, more relative indicators must be included in the model to explain online identity theft. It means that maybe other routine online activities and other types of victimization can predict identity theft much better than this research. Moreover, Reyns and Randa (2019) employed structural equation modeling (SEM) for data collected in a university in the US. This research found a direct relationship between identity fraud and low self-control, peer deviance and hacking victimization as well as an indirect relationship to personal deviance. As a result, routine lifestyle routine activities and low self-control describe identity fraud.

Therefore, the present study focuses on identity theft to test the effects of four types of identity theft as the dependent variable and also 92 risk and protective behaviors to indicate much of what explains identity theft victimization.

3.3 Research Model and Hypothesis

The increasing trend of identity theft indicates that consumers need to consider all forms of identity theft protection. It is unclear what behaviors are the most influential in the likelihood of this crime occurring. This research makes contributions in terms of the six independent variables and one dependent variable. The dependent variable is the occurrence of identity theft, and the independent variables include: physical security, online security and account monitoring, which are associated with protective behavior. Also, offline risk, online risk and cybercrime victimization, which are associated with risk behavior, are considered as shown in Figure 3.1.

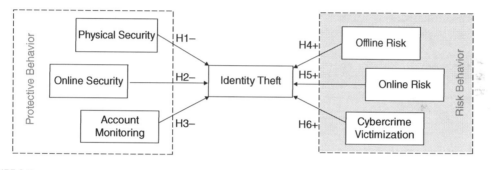

FIGURE 3.1
Conceptual model.

H1: "Physical security" has a negative impact on identity theft..

Physical security: This component explains the security activities anticipated to block unauthorized members (e.g., hackers or random intruders) from gaining physical access to resources or saved data; in addition, it instructs how to plan structures that resist the harm of assumed animus and malicious activities. Following are the measures of this component adopted from Milne, Archer, Lewis and Pannah (Milne, 2005; Archer, 2011; Lewis, 2011a; Pannah, 2011): 1) use a locked mailbox; 2) shred documents; 3) lock up financial documents; 4) ensure no one is watching at an ATM or when filling out a form; 5) destroy hard drives, thumb drives, media cards, tapes, CDs, or similar materials before discarding; 6) register phone numbers with the national do-not-call registry to stop unwanted telemarketing phone calls; 7) watch in-store credit/bank/store card transactions closely to ensure that the store cashier is not copying the card; 8) collect all receipts from transactions; 9) check items in billing statements; 10) scan documents and store electronic copies; 11) verify the reputation of a vendor; 12) shield the key pad when entering PIN codes for debit or credit cards; 13) lock your computer when it is not in use; and 14) do not leave garbage out overnight but place it by the curb near the time it is to be picked up.

H2: "Online security" has a negative impact on identity theft.

Online security: Consumers can take certain computer-based steps to secure their confidential information. These steps are not specifically for online shopping only but for all online activities.

Following are the measures of this component adopted from Milne, Winterdyk and Thompson, Higgins et al., Archer, Pannah, Lewis, Holt and Turner, and Reyns and Henson (Milne et al., 2004; Winterdyk and Thompson, 2008; Higgins et al., 2010; Archer, 2011; Pannah, 2011; Lewis, 2011b; Holt and Turner, 2012; Reyns and Henson, 2015): 1) use a separate personal e-mail account and work e-mail account; 2) have a separate e-mail account just for registering on websites; 3) encrypt e-mail; 4) choose not to receive mail and e-mail offers and request that customer information be removed from lists; 5) have a virus checker installed on the computer and update it; 6) frequently scan computer for spyware; 7) clear the computer's cache after browsing; 8) ensure that online forms are secure before filling out information (check for the "padlock" icon at the bottom bar of the screen); 9) when given the chance, opt out of third party information sharing; 10) remove name and address from any lists used for marketing purposes; 11) upgrade Web browser to the newest version; 12) refuse to give personal information to a website; 13) have phishing detection turned on in browser; 14) set up browser to reject unnecessary cookies; 15) clear cookies after using internet or do not save cookies; 16) always look for and read privacy statements on the Web; 17) configure the computer to activate a password-protected screen saver after a set period of inactivity; 18) install a personal firewall (software or hardware); 19) install Spybot; 20) encrypt sensitive information (such as name, SSN, birth date) when storing it on the computer; 21) power off computer rather than leaving it running; 22) contact the organizations you deal with to limit security risks; 23) type the URL instead of using hyperlinks to navigate a vendor's page; 24) use Anonymizer while browsing the Web; 25) use different passwords; 26) use a combination of letters, numbers and symbols in password; 27) set computer to lock out users from login after three incorrect passwords are entered; 28) change login passwords at least every 60 days; and 29) use login passwords which are at least 12 characters long.

H3: "Account monitoring" has a negative impact on identity.

Account monitoring: Account monitoring is a preventive process. In fact, regular monitoring of accounts and setting up banking alerts help customers quickly identify fraudulent activity. Following are the measures of this component adopted from Milne, Winterdyk and Thompson, Higgins et al., Pannah and Lewis (Milne, 2005; Winterdyk and Thompson, 2008; Higgins et al., 2010; Pannah, 2011; Lewis, 2011b): 1) monitor bank account; 2) monitor credit card; 3) periodically request a new account number; 4) monitor check images through the bank's e-mail; 5) choose electronic statements and use online bill payment services for transactions; 6) use a temporary credit card; 7) use debit cards for transactions rather than credit cards; 8) use a prepaid credit card to shop; 9) get a credit report; 10) check Land Registry; and 11) authorize Credit Tip Off Service (CTOS), Central Credit Reference Information System (CCRIS) or similar companies to proactively limit or prevent release of personal data without permission.

H4: "Offline risk" has a positive impact on identity theft.

Offline risk: In contrast to other studies on identity theft, this study considers offline risk as an independent variable that could lead to identity theft when physical security is absent. There are a number of ways in which consumers are victimized by physical approaches when the intruder succeeds in accessing personal information fraudulently in actual situations according to Lombardi (2006). Also (Garg et al., 2012) conducted risk perception studies related to offline risks that are very different from online risks. Consequently, this research identified measures based on Milne (2005), Pannah (2011), Winterdyk and Thompson (2008), and Lewis (2011a) that influence identity theft when customers are offline. The following are the measures of this component: 1) giving personal information over phone or cell phone; 2) carrying extra credit cards in the wallet when no need; 3) carrying social security card in wallet or purse; 4) carrying checkbook while shopping or traveling; and 5) making purchases over the phone or cell phone.

H5: "Online risk" has a positive impact on identity theft.

Online risk: Consumers online are collectively and frequently faced with threats of identity theft during online shopping. Tracking tools such as Web-bugs are employed to steal sensitive data, which makes the opportunity riper for identity theft (Jakobsson and Myers, 2006). Risky behaviors cannot be expressed as actions attributed to consumers online that compromise their online security. Although internet users are increasingly gaining more awareness of the online threats involved in passing their information to online enterprises, they still compromise their online safety by not taking the appropriate precautionary technical steps, or learning about the ways in which websites save their information. The following are the measures of this component, adopted from Pannah (2011), Higgins et al. (2010), Winterdyk and Thompson (2008), Archer (2011), Lewis (2011a) and Holt and Turner (2012): 1) open an e-mail without a subject; 2) read spam e-mail; 3) set images to automatically download in e-mail; 4) click on links in an e-mail without knowing the sender; 5) open e-mail attachments without knowing the sender; 6) click links and fill out forms when in e-mails from financial institutions; 7) have browser safety settings (JavaScript/cookies) set at low; 8) participate in a blog; 9) use public wi-fi; 10) use peer-to-peer file sharing networks (e.g., music, video, and software sharing); 11) keep profiles open on social media and cloud-based services (Facebook, Dropbox...); 12) ignore system (e.g., Windows) updates; 13) log into online accounts using public computers; 14) use an unsecured home network; 15) post your identity card number, birth date, address, phone number, bank account or credit card number or other personal information to an unknown site; 16) accept unknown "friends" on social media and cloud-based services (Facebook, Dropbox...); 17) use identity card number for registering on a website; 18) make purchases using public computers; 19) download unknown files on social media and cloud-based services (Facebook, Dropbox...); 20) use illegal copied software or pass it to others; 21) use, make, or give to another person "pirated" media (music, TV show or movie); 22) use a dictionary word as password; 23) save passwords on your computer/mobile device; 24) use personal information such as your birthday, identity card number, or consecutive numbers as password or login; and 25) use an alternative password to get into others' accounts or files on devices.

H6: "Cybercrime victimization" has a positive impact on identity theft.

Cybercrime victimization: Individual users of computers and the internet should learn about the probable threats, and their potential consequences, in order to take basic protective measures to lower the possibilities of victimization. In fact, the risk measures related to malware infection increase the possibility of identity theft for customers (Holt and Turner, 2012). In many cases, malware is employed by identity thieves to access computer systems or information illegally (Chu et al., 2010). The following are the measures of this component, adopted from Holt and Turner (Holt and Turner, 2012): 1) someone threatens others or makes them worry by posting a message about you; 2) receive a message via e-mail or instant message that makes you feel threatened or worried; 3) computer slowing down or not running as fast as it used to; 4) computer freezing or crashing, requiring the system to be shut down or reset; 5) the homepage is changed without you changing the computer's settings; 6) a new program appears on the computer that was not installed; and 7) send messages to other people to threaten them.

3.4 Method

The following section describes the questionnaire design, and the methods of data collection and sampling. Also, data analysis and the model evaluation method are presented.

3.4.1 Ethics Statement

Taking part in this research was entirely voluntary, and all those involved were informed of their right to drop out at any time without having to provide a reason. All individuals provided prior written consent on the first page of the questionnaire to publish these case details. Moreover, this study employed Survey Monkey for survey distribution and just received the responses. E-mail addresses and other identifying information were not included in the data collection because they were not necessary. Surveys were submitted anonymously and were de-identified by the researcher. There was no requirement to collect the consent form because, based on the first page of the questionnaire, respondents had indicated their voluntary participation in the survey.

3.4.2 Data Collection

The rationale for using university students in this study is because Malaysia has been ranked as the country with the highest percentage of "digital natives" (Measuring the Information Society 2013 report, a pioneering and comprehensive research on global internet usage). Constraints of budget and time influenced the decision to limit the study to only one location (Chamhuri and Batt, 2013).

The stratified random sampling and cluster sampling are utilized in this research. For the cluster sampling step, the population is firstly divided into several clusters, and then each of those clusters is composed of secondary units. Some of the clusters are then picked from the population. Lastly, the result is applied to the entirety of the secondary units of those picked clusters (Xiangke et al., 2012).

Malaysia comprises 13 states, 11 in west Malaysia and two in east Malaysia. The study location of the Klang Valley was chosen for some important reasons: a) the Klang Valley is in the state of Selangor and next to the Federal Territory and this area encompasses some of the largest cities in Malaysia such as Kuala Lumpur (the Malaysian Federal Capital), Putrajaya (the Malaysian administrative center), Shah Alam, and Klang; b) within this region is a substantial population that is a good mix of potential respondents with different education levels; c) it is also a region with very high internet penetration; d) the majority of the potential respondents are of middle income class; e) and the Klang Valley has the highest concentration of higher learning institutions, both public and private (Samah et al., 2013).

When choosing the university from among Malaysia's universities, stratified random sampling was considered, while systematic random sampling was considered when choosing the university students. According to an official declaration (Facts, 2011), a population of about 162,000 students was recorded in six public universities in the area. Cattell (1977) recommended that the ratio of the sample size to the number of items should be in the range of 3:6. With 386 respondents and 92 items, it seemed satisfactory to have a ratio of 4:2 in the current study. The researcher designed an online questionnaire through Survey Monkey, and e-mail addresses were chosen randomly from the list of students from various universities, in relation to the proportion of each university. University A provided all students' e-mails and the researcher selected the respondents randomly; Universities B and C selected the student e-mails at random and the researcher sent the questionnaire to them. Universities D, E and F did not submit the students' e-mails to the researcher, but instead they randomly distributed the link for the questionnaire to their students. Based on Hu et al. (2011), the usual response rate for online questionnaires is less than 40%, so the survey was sent to 1,000 e-mails to achieve the required sample size. The proportion of each university was (A = 18%, B = 17%, C = 15%, D = 18%, E = 25%, and F = 7%).

3.4.3 Instrument Development

This study adopted questions from published papers, and respondents were asked to indicate their responses on a five-point Likert scale where 1 = Never, 2 = Rarely, 3 = Sometimes, 4 = Often, 5 = Almost Always. The dependent variable of this research is the occurrence of financial identity theft that is evaluated by four choices: a) opened new credit accounts using my name and identity card number; b) accessed my existing accounts (Hoofnagle, 2007); c) took loan(s) in my name (Ramaswamy, 2006); and d) used my credit card for shopping (Hoofnagle, 2007).

Physical security, online security, account monitoring and online risk are components that are adopted from current models. However, new measures are considered in this research for these components, based on the literature. Meanwhile, offline risk and cybercrime victimization are two new components in the proposed model of this study. To reduce measurement error, all items in the model were developed based on previous studies in the field, and previously tested instruments (Milne, 2005; Winterdyk and Thompson, 2008; Milne et al., 2009; Higgins et al., 2010; Archer, 2011; Pannah, 2011; Holt and Turner, 2012).

A panel of experts was established to determine the validity of the research instrument. Then a pre-test was conducted with 33 respondents before the main stage of the data collection. This was to ensure that the concepts, wordings and measurements used in the instruments were clear, meaningful and understandable for the participants, and that the instrument was reliable. Some minor improvements and modifications were made after the pre-test based on the suggestions and comments from the respondents. This study used a reliability coefficient of 0.6 or higher as the standard for accepting the questionnaire (Malhotra et al., 2013). The alpha coefficients for the instruments of the pre-test ranged from 0.61 to 0.88, and the final test ranged from 0.76 to 0.86. The results showed acceptable reliability scores.

3.5 Result

The current research utilized descriptive and inferential statistics. The data collected from the survey were analyzed utilizing the statistical software SPSS 19 and Analysis of MOment Structures 18.0 (AMOS).

3.5.1 Demographics

The target population in this study involved a total of 372 students in Malaysia. The primary analysis of the respondents' demographic information represents the high frequency of online shopping among students, as 73.5% of the respondents engaged in online shopping monthly, weekly or daily. Also, 68.3% of them had more than one year's access to the internet for online shopping or using online services. This indicated that respondents had sufficient experience in the domain of e-commerce to understand the questions and concepts they had evaluated. Furthermore, it was found that undergraduates comprised the majority of participants, with n = 206 (55.4%). According to the data, 60% (n = 42) of those who suffered identity theft were male, while 40% (n = 28) were female. Moreover, 75.7% (n = 53) of the victims of this cybercrime were local students, while 24.3% of them were international students. Table 3.1 demonstrates the overall means and standard deviations evaluated from the six scales. It can be concluded that all mean scores are more than midpoint (2.5).

According to Table 3.1, the most important construct in selecting protective behavior is account monitoring (MO) as (M = 3.51), demonstrating that university students generally consider security for their account. On the other hand, the least important construct in selecting protective behavior was offline risk (OFR) (M = 2.63), which shows that respondents do not pay attention to risk behavior when they are offline.

TABLE 3.1

Descriptive Statistics on Scales.

Scale	PHS	ONS	MO	OFR	ONR	CV
Mean	2.75	3.36	3.51	2.63	3.07	3.13
Std. Deviation	1.12	1.07	1.04	1.27	1.20	1.08

3.5.2 Exploratory Factor Analysis

It is necessary to test the fitness of the data set for factor analysis before the extraction of constructs. The Kaiser, Meyer, Olkin (KMO) index in this study was 0.92; also, the Bartlett's Test was significant ($p < 0.05$) (Hair et al., 2010). Pett et al. (2003) stated that the cumulative percentage of variance is a disparity in factor analysis and generally is as low as 50% – 60%. In this study, the cumulative percentage of variance was 64%, and had a total of six constructs. This study employed exploratory factor analysis (EFA) on the 92 items by utilizing principal components with maximum likelihood and Promax rotation, while the Eigenvalues were greater than one for three different times. After examining the main loadings comprising each factor, and eliminating 38 items that exhibited a coefficient value of less than 0.3 according to Gaskin (2012) and Williams (2010), six components were figured out. Also, according to McMillan and Schumacher (2014), the six constructs have satisfactory reliability estimates. The Cronbach's alpha for the instrument was $\alpha = 0.85$, and the subscales were more than 0.7.

3.5.3 Confirmatory Factor Analysis

Indicator variables were chosen on the basis of previous studies, and factor analysis was employed to determine if they loaded as predicted on the expected number of factors. According to Hair et al. (2010), if there are three or four indices among the measure fit indices, including one absolute index and one incremental index, they fulfill the criteria, and adequate evidence for the model fit is provided. Table 3.2 represents the goodness of fit index resulting from the confirmatory factor analysis (CFA) model for the six constructs. As χ^2/df is less than 5, it meets the criteria. Additionally, the Root Mean Square Error of Approximation (RMSEA) just fit the .08. Meanwhile, the Goodness of Fit Index (GFI) and the Normed Fit Index (NFI) meet the criteria, which are all greater than 0.90 (Hair et al., 2010). Also, each item was statistically valid for the construct, with regard to a significant result for convergent validity (AVE > .5 & CR > .7) (Pedhazur and Schmelkin, 2013). Also, the average variance extracted (AVE) from two constructs is higher than the square of the correlation between the two constructs, so discriminant validity exists (Hair et al., 2010). These analyses confirm that the measurement model of this study maintains both validity and reliability.

TABLE 3.2

Goodness of Fit Indices.

Construct	Chi-squares	df	χ^2/df	GFI	NFI	RMSEA
PHS	144.7	31	3.3	.93	.95	.070
ONS	203.4	65	3.1	.92	.93	.076
MO	88.08	27	2.5	.95	.95	.078
OFR	2.82	2	1.43	.99	.99	.034
ONR	88.79	35	2.5	.95	.96	.064
CV	42.3	11	3.8	.96	.97	.080

3.5.4 Structural Model and Hypotheses Testing

After general estimates for the relationships of six independent variables, a structural equation modeling (SEM) technique was used (Kaplan and Depaoli, 2012) to test the hypothesized model as suggested in the literature. Standardized regression weights were used for hypothesis testing when it was necessary to test the consequence of independent variables on the dependent variable. A p-value of 0.05 or less was utilized as the criterion (Hair et al., 2010) to decide if the degree of prediction was significant. The hypothesized model is displayed in Figure 3.2 and Table 3.3 summarizes the outcomes of testing the hypotheses.

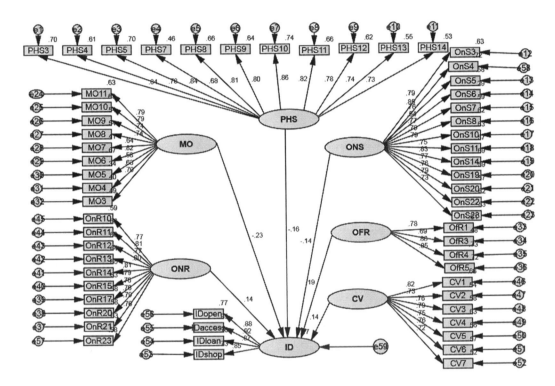

FIGURE 3.2
Structural model.

TABLE 3.3

Summary of Hypotheses and Findings.

	Hypothesis	Standardized Regression Weights (λ)	P	Result
H1	PhS→Identity Theft	−0.157	.002	Supported
H2	OnS→Identity Theft	−0.141	.006	Supported
H3	MO→Identity Theft	−0.227	***	Supported
H4	OfR→Identity Theft	0.187	***	Supported
H5	OnR→Identity Theft	0.136	.009	Supported
H6	CV→Identity Theft	0.142	.007	Supported

3.6 Discussion

The research model indicated that offline risk and account monitoring are the most influential factors in the occurrence of identity theft. Results of this study show that account monitoring is the most influential construct that decreases the likelihood of identity theft. Results of this research show that Malaysian youths are well informed about account security. Also, Malaysia is a pioneer in youth savings programs and child development accounts among developing countries. Bank Simpanan National (BSN), a development bank in Malaysia, participates in educating the young on the importance of savings and financial decision making (Masa, 2009). The results of this study show that customers who monitor and check images sent by the bank's e-mail are more secure against identity theft. By checking e-mail, the check payee, the amount, and when it was cashed can be verified and in case of fraud it can be reported quickly to the bank.

Moreover, using online banking has now become very much part of Malaysian lifestyle and one of the innovative products of financial institutions in this country is electronic statements (Bekhet and Al-Alak, 2014), which have replaced paper statements. Such electronic statements help to significantly minimize the presence of sensitive confidential information in easily accessed mailboxes, where it can fall into the wrong hands. Payments and receipts conducted online enjoy greater security compared to checks sent by mail. Furthermore, there is guaranteed protection should unauthorized transactions occur during the process of making or receiving payments using a bank website.

Besides, the results of various studies affirm that Malaysia commenced the issue of temporary credit cards to businesses. This card was one way to prevent identity theft because the number on the card is issued by a credit card company for online transactions and is only used once. The advantage of using a temporary credit card number is that if it is compromised, the holder only has to cancel that number instead of the main account number, meaning that the temporary credit card number can help keep the real card safe. However, credit cards provide greater protection and the risk is less as funds are not taken directly from the holder's personal bank account, as is the case with a debit card. If withdrawals are fraudulently made from a debit card, checks can be bounced and accessibility to cash is blocked while the bank is investigating an unauthorized withdrawal report. In addition, in the case of credit cards, there is usually a 90-day period from the date of an unauthorized transaction during which the incident may be reported, while in the case of debit cards, banks require two days' notice. In light of this, it is in fact true to say that using a credit card will reduce the incidence of identity theft. Some financial institutions issue prepaid credit cards that are preloaded, much like gift cards. However, the security of such cards is not as high as that of credit cards, although prepaid credit cards would lessen the use of credit cards and thus minimize the chances of credit card disclosure.

A credit report is fundamentally a summarized statement of financial activities such as loans, repayment records, new and closed accounts, outstanding and overdue bills, among other such activities. A bank or an agency would release such credit reports. The monitoring of such services can be useful to identify problems, for example, a new credit account is opened by someone with your stolen information. In general, Malaysian financial institutions maintain such reports on their creditors and borrowers and make them available to the Credit Bureau of Bank Negara Malaysia on a monthly basis. Currently, the detailed reports of almost nine million consumers are in the CCRIS and CTOS. The processing of the overall data is done by Bank Negara Malaysia, which makes available credit reports that can be accessed by all financial institutions whenever required.

In contrast to CCRIS, which is managed by Bank Negara Malaysia (BNM), CTOS is owned and managed by a more than 20-year-old Malaysian firm, which collates data on individuals and companies available from various sources in the public domain. CTOS is of particular use to businesses that need background checks on possible business associates. To businesses allowing credit terms, such background information from CTOS and CCRIS is crucially beneficial to protect their interests. Customers who authorize CTOS or CCRIS to proactively limit or prevent release of personal data without permission gain from a reliable credit information system as it minimizes the impact of banks monopolizing credit. This is in fact an approach that leads to better control in accessing credit. The conclusion therefore could be that the government and Bank Negara Malaysia should be diligent in reviewing the operational aspects of domestic banks so that these financial institutions make available sufficient technological support and secure technologies (e.g., firewalls, two-factor authentication, secure socket level, etc.) prior to granting approval for the launching of new internet banking services (YenYuen and Yeow, 2009). As a result, local banks should pay greater attention to the provision of high level service, by reassessing their professional practices and ensuring their consistency with consumer needs and demands.

On the other hand, the result of maximum likelihood (ML) estimation shows that customers who engage in offline risky behavior are more exposed than others to identity theft. According to Table 3.1, offline risk was selected by respondents as the least important; this shows respondents do not pay attention to risk behavior when they are offline. There are several reasons to explain this. In Malaysia, it is compulsory for all citizens aged 12 years and above to have with them their National Identification Card (NIC or MyKad) (Loo et al., 2011). However, customers are advised to limit what they carry and to leave their social security cards at home. In fact, the social security card is the absolute worst item to carry around as it poses a great risk of being used in identity theft every day.

It is unfortunate that Malaysians appear to be rather careless with their MyKad and it has resulted in an issue that affects the security of their personal data and privacy particularly in the domain of cyberspace. A total of almost 68,839 Malaysians misplaced/lost their MyKad in 2011 alone, which means more than 1,000 people lost their cards daily. The many reasons given included that they were misplaced and sheer carelessness (Hazelah et al., 2011).

Carrying a checkbook when there was no need to do so was found to be another risk behavior. Checks when misplaced can lead to various undesirable results as they contain name, address, bank account number, bank routing number, and bank name. Such sensitive information can allow thieves to fraudulently access the checking account and siphon funds from it to their personal accounts. Besides, personal information should not be given over the phone or cell phone unless it is first determined how it is going to be used and how it will be protected.

In another study in Malaysia, Zendehdel and Paim (2012) reported that e-commerce has increased the likelihood of negative consequences of some risks in the offline environment. While the relationship between offending and victimization is well recognized in research on street crimes, there have been few explorations of this issue for virtual offending. Meanwhile, other statistics on Malaysia show the same result (Raus et al., 2013). Young adults are at an age when they are learning new skills, acquiring new experiences and experimenting with various lifestyle changes. In extending e-commerce for e-banking and shopping and focusing on 106% penetration rate of multiple subscriptions among young adult Malaysians (Goi and Ng, 2011), it is possible that personal information is released orally on mobiles when customers order merchandise. Usually when people are talking by phone, they pay little attention to where they are or who is around them. Giving personal information over the phone is a risky behavior because there is the possibility of thieves eavesdropping.

It is noticeable that public awareness campaigns that demonstrate the connection between individual behavior and risk of identity theft may improve this form of victimization. Also, as a practical contribution for public policy makers, the findings of this study can be used to educate and motivate customers—of all ages—to appreciate the value of protective measures that should be taken to protect their identities from being stolen. This may need simultaneous attempts by individuals, businesses, customer groups and the government working together. This is because without customer awareness and knowledge of the steps that should be taken offline and online to prevent identity theft, any attempt to protect the privacy of personal identities and prevent identity theft will be ineffective and unsuccessful.

3.7 Conclusion

Although the prevalence and impact of identity-based crimes have grown significantly in the last decade, relatively less is known about how individuals can protect themselves from experiencing such an incident. This present study attempted to fill this gap by applying theoretical integration to investigate the extent to which risk behavior and protective behavior influence identity theft. For the first time this study covers offline as well as online identity theft victimization in research and considers many more predictors compared to what were considered in past studies. Also, contrary to previous studies, this research considers four types of identity theft as dependent variables to indicate much of what explains identity theft. This study proposed a new model for protective behavior concepts, as well as risk behavior concepts, to minimize the occurrence of identity theft for e-commerce customers. This process includes several ways to discover a subset of the total set of recorded parameters, showing good predictive capability. SEM was used to determine how 92 human risk and protective behaviors influence the occurrence of identity theft. The results indicated that offline risk and account monitoring are the most influential on identity theft prediction, and the best predictor.

Regarding the age of university students, the importance of increasing awareness is illustrated because adulthood is the time to experience new things and experiment with changes. Consequently, they have issues with the protection of their personal data and privacy within cyberspace. The outcomes of this study could enable authorities like policy makers to set up policies and rules to better influence users on prevention efforts.

References

Adam, M. E., Yousif, O., Al-Amodi, Y. & Ibrahim, J. 2011. Awareness of Social Engineering among IIUM Students, *World of Computer Science and Information Technology Journal*, 5, 121–130.

Albrecht, C., Albrecht, C. & Tzafrir, S. 2011. How to Protect and Minimize Consumer Risk to Identity Theft. *Journal of Financial Crime, 18*, 405–414.

Archer, N. 2011. Consumer Identity Theft Prevention and Identity Fraud Detection Behaviours. *Journal of Financial Crime, 19*, 20–36.

Bekhet, H. A. & Al-Alak, B. A. M. 2014. Modelling Client Usage of e-Statements: An Empirical Study in Malaysia. *International Journal of Banking, Accounting and Finance, 5*, 309–328.

Bernama. 2013. *Look Out For Cyber Cheats*. Bernama, August 15 2013.

Cattell, R. B. 1977. *Scientific use of factor analysis in behavioral and life sciences*.

Chamhuri, N. & Batt, P. J. 2013. Exploring the Factors Influencing Consumers' Choice of Retail Store When Purchasing Fresh Meat in Malaysia. *International Food and Agribusiness Management Review, 16*, 99–122.

Chu, B., Holt, T. J. & Ahn, G. J. 2010. *Examining the Creation, Distribution, and Function of Malware On Line*. Washington, DC: National Institute of Justice. Retrieved from www. ncjrs. gov. /pdffiles1 / nij/grants/230112. pdf.

Facts, Q. 2011. Malaysia Educational Statistics. (July 2011). Retrieved July 12, 2012. Ministry of Education.

Garg, V., Camp, L. J., Connelly, K. & Lorenzen-Huber, L. 2012. *Risk Communication Design: Video vs. Text*. Vigo, Spain: Privacy Enhancing Technologies/Springer, 279–298.

Gaskin, J. (2012), "Exploratory Factor Analysis," *Gaskination's Statistics*. http://youtube.com/ Gaskination.

Goi, C.-L. & Ng, P. 2011. Perception of young consumers on mobile phone applications in Malaysia. *World Applied Sciences Journal, 15*, 47–55.

Hair, J., Black, W. & Babin, B. 2010. *RE Anderson Multivariate Data Analysis: A Global Perspective*. Princeton, NJ: Pearson Prentice Hall.

Hazelah, A., Ismail, N. N. & Hashim, R. 2011. Identity Theft Awareness among City Dwellers in Malaysia. *Journal of Information Assurance & Cybersecurity, 11*, 1–9.

Higgins, G. E., Hughes, T., Ricketts, M. L. & Fell, B. D. 2010. Self-Protective Identity Theft Behaviors of College Students: An Exploration Using the Rasch Person-Item Map. *Southwest Journal of Criminal Justice, 7*, 24–46.

Holt, T. J. & Turner, M. G. 2012. Examining Risks and Protective Factors of On-Line Identity Theft. *Deviant Behavior, 33*, 308–323.

Holtfreter, K., Reisig, M. D., Pratt, T. C. & Holtfreter, R. E. 2015. Risky Remote Purchasing and Identity Theft Victimization among Older Internet Users. *Psychology, Crime & Law, 21*(7), 681–698.

Hoofnagle, C. 2007. Identity Theft: Making the Known Unknowns Known. *Harvard Journal of Law & Technology, 21*, 98–122.

Hu, X., Primack, B. A., Barnett, T. E. & Cook, R. L. 2011. College Students and Use of K2: an Emerging Drug of Abuse in Young Persons. *Substance Abuse Treatment, Prevention and Policy, 6*, 7–16.

Jakobsson, M. & Myers, S. 2006. *Phishing and Countermeasures: Understanding the Increasing Problem of Electronic Identity Theft*, Princeton, NJ: John Wiley & Son.

Kahn, C. M. & Roberds, W. 2008. Credit and Identity Theft. *Journal of Monetary Economics, 55*, 251–264.

Kaplan, D. & Depaoli, S. 2012. Bayesian Structural Equation Modeling. In: H. Hoyle (ed.), *Handbook of Structural Equation Modeling*. New York: Guilford Press.

Lewis, J. L. 2011a. *Exploring the Identity-Theft Prevention Efforts of Consumers in the United States*, United State: BiblioBazaa.

Lewis, J. L. 2011b. *Exploring the Identity-Theft Prevention Efforts of Consumers in the United States*. ProQuest LLC.

Lombardi, R. 2006. *Myths about Identity Theft Debunked by Experts*. IT World Canada

Loo, W., Yeow, P. H. & Chong, S. 2011. Acceptability of Multipurpose Smart National Identity Card: An Empirical Study. *Journal of Global Information Technology Management, 14*, 35–58.

Malhotra, N. K., Birks, D. F. & Wills, P. 2013. *Essentials of Marketing Research*. London: Prentice Hall.

Masa, R. 2009. *Innovations in Youth Saving and Asset Building around the World*. CSD Research Brief.

Mcmillan, J. H. & Schumacher, S. 2014. *Research in Education: Evidence-Based Inquiry*, Virginia: Pearson Higher Ed.

Messner, S. F. & Krohn, M. D. 1989. *Theoretical Integration in the Study of Deviance and Crime: Problems and Prospects*. SUNY Press.

Milne, G. R. 2005. How Well Do Consumers Protect Themselves From Identity Theft? *Journal of Consumer Affairs*, 37, 388–402.

Milne, G. R., Labrecque, L. I. & Cromer, C. 2009. Toward an Understanding of the Online Consumer's Risky Behavior and Protection Practices. *Journal of Consumer Affairs*, 43, 449–473.

Milne, G. R., Rohm, A. J. & Bahl, S. 2004. Consumers' Protection of Online Privacy and Identity. *Journal of Consumer Affairs*, 38, 217–232.

Mohamed, D. B. 2013. Combating the Threats of Cybercrimes in Malaysia: The Efforts, the Cyberlaws and the Traditional Laws. *Computer Law and Security Review: The International Journal of Technology and Practice*, 29, 66–76.

Norberg, P. A., Horne, D. R. & Horne, D. A. 2007. The Privacy Paradox: Personal Information Disclosure Intentions versus Behaviors. *Journal of Consumer Affairs*, 41, 100–126.

Pannah, E. 2011. *Cybersecurity in Electronic Commerce | Effect of Safeguarding Personal Data on Identity Theft*. University of Maryland University College.

Pedhazur, E. J. & Schmelkin, L. P. 2013. *Measurement, Design, and Analysis: An Integrated Approach*. Hillsdale, NJ: Psychology Press.

Pett, M. A., Lackey, N. R. & Sullivan, J. J. 2003. *Making Sense of Factor Analysis: The Use of Factor Analysis for Instrument Development in Health Care Research*, Thousand Oaks, CA: Sage.

Ramaswamy, V. M. 2006. Security Identity-Theft Toolkit. *CPA Journal*, 76, 101–167.

Raus, M. I. M., Tah, I. H. M. & Yahya, S. 2013. Personal Information Disclosure in Facebook: The Awareness of UiTM Pahang Students. *International Journal of Future Computer and Communication*, 2, 258–262.

Reyns, B. W. 2013. Online Routines and Identity Theft Victimization Further Expanding Routine Activity Theory beyond Direct-Contact Offenses. *Journal of Research in Crime and Delinquency*, 50, 216–238.

Reyns, B. W. & Henson, B. 2015. The Thief with a Thousand Faces and the Victim with None Identifying Determinants for Online Identity Theft Victimization With Routine Activity Theory. *International Journal of Offender Therapy and Comparative Criminology*, 60, 1119–1139. 0306624X15572861.

Reyns, B. W. & Randa, R. 2019. No Honor among Thieves: Personal and Peer Deviance as Explanations of Online Identity Fraud Victimization. *Security Journal*, 33, 228–243.

Samah, A. A., Ahmadian, M., Gill, S. S. & Hendijani, R. B. 2013. Residents' Attitude towards Educational Tourism in Malaysia. *Asian Social Science*, 9, 14–18.

Seda, L. 2014. Identity Theft and University Students: Do They Know, Do They Care? *Journal of Financial Crime*, 21, 461–483.

Shah, M. & Okeke, R. I. A Framework for Internal Identity Theft Prevention in Retail Industry. *2011 European Intelligence and Security Informatics Conference*, Athens. IEEE, 366–371.

Symantec. 2014. Symantec 2013 [Online]. Available: http://www.symantec.com/security_response/publications/threatreport.jsp#preview_2_column_1 10/20/2014].

Tanner JR, J. F., Hunt, J. B. & Eppright, D. R. 1991. The Protection Motivation Model: A Normative Model of Fear Appeals. *The Journal of Marketing*, 5, 36–45.

Thornberry, T. P. 1989. *Reflections on the advantages and disadvantages of theoretical integration. Theoretical integration in the study of deviance and crime: Problems and prospects*. New York: State University of New York Press, 51–60. ISBN: 978-0791400012.

Wang, W. J., Yuan, Y. & Archer, N. 2006. A Contextual Framework for Combating Identity Theft. *Security & Privacy, IEEE*, 4, 30–38.

Williams, B., Onsman, A. & Brown, T. 2010. Exploratory Factor Analysis: A Five-Step Guide for Novices. *Journal of Emergency Primary Health Care*, 8, 1–13.

Winterdyk, J. & Thompson, N. 2008. Student and Non-Student Perceptions and Awareness of Identity Theft. *Canadian Journal of Criminology and Criminal Justice, 50,* 153–186.

Xiangke, P., Ge, G., Yubo, F. & Mian, W. 2012. Stratified Cluster Sampling Under Multiplicative Model for Quantitative Sensitive Question Survey. *Interciencia, 37,* 833–837.

YenYuen, Y. & Yeow, P. H. 2009. *User Acceptance of Internet Banking Service in Malaysia. Web Information Systems and Technologies.* Berlin: Springer.

Zendehdel, M. & Paim, L. H. 2012. Perceived Risk of Security and Privacy in Online Shopping: A Study of Malaysia Context. *Life Science Journal, 9,* 983–987.

4

Organization Security Policies and Their After Effects

Premkumar Chithaluru and Ravi Prakash

University of Petroleum & Energy Studies, Dehradun, India

4.1 Introduction

Globally, billions of dollars are spent on security systems and human resources to protect an organization's properties, especially in the industrial sector. Over the years, the efficiency of the technologies has increased given that trillions of dollars are spent internationally on different forms of manufacturing, some essential and some not so important. But the fact remains that with a certain amount of production, business has a massive investment and there is a perceived need to secure certain properties. Nonetheless, most companies do not feel the need to invest in defense because it is not quantifiable and investment returns are practically zero (Aksulu and Wade 2010; Al-Mukahal and Alshare 2015; Albrechtsen 2007).

One of the factors in industry's apathy for defense (surprising as they are trying to protect their own assets) is the lack of a particular industry's typical asset protection activities. The requirements provide consistent procedures for a specified asset, and programs that are successful in defending the assets from unwanted interference (Alter 2008a).

Therefore, visualizing a set of standards to protect the properties is essential for protection managers (Alter 2008b). Different industries have different practices in the absence of guidelines but do not adopt a common practice that is best suited to the enterprise.

4.1.1 What Does Security Policy Mean?

A security policy is an organization's written document detailing how to defend the institution from threats (Alter 2013), like computer security risks, and how to handle situations as they arise.

A security policy has to recognize all the properties of an organization and all the potential threats to those assets. Employees of the business must be kept updated on the organization's security policies. The policy itself should also be periodically updated (Anderson and Agarwal 2010).

A security approach will set out the key things which should be verified inside an endeavor. This could incorporate the association's system, its physical form, amongst others. The potential dangers to these things should be recorded as well. If the document focused on cyber security, risks could include those from inside, such as the risk of disgruntled employees stealing important information or releasing an internal virus on the company's network (Angst et al. 2017); alternatively, a hacker from outside the company may enter the system and cause data loss, alter data, or steal information. In the end, there could be physical damage to computer systems.

When the risks are established, it is necessary to determine the likelihood that they will actually occur. A business also needs to determine how to prevent such risks. A few protections could be the implementation of certain workplace rules, as well as strong physical and network protection. There must also be a roadmap of what to do if a hazard really materializes (Aurigemma and Leonard 2015). The security policy should be distributed to everybody in the business, and the data protection process needs to be periodically checked and modified when new people come on board.

4.1.2 Why Do You Need a Security Policy?

Who is liable for the security of knowledge about an organization? Maybe the Evaluation and Analysis department? In the Management Information System (MIS), the responsibility for the protection of confidential information belongs not only to individual employees or departments (Backhouse et al. 2006; Bandara et al. 2015; Banerjee et al. 1998), but also to the agency itself. Ultimately, it is down to top administrators, who are answerable for ensuring the eventual benefits of the association, and for guaranteeing that a worthy and compelling security methodology is executed and set up as a regular occurrence.

Despite the fact that strategies don't take care of issues themselves, and can possibly convolute things unless they are plainly composed and actualized, the approach decides the objectives on which every single corporate activity ought to be based (Barlow et al. 2013). The security strategy applies essentially to straightforward, deliberate, and well-characterized arrangements, guidelines, and methods that oversee access to the arrangement of a system and the data contained inside. Security strategy policy reports and procedures as well as explicit representatives and their roles should all be included. It is likewise a persuasive message to the outside world about the organization's devotion to assurance.

4.1.3 How to Develop Policy

The discoveries of a hazard appraisal as characterized in Chapter 2 must be centered on a practical security strategy. Discoveries from a hazard appraisal offer arrangement creators an exact image of their association's explicit security needs (Basin et al. 2013). Such information is significant as it provides powerful details of arrangements to be requested from the leaders:

- Describe sensitive data and basic frameworks.
- Incorporate city, state and government legislation, just as a pertinent moral gauge. Identify internal insurance objectives and targets.
- Set a schedule for meeting objectives and goals.
- Ensure that procedures are set up to meet the goals and objectives.

Along these lines, it is critical to incorporate both lawful and administrative inquiries, operational highlights, contract necessities, ecological issues and client remarks into strategy improvement (Baskerville et al. 2014). Successful security techniques blend these and different variables into a basic arrangement of objectives and goals that guide laborers while they execute their undertakings.

In spite of the fact that settling corporate approaches is ordinarily a job reserved for top-level leaders, a venture-wide practice ought to be adding to the arrangement improvement. While every worker does not really need to join every security strategy arranging session, top-level directors ought to include in the data gathering process individuals from all activity levels and types (similarly to when conceptualizing during hazard assessment) (Baskerville and Siponen 2002). Non-regulatory staff have an exceptional understanding that is important when speaking with approach creators and that clearly cannot be replaced through some other procedure. Meeting consistently with laborers to find out about critical issues affecting their employment is a major advance towards accomplishing traction at all levels of the association.

While it is important get however much feedback from future clients as could reasonably be expected, it is likewise significant that points of view from outside the association are heard during the periods of approach improvement in the data gathering. Why? For what? Because leaders should know about security courses of action that are being created by different associations that might conceivably influence them and the methodologies that they will execute. As an example, if every school apart from one in a network adds encryption programming to verify correspondence sent over the Internet (Bauer and Van Eeten 2009), it will be extremely trying for the single school that does not have the encryption key to associate with its accomplices. The contention is that just as security arrangements should include an inner joint effort, they frequently need it remotely as well—a message that ought not to be overlooked, particularly by those associations that utilize site-based administration.

Hazard evaluation by an office encourages approach producers to focus on the particular security prerequisites of their program. However, paying little heed to those ends, the accompanying general issues in any security strategy ought to be addressed expressly and compactly (Ligatti et al. 2009):

- What is the clarification of the strategy?
- Who made this strategy?
- Who upheld the approach?
- Whose authenticity does the enactment support?
- What laws or guidelines are engaged, assuming any, un the strategy?
- Who will authorize this strategy?
- How will the procedure be actualized?
- What impacts the approach?
- What internal properties should be secured?
- What do customers truly need to do?
- How should vulnerabilities and infringement of insurance be accounted for?
- What are the arrangement's effect date and expiry date?

Policies should be designed in such a way as to make sense for their expected audience. After all, requirements which have not been followed foreshadow targets which will not be met (Bijlsma-Frankema and Cristina Costa 2010). Reader-friendly policy ideas include, for example:

- Be concise
- Focus on goals and implications, then clarify the basic reasoning where necessary

- Don't soften the message
- You are not asking but explaining, so do not recommend, imply or insinuate unless that is actually what you plan to do
- Use clear, descriptive words when practicable

4.1.4 How Can Policy Operation Be Made Truthful?

Apart from keeping rules straightforward, brief and instinctive, endeavors are being made to make them as simple as feasible for laborers to meet. Note, the point is not to tell the laborers "how it is" as much as to get everybody to help with the effort (Boss et al. 2009, 2015; Bulgurcu et al. 2010). Through making things as basic as conceivable it turns into a down to earth objective for workers to commit to. Explicit approaches which increase the odds of really actualizing your strategies in the work environment include:

- Clearly delegate security obligations to a motivated and dedicated director: one who will view insurance as a necessity. It is important that such staff must be permitted to praise and censure laborers at all levels of the hierarchy (Burns et al. 2017).
- Conduct workforce readiness training closely matching the security procedure criteria and staff needs: recognize that most users have never been instructed to utilize PCs appropriately—and understand what little experience they have. Really attempt to comprehend their interests and tell them the best way to turn their gadgets on. We may have learned, all things considered, how to utilize a solitary bit of programming for a specific application. Along these lines, the majority of the workers have little information on security issues and there is no reason to anticipate that that should improve unless the association is making a valiant effort to address the circumstances. The security organizations are not running with sufficient staff to make wellbeing of the executives a component of the workplace, which makes the remainder of the activity a vital exercise—and this rationale will not shield a program from very down-to-earth threats (Burton-Jones et al. 2015).
- Communicate corporate needs and desires to representatives: make a genuine attempt to get the message out to laborers, yet do not be too severe about it. As in any showcasing effort, purchaser receptivity should reward development and consistency (Cairney 2013). As compelling techniques for communicating security norms to laborers, the accompanying proposals are suggested:

  - Hold booster classes for security.
  - Develop a work environment support foundation (e.g., a Support Desk with qualified and promptly accessible advisors).
  - Frequently and freely recognize excellent conduct.
  - Create and appropriate reference materials (for example, agendas, leaflets, and rundowns—remember that succinct and accessible material is more important than unedited technical material when it comes to security).
  - Review the course reading for laborers to ensure it includes security methodology.
  - Hold security records accessible throughout the workplace (for example signs, FYI notes and email transmissions).

Equally enforce wellbeing guidelines at all levels of the association: every worker in the program will perceive that they are legitimately liable for security. Managers need to state "go with the plan," trust it, and demonstrate it themselves. The organization's standards make a difference to all (Chan et al. 2005). The organization's security is not only a moral good—at this point the structure should be protected from start to finish by the plan!

4.1.5 Personnel Issues

One of the goals of a good security policy is to reduce the need for confidence in the system. While this may seem like an overly pessimistic concept, it genuinely serves to protect both the workers of the company as well as the enterprise itself. But before the security benefits can be achieved, workers need to be properly informed regarding their positions, duties and organizational expectations (Chatterjee et al. 2015).
Workers' needs should be communicated and recorded as a hard copy:

- What utilization of apparatus is and is not working?
- What will be the arrangements for infringement of the guidelines?
- Workers should be informed that it is critical to follow their procedures.

Security will be checked through audits. (Clients who do their part ought to be praised, while those individuals who are lingering behind might be censured or retrained.)
Workers ought to be reminded that:

- Organizational administrations, similar to gadgets, have a place within an association.
- Privacy necessities for data stored on or traded with the association's gear ought not to be required.

Workers ought to be required to consent to a security arrangement so that they are aware of their commitments and to guarantee familiarity with the assurance strategy (Chen et al. 2012). This requires:

- Workers having a chance to peruse and examine the strategies and guidelines they must follow.
- A suitable stage for explaining questions or worries about the principles of the association to be given to all representatives.
- Until an archive has been created and stored in a protected area, laborers ought not to be permitted access to the framework.

Every single new representative ought to be relied upon to meet the association's security prerequisites and strategies. When recruited, new employees should be taught and educated on safety policies as part of their formal orientation to impress upon them the value of protection.

4.1.6 Security Policy of Outsiders

Outsiders (for example, upkeep laborers, providers, and crisis help) and those from different offices (e.g., government elements, other instructive foundations, and contractual workers) with connections to your system should likewise consent to arrangements permitting them to acknowledge and hold the information private. Be that as it may, be mindful not to impart more to outsiders about your security activity than is required (Chen et al. 2015). Indeed, even apparently innocuous admonitions about what to foresee from your barrier will give an edge to an expert programmer in misusing your gadget. Then again, confine security briefs to those required to adhere to them to avoid violation of your security:

- Reassure them that you will be concerned about protecting your device properties.
- Make sure they treat your assets safely.

4.2 Background

Although manpower plays an important role in the overall security scenario, it is difficult in today's world to imagine a circumstance in which manpower-aided infrastructure is not deemed collateral for any successful safety (Chen and Mariam Zahedi 2016). Difficult technologies cannot fully replace manpower; since both have their fundamental flaws and also strengths, it is vital to have a proper mix of technology and manpower.

This chapter attempts to portray the technology available, both important technology as well as that which is specialized for a particular industry. Although certain technical inputs are important, the option of advanced equipment depends on the understanding of the hazard, the form of product being generated and the importance of the commodity being created. Much also depends on the management's propensity to invest in protection, particularly as one visualizes that there is no return on investment in security and returns cannot be quantified. The equipment listed here covers a wide range of products and their needs emerge in terms of the type of product or industry that one retains in terms of its criticality (Cheng et al. 2013).

4.2.1 Types of Information Security Policies

Management needs to define three kinds of information security policies to create a complete information security policy (Swanson and Guttman 1996).

   I. Enterprise Information Security Policy (EISP)

  II. Issue-specific security policies (ISSP)

 III. Systems-specific security policies (SysSP)

     I. **Enterprise information security policy (EISP)**

     An organizational information security strategy lays out the strategic direction, reach and language for the security initiative of the company, and provides responsibility for various information management fields. The EISP offers guidance for the information security program's creation, deployment and management prerequisites.

    II. **Issue-specific security policies (ISSP)**

     Issue-specific policies include detailed instructions and clarification on the use of a tool, such as a procedure or equipment used by the company, to all members of the organization. The ISSP of each organization will address specific technology-based systems, which often need to be modified.

III. **System-specific security policies (SysSP)**

Specific security measures for the device do not match such regulation styles. These can often be designed to act as specifications or protocols that can be used to install or manage processes such as configuring a network firewall and running it. The specific security practices of the networks can be classified into two groups:

- **Management guidelines SysSP:** A management guidance manual SysSP is developed for management and provides advice on the deployment and integration of technologies as well as a summary of the reasonable behavior that persons in the enterprise will follow in order to promote information security (Choudhury and Sabherwal 2003).

- **SysSP technical specifications:** The management policy is formulated in collaboration with the boss and the system administrator; the system administrator may need to develop a different kind of management policy (Chu et al. 2015). For example, if the ISSP might allow user passwords to be updated on a quarterly basis, system administrators might put a technological control inside a particular system request to impose this policy.

4.2.2 Development of Information Security Policy

The implementation of information security policies consists of a two-part project: the policy is designed and implemented in the first phase, and the compliance mechanisms are generated in the second part in order to ensure that the policy is consistently used within the organization. Projects for policy development should be well prepared and supported, properly organized, and completed on time and within budget (Chu et al. 2018). The Security Systems Design Life Cycle (SecSDLC) can be used to direct the policy development programs.

Exploration stage: The policy development team should: seek senior management (CIO) assistance in this process.

- If the project gets senior management sponsorship, it has a better chance of success.
- The more the top management participates, the quicker it will be to execute.
- Represent the project policy objectives well.
- Involve the same persons who will be impacted by the proposed policies.
- The committee should be made up of the legal department, human resources department and end-user members.
- Obtain a project manager capable of leading the project from start to finish.

Analyzing stage: The following tasks should be included in this phase:

- Undertaking a fresh or latest risk assessment or IT audit documenting the organization's current information security needs.
- Selection of main resources of information and existing policies.

Design stage: This step should include a strategy for how to execute the policy and how to validate delivery. Organization leaders shall accept and read the regulations.

Implementation stage: The policy development department is drafting the regulations during this process. The department will ensure the regulations are enforceable as written documents, and that they are published, interpreted, and accepted by those to whom they refer.

Maintenance stage: In this process, the policy development team manages and updates policy if needed to ensure that it stays successful. The program should be linked to a framework through which problems associated with it can be freely recorded. It should be checked regularly, too.

4.2.3 Approaches to the Implementation of Information Security Policy

There are two ways to achieve the application of an information security policy: the top-down strategy and the bottom-up approach (Chua et al. 2012).

The bottom-up strategy is implemented by executives and technicians. The system administrators are trying to enhance their applications in this strategy. Systems and network engineers provide extensive expertise that can greatly improve the security of information in the enterprise.

We know the risks that can be dangerous to their processes, and we know what measures and strategies are required to secure their technologies. This strategy is rarely successful as preparation is not organized by the top management, such as collaboration between agencies and the creation of an appropriate budget.

There is structured coordination in the top-down strategy, which starts from top management, and a dedicated leader that provides funding and recommends the mechanism for execution. Top management has adequate money, provides guidance and creates strategies, protocols and processes.

4.2.4 Policies, Standards and Practices

Policies are a set of rules that set out permissible and unacceptable conduct within an organization (Cram et al. 2016b). Policies guide how to allow use of the technology. The information security strategy consists of high-level comments relating to information privacy throughout the company and it should be produced by the senior management. The legislation outlines the roles and responsibilities of the police, and the type of information that needs defense. We should not state exactly which program or machinery is operating properly. In other documentation called standards, procedures, guidelines and practices this type of information should be stated.

Requirements are detailed statements about what needs to be done to abide with the policies. Standards endorse and promote the development of a cyber-security strategy. These promote making sure of the organization's compliance integrity. The guidelines usually describe the security controls involved with introducing particular technology, hardware, or applications.

- Procedures, processes and protocols define how the directives will be followed by workers.
- Preferred measures enforcing expectations are the guidance. Guidelines should be seen, according to Cram et al. (Cram et al. 2016a), as best practices which are highly recommended. For example, a requirement may allow passwords to be ten characters, and a supporting recommendation could clarify that making sure the password expires after 30 days is also best practice.
- Instructions are step-by-step guidance for regulation, protocols and procedures execution. For example, a protocol can specify how to install Windows securely by providing detailed steps to be taken to protect the operating system, so that the procedure, requirements and instructions involved are followed.

4.2.5 Governance of Information Security

In order to satisfy Cronan and Douglas (Cronan and Douglas 2006), cyber-security regulation is characterized as a series of actions on how computer protection can be handled at the management level. Information security, which includes maintaining the secrecy, credibility and quality of corporate data, helps to reduce the numerous threats that may be detrimental to business information by implementing appropriate security measures. There are various security standards and protocols that need to be addressed in order for organizations to adopt an appropriate set of controls to handle information security effectively. Such safety requirements and recommendations come from both internal and external channels within an enterprise.

In order to properly handle information security, it is important to address all internal and external security requirements, and to prevent possible effects of any weakness in information security. Such security requirements include IT system specifications, civil, administrative, and contractual requirements, as well as knowledge protection, privacy, and quality requirements as understood by the company. Together with guidelines on agreed safety standards, such as BS 7799 and other best practices, these requirements provide the foundation for an effective approach to information security (Crossler and Bélanger 2009; Crossler et al. 2013, 2014).

With respect to formal criteria and protocols, information security policies and best practices are important since they have helped to promote the ideals of global information protection and to help develop partnerships between organizations and their stakeholders. BS 7799 is an example of such a norm that provides guidance on how organizations should manage information security, by providing information security advice focused on ten broad categories of security control. The norm is seen as a starting point for organizations to focus on an effective strategy for information security. Governments around the world have decided to create various regulatory and procedural standards with a view to inspiring, promoting and strengthening efforts to secure private records. There are different kinds of legal requirements which should be fulfilled by organizations. These include different specific fields and also country-specific laws and statutes (Culnan and Williams 2009).

With respect to internal specifications, IT architecture concerns relevant to information security help to define criteria to protect the critical infrastructure that makes up the information support. Company information issues related to information security help identify certain criteria essential to safeguarding the secrecy, credibility, and availability of critical company information data. Such issues are resolved through a risk assessment that aims to recognize and evaluate various risks. First, a risk management procedure is carried out, in which appropriate security measures are identified and enforced with the goal of minimizing these possible risks (Cuppens et al. 2013).

There are two essential approaches of information technology governance that help to achieve a successful corporate governance approach for resolving the business information danger. Next, there is a side of governance that requires executive and committee leadership. We are required to set the course and policy for the information security, overseeing their organization's information security activities. Through coordinating the information security activities of an organization, the CEO and the board will adopt a corporate information security strategy that reflects their dedication to information security and promotes the organizational purpose, goals and strategies for information security. When monitoring the information security activities of a company, executive management and the board must have periodic reports from multiple administrators in corporate organizations to closely analyze and evaluate their procedures and practices so that they can be reviewed against rules or laws and strengthened if appropriate. First, there is the operations aspect that concerns how an organization's protection policy will be handled and executed. It is how numerous department heads and other administrators are dedicated to enforcing the organizational information security strategy with the aid of traditional procedure codes. An outline of the Code of Practice is BS 7799, which includes appropriate security safeguards that can safeguard the secrecy, credibility, and quality of company information and advice, and incorporate information security into the day-to-day operations and functions of the organization (D'Arcy and Devaraj 2012).

ISO 27001 certification gives the existing information security system extra security, without altering the structure of information security processes. ISO 27001 respects transparency, quality and honesty as fundamental principles in its specifications. The implementation of ISO 27001 requirements can be of great help to organizations; it can promote the development of a robust structure that provides the organization and the knowledge assets with protection. The ISO 27001 standard can help in the assessment, implementation and maintenance of a cyber-security human resources system (D'Arcy and Greene 2014).

In fact, a new standard costs a lot of time to introduce. Yet obtaining ISO 27001 certification for organizations would help to reduce the money spent on IT security operations, as well as helping to improve compliance procedures, while minimizing or even eliminating reliance on third-party providers. Therefore, if its members recognize the need for a cyber-security control system, companies will maximize the benefits.

It can also be very useful to look for ISO 27001 certificates for organizations because it can help top management improve the way they comply with information security within the organization. The framework includes criteria of processes and procedures to be implemented by the administration to ensure effective management of the information system.

4.3 Success Factors of Security Policies in Organizations

The implementation of an information security policy may not only render the company safer or minimize the risks of an inappropriate use of any knowledge tools of the organization. There are some variables that must be monitored, which direct the successful implementation of an information security policy (D'Arcy and Herath 2011). There are numerous critical factors which play an important role in improving organizational information security. Some considerations that are required include knowledge and preparation, resources for management, strategy, implementation of information security policies and organizational purpose. Those factors are further described below.

4.3.1 Awareness and Training

It is easy to achieve information security in organizations by raising awareness and providing training to all employees. Safety preparation and understanding are the knowledge and instructions given to all members of the organization to promote their effective execution of their duties (D'Arcy et al. 2014).

Training, according to D'Arcy and Hovav (D'Arcy and Hovav 2007), is to teach users what they should or should not do, and also how to do it. Safety consciousness relates to a situation where all workers in a company are conscious of their safety priorities and purpose, or are active in it.

Safety knowledge allows staff to become aware of potential threats that endanger the security of the organization's information, how those threats can arise, and how to manage information safely from the company.

Most organizations tackle most compliance issues that arise from their own workers (the mistakes of the employees). This is regarded as dangerous insider danger. The safety training has to be adapted to the needs of the users (D'Arcy et al. 2009).

Based on the technical context, the instructions for consumers can be tailored according to Siponen and Vance (Siponen and Vance 2010). This approach involves general user preparation, administrative user training and professional user training.

Registered consumer awareness: The only way to ensure the registered users read and understand the rules is through instruction on those policies. Such a course allows users to ask questions, and they can get feedback as well. Such general consumers also get guidance on how they can safely conduct their tasks, such as good security habits and password protection.

Management user training: Managers need a more intimate type of training, in small groups and with more engagement and conversation.

Professional consumer training: This is professional instruction for IT workers, which ensures the preparation can include the recruiting of a contractor or outside training organizations.

4.3.2 Management Support

Business assistance plays a key role in the successful execution of cyber security. In many organizations, though, the need for encryption is evoked by the IT manager or the person in charge of cyber security.

Senior management is often of the belief that everything relating to information security is the duty of the IT departments. That is because of the senior management.

Senior management has to be persuaded to recognize the importance of cyber security in companies, so they will provide an appropriate budget to try to enforce the cyber-security policies. Executive involvement is very necessary because if the top management truly recognizes the organization's need for information security, attempts will be taken to implement it and more personnel will be engaged.

4.3.3 Budget

The budget is also essential because enforcing cyber security in companies requires adequate budget to ensure effective security of information. According to Bjorck, the budget can be described as a financial facility capable of calculating costs and assessing access to the resources needed to ensure the successful implementation of information security. A proposal can include technological expenses and the cost of education. Maintenance expenses include all the resources necessary to ensure the protection of devices, for example, antivirus that defends against malware, cyber threats, and firewalls to secure network connections. For starters, the security expense includes all the funds used to plan the protection curriculum for the workers. Protection awareness can include hiring an outside professional or teaching agency.

4.3.4 Information Security Policy Enforcement

The cyber-security strategy helps with defining important assets of the company. It also helps companies deliver a good result. It is crucial that the proposal is descriptive, simple to understand and consistent. Policies often need to be checked and revised.

According to Madigan, in order to enforce the rules of organizations, it is necessary to ensure that all workers recognize the regulations, to check if the policies are being followed, and to have some clear procedures for coping with events in the case of policy violations. Canavan makes clear that cyber-security policies can only be implemented through the deliberate execution process. When a company decides to implement an information security program, it needs workers to follow the rules and be aware of their actions and obligations.

4.3.5 Organizational Mission

Setting goals and objectives is essential for each organization because it will help to begin implementing cyber security. According to McKay, if the aims and priorities of the organization are not met, the company would tend to have problems securing the details, so personnel will not be interested and will not follow guidelines in the cyber-security policies.

4.4 Case Studies of Security Policies in Organizations

The study found that the community has a strategy on cyber security that lets the company handle cyber security effectively. The local government recognizes that a cyber-security strategy is an essential tool that organizations should have in order to manage a good information protection execution.

One of the questioners stated: "We treat a lot of sensitive details regarding people in the public sector that we need to ensure safe handling." During an awareness session, the cyber-security strategy is introduced and demonstrated to the senior management and chief executives of each group. After the workshop, it is the duty of each leader of each division to coordinate and disseminate all information relating to the information security policies to end users within each group.

CASE STUDY 1

The town has one method of information security that helps to protect information in particular. One person interviewed explained: "We only have one data safety policy which generally covers information. They support the same level of protection no matter the type of cyber threat.

"The municipality's information security policy document is accessible, ensuring that workers may memorize sections of the regulation. Some of the questioners clarified that our organization's information security policy is written for everyone to understand and obey the spirit of the policy. It is also put on a very simple, internal (intranet) and external (website) location on the net."

CASE STUDY 2

The security manager with the help of the IT department is the person responsible for creating the information security policy. For their research, the municipality uses ISO 27001 and ISO 27002 standards as guidelines. Through beginning from top management and ending with the end users, the company gives a lot of priority to its information security policy. Some of the questioners stated: "The top management of our company recognizes the need, the importance of providing a cyber-security policy, supports and implements the ongoing process of its enforcement."

The impression of top management on introducing a cyber-security policy is that: "It's a process that requires to [be] execute[d] in such a broad workforce," some of the interviewees added. Thus the municipality's top management recognizes the need for confidentiality of records.

The information security strategy is the core of the manuals directed at the company. The organizations should have a framework and processes within which the policy will operate, and how they are created should be taken into consideration by company. Which processes should be called policy? For example, each company is liable for organizational policy (which presumably often involves other than information-related compliance), security policy (which deals with security issues), and information security policy. The essential thing is that the management will show its expectations regarding security of knowledge. The technical support offered by the Swedish Civil Contingencies Agency covers cyber security only and there are also guidelines about what should be shown in cyber-security policies.

The legislation should not include any specific rules of behavior without communicating the expectations of the leadership and should, therefore, structure the other articles of incorporation. A strategy should be concise and available to all. For starters, more details and descriptions can be shared on the internal site. The strategy reflects the general purpose of the administration. Once it comes to cyber-security policies, where it relates to all security work, it can be named as an information security policy or security policy. The strategy should be formulated at an earlier stage, at or before the same period as the operations decide the security and safety processes. Identifying all existing policy records is important in order to know what information you need to operate with. This gives some idea of the work needed for preparing the necessary regulatory documentation and bringing order to policy statements. The working group can then revise and compose policy documents in the sequence that suits the organization's information security requirements. In addition, the first approach is to control the defense of the most sensitive information in those fields where the threats are highest.

A cyber-security strategy should include:

- The goals of administrators, including why information security is essential.
- A clear explanation of how these goals will be met.
- A short description of responsibilities.
- Details of internal information security.
- An explanation of key concepts.
- Who is accountable for the strategy and how it is checked and updated.

The administration should be actively involved in policy making. After all, it is the administration who sends out the communication and it is essential that they accept responsibility for the program. Nonetheless, is it the person responsible for information security or the members of Local Implementing Structures (LIS) committees who is accountable for policy development? Although the manual is held by the administration, information security professionals will develop the information security strategy so that it fits the cyber-security job intentions. Once the policy has been implemented, the company will coordinate protection awareness and information sharing to educate all staff regarding policy and how essential it is for the regulation organization.

Those who would formulate regulations, and above all other governing documents, must be familiar with the process of creating and forming regulatory structures within the company. Many organizations have some kind of formalized structure with such a specified hierarchy of policy documents, internal planning and referrals and standardized models for how policy documents will look. Legal experience of the company should be included in the elaboration of documents. Definitions of information security strategies can be contained in the supporting documents for the technique.

Organizations need to secure the details about the company in a way that fits their corporation. We need to reach business goals, and to have trust in them for clients, customers, investors, the public and staff. We also actively work with details so that all of their knowledge is always secure, reliable and available. They have chosen a common and structured way of working with information based on Swedish and international (LIS Information Security Management) standards. The companies get the correct level of information protection with the help of LIS, while their workers get assistance in their daily work.

Information security work should be continuous and long-term, covering all aspects of their business and all the information assets they own or manage. People should be provided with regular instruction to learn how the management of knowledge operates. Everyone has a duty in the role of defense. Anyone who finds information security vulnerabilities will pay attention to their boss or security function. Staff must also disclose incidents that could pose damage to our knowledge properties.

Confidentiality regarding the details is an organizational obligation. Definitions (based on "Terminology Details," SIS HB550 Issue 3, SIS publishing):

- Data Resources are doing anything that includes information and carries knowledge.
- The protection of information relating to properties, the ability to maintain the requisite confidentiality, honesty and transparency are all facets of information security.
- Each unauthorized person may not view or reveal confidential information. The content of an access to information, but sometimes also the secret of the existence of assets.
- Accurate information ensures the records cannot be changed by authorization; not by mistake and not by failure.
- Available information helps authorized users to use information if required and as much as appropriate.
- The Information Security Management System (ISMS) is a mechanism that aids organizations in developing, enforcing, running, tracking, evaluating, sustaining and enhancing the organization's optimal information security standard.

The head of security checks and updates the information security strategy each year. You can get a guide to dealing with the laws and guidance in the right way. Guides may also be published in places where legislation or instructions are not in force. Descriptions of the method and directions show in detail how the work should be done. For example, these protocols can determine how and when to create copies, or how to track and manage event logs.

4.4.1 Organizational Objectives and Goals as Derived from the Case Studies

Many companies do not pay attention to information security until something goes wrong, but when a data breach arises, they pay attention immediately, and a lot of effort is taken to rebound from it. When organizations do not recognize the need for information security, they cannot establish goals and objectives.

Siponen states that companies need to set goals and objectives in order to make information security an effective operation. They decide what they want to do for the community, and describe what they want to accomplish by setting goals and objectives. For the area county council, this is the same; they decide what they want to do, what they want to do and make their information security stronger. They appreciate the need for information security for those two organizations: they handle a lot of sensitive information which needs to be protected. Their goals and objectives are to ensure that their organizations successfully enforce information security and an information security strategy. They aim to protect their information by coordinating technology knowledge and preparation to provide all their staff with details about information security and information security policies.

4.5 Conclusion

This chapter deals with performance factors related to the organization's introduction of information security with an emphasis on the role of top management in enforcing an information security strategy in organizations. The impact of any loopholes in the organizational security has been discussed in a qualitative manner.

References

Aksulu, Altay, and Michael R. Wade. 2010. "A comprehensive review and synthesis of open source research." *Journal of the Association for Information Systems* 11(1): 6.

Al-Mukahal, Hasan M. and Khaled Alshare. 2015. "An examination of factors that influence the number of information security policy violations in Qatari organizations." *Information & Computer Security*.

Albrechtsen, Eirik. 2007. "A qualitative study of users' view on information security." *Computers & Security* 26(4): 276–289.

Alter, Steven. 2008a. "Defining information systems as work systems: implications for the IS field." *European Journal of Information Systems* 17(5): 448–469.

Alter, Steven. 2008b. "Service system fundamentals: Work system, value chain, and life cycle." *IBM Systems Journal* 47(1): 71–85.

Alter, Steven. 2013. "Work system theory: overview of core concepts, extensions, and challenges for the future." *Journal of the Association for Information Systems 72.*

Anderson, Catherine L. and Ritu Agarwal. 2010. "Practicing safe computing: a multimedia empirical examination of home computer user security behavioral intentions." *MIS Quarterly 34*(3): 613–643.

Angst, Corey M., Emily S. Block, John D'Arcy, and Ken Kelley. 2017. "When do IT security investments matter? Accounting for the influence of institutional factors in the context of healthcare data breaches." *MIS Quarterly 41*(3): 893–916.

Aurigemma, Salvatore and Lori Leonard. 2015. "The influence of employee affective organizational commitment on security policy attitudes and compliance intentions." *Journal of Information System Security 11*(3).

Backhouse, James, Carol W. Hsu, and Leiser Silva. 2006. "Circuits of power in creating de jure standards: shaping an international information systems security standard." *MIS Quarterly* 413–438.

Bandara, Wasana, Elfi Furtmueller, Elena Gorbacheva, Suraya Miskon, and Jenine Beekhuyzen. 2015. "Achieving rigor in literature reviews: Insights from qualitative data analysis and tool-support." *Communications of the Association for Information Systems 37*.

Banerjee, Debasish, Timothy Paul Cronan, and Thomas W. Jones. 1998. "Modeling IT ethics: A study in situational ethics." *MIS Quarterly* 31–60.

Barlow, Jordan B., Merrill Warkentin, Dustin Ormond, and Alan R. Dennis. 2013. "Don't make excuses! Discouraging neutralization to reduce IT policy violation." *Computers & Security 39*: 145–159.

Basin, David, Vincent Jugé, Felix Klaedtke, and Eugen Zălinescu. 2013. "Enforceable security policies revisited." *ACM Transactions on Information and System Security (TISSEC) 16*(1): 1–26.

Baskerville, R., Spagnoletti, P. and Kim, J. 2014. "Incident-centered information security: Managing a strategic balance between prevention and response." *Information & Management, 51*(1): 138–151.

Baskerville, Richard and Mikko Siponen. 2002. "An information security meta-policy for emergent organizations." *Logistics Information Management.*

Bauer, Johannes M. and Michel JG Van Eeten. 2009. "Cybersecurity: Stakeholder incentives, externalities, and policy options." *Telecommunications Policy 33*(10–11): 706–719.

Bijlsma-Frankema, Katinka M. and Ana Cristina Costa. 2010. "Consequences and antecedents of managerial and employee legitimacy interpretations of control: a natural, open system approach." *Organizational Control* 396–434.

Boss, Scott, Dennis Galletta, Paul Benjamin Lowry, Gregory D. Moody, and Peter Polak. 2015. "What do systems users have to fear? Using fear appeals to engender threats and fear that motivate protective security behaviors." *MIS Quarterly (MISQ) 39*(4): 837–864.

Boss, Scott R., Laurie J. Kirsch, Ingo Angermeier, Raymond A. Shingler, and R. Wayne Boss. 2009. "If someone is watching, I'll do what I'm asked: Mandatoriness, control, and information security." *European Journal of Information Systems 18*(2): 151–164.

Bulgurcu, Burcu, Hasan Cavusoglu, and Izak Benbasat. 2010. "Information security policy compliance: an empirical study of rationality-based beliefs and information security awareness." *MIS Quarterly 34*(3): 523–548.

Burns, A. J., Clay Posey, Tom L. Roberts, and Paul Benjamin Lowry. 2017. "Examining the relationship of organizational insiders' psychological capital with information security threat and coping appraisals." *Computers in Human Behavior 68*: 190–209.

Burton-Jones, Andrew, Ephraim R. McLean, and Emmanuel Monod. 2015. "Theoretical perspectives in IS research: from variance and process to conceptual latitude and conceptual fit." *European Journal of Information Systems 24*(6): 664–679.

Cairney, Paul. 2013. "Standing on the shoulders of giants: how do we combine the insights of multiple theories in public policy studies?" *Policy Studies Journal 41*(1): 1–21.

Chan, Mark, Irene Woon, and Atreyi Kankanhalli. 2005. "Perceptions of information security in the workplace: linking information security climate to compliant behavior." *Journal of Information Privacy and Security 1*(3): 18–41.

Chatterjee, Sutirtha, Suprateek Sarker, and Joseph S. Valacich. 2015. "The behavioral roots of information systems security: Exploring key factors related to unethical IT use." *Journal of Management Information Systems* 31(4): 49–87.

Chen, Yan, K. Ramamurthy, and Kuang-Wei Wen. 2012. "Organizations' information security policy compliance: Stick or carrot approach?" *Journal of Management Information Systems* 29(3): 157–188.

Chen, Y. A. N., K. R. A. M. Ramamurthy, and Kuang-Wei Wen. 2015. "Impacts of comprehensive information security programs on information security culture." *Journal of Computer Information Systems* 55(3): 11–19.

Chen, Yan and Fatemeh Mariam Zahedi. 2016. "Individuals' internet security perceptions and behaviors: polycontextual contrasts between the United States and China." *MIS Quarterly* 40(1).

Cheng, Lijiao, Ying Li, Wenli Li, Eric Holm, and Qingguo Zhai. 2013. "Understanding the violation of IS security policy in organizations: An integrated model based on social control and deterrence theory." *Computers & Security* 39: 447–459.

Choudhury, Vivek and Rajiv Sabherwal. 2003. "Portfolios of control in outsourced software development projects." *Information Systems Research* 14(3): 291–314.

Chu, Amanda MY, Patrick YK Chau, and Mike KP So. 2015. "Developing a Typological Theory Using a Quantitative Approach: A Case of Information Security Deviant Behavior." *CAIS* 37: 25.

Chu, Amanda MY, Mike KP So, and Ray SW Chung. 2018. "Applying the randomized response technique in business ethics research: The misuse of information systems resources in the workplace." *Journal of Business Ethics* 151(1): 195–212.

Chua, Cecil Eng Huang, Wee-Kiat Lim, Christina Soh, and Siew Kien Sia. 2012. "Enacting clan control in complex IT projects: A social capital perspective." *MIS Quarterly* 577–600.

Cram, W. Alec, M. Kathryn Brohman, and R. Brent Gallupe. 2016a. "Hitting a moving target: a process model of information systems control change." *Information Systems Journal* 26(3): 195-226.

Cram, W. Alec, Kathryn Brohman, and R. Brent Gallupe. 2016b. "Information systems control: A review and framework for emerging information systems processes." *Journal of the Association for Information Systems* 17(4): 2.

Cronan, Timothy Paul, and David E. Douglas. 2006. "Toward a comprehensive ethical behavior model for information technology." *Journal of Organizational and End User Computing* 18(1): I.

Crossler, Robert E., and France Bélanger. 2009. "The Effects of Security Education Training and Awareness Programs and Individual Characteristics on End User Security Tool Usage." *Journal of Information System Security* 5(3).

Crossler, Robert E., Allen C. Johnston, Paul Benjamin Lowry, Qing Hu, Merrill Warkentin, and Richard Baskerville. 2013. "Future directions for behavioral information security research." *Computers & Security* 32: 90–101.

Crossler, Robert E., James H. Long, Tina M. Loraas, and Brad S. Trinkle. 2014. "Understanding compliance with bring your own device policies utilizing protection motivation theory: Bridging the intention-behavior gap." *Journal of Information Systems* 28(1): 209–226.

Culnan, Mary J. and Cynthia Clark Williams. 2009. "How ethics can enhance organizational privacy: lessons from the Choicepoint and TJX data breaches." *MIS Quarterly* 673–687.

Cuppens, Frédéric, Nora Cuppens-Boulahia, and Yehia Elrakaiby. 2013. "Formal specification and management of security policies with collective group obligations." *Journal of Computer Security* 21(1): 149–190.

D'Arcy, John and Sarv Devaraj. 2012. "Employee misuse of information technology resources: Testing a contemporary deterrence model." *Decision Sciences* 43(6): 1091–1124.

D'Arcy, John, and Gwen Greene. 2014. "Security culture and the employment relationship as drivers of employees' security compliance." *Information Management & Computer Security*.

D'Arcy, John and Tejaswini Herath. 2011. "A review and analysis of deterrence theory in the IS security literature: making sense of the disparate findings." *European Journal of Information Systems* 20(6): 643–658.

D'Arcy, John, Tejaswini Herath, and Mindy K. Shoss. 2014. "Understanding employee responses to stressful information security requirements: A coping perspective." *Journal of Management Information Systems* 31(2): 285–318.

D'Arcy, John and Anat Hovav. 2007. "Deterring internal information systems misuse." *Communications of the ACM* 50(10): 113–117.

D'Arcy, John, Anat Hovav, and Dennis Galletta. 2009. "User awareness of security countermeasures and its impact on information systems misuse: A deterrence approach." *Information Systems Research* 20(1): 79-98.

Ligatti, Jay, Lujo Bauer, and David Walker. 2009. "Run-time enforcement of no safety policies." *ACM Transactions on Information and System Security (TISSEC)* 12(3): 1–41.

Monfelt, Y., Pilemalm, S., Hallberg, J., and Yngström, L. 2011. The 14-layered framework for including social and organizational aspects in security management. *Information Management & Computer Security*

Siponen, Mikko, and Anthony Vance. 2010. "Neutralization: new insights into the problem of employee information systems security policy violations." *MIS Quarterly* 487–502.

Swanson, M., and B. Guttman. 1996. Generally accepted principles and practices for securing information technology systems. National Institute of Standards and Technology, Technology Administration, US Department of Commerce.

Wong, C. 2011. Clifford R. Shaw and Henry D. McKay: The Social Disorganization Theory.

5

Cyber-Attacks and Their Impact on Real Life: What Are Real-Life Cyber-Attacks, How Do They Affect Real Life and What Should We Do About Them?

Premkumar Chithaluru, Rohit Tanwar, and Sunil Kumar

University of Petroleum & Energy Studies, Dehradun, India

5.1 Introduction

Due to the rapid growth and widespread use of IT, cyberspace has become an integral part of states, cultures and individual lives. Cyberspace has already posed a growing number of possible risks and difficulties alongside its leisure opportunities. To seek superiority in cyberspace, cyberspace policies and strategies have been formulated by most ICT (Information and Communication Technology) developed nations. In order to comprehend cyberspace, we must utilize the layered pattern as follows:

1. The physical framework and infrastructure that constitute the cyber playing field;
2. The logical building blocks to sustain and provide the digital platform;
3. The data content put away, transferred or processed.

There is much that challenges the state in this new world, but boundaries are permeable in the cyber domain, and evidence, thoughts, and correspondence can be distributed with little respect for region or authority. This means that the state's usual tools are often not applicable for cyber-arena usage. But the state adjusts. States are working to develop and deploy new control instruments, and they obviously gain by developing supportive coders in the network-space in many cases. In quite a few countries cyber-warfare has become an important part of military growth. As well as nation-states, non-state actors have done enormous damage to countries and societies with the insecurity and interconnectivity of cyberspace.

5.1.1 Definition of Cyber-Attacks

In the early 1950s, the term applied to cyber computing—equipment perception, animal control and movement. In the 1990s, a modern technology-based concept was coined, with "cyber" standing for "machine controlled." The word "cyberspace" was used to apply to an abstract physical space that certain citizens wanted to believe occurred in the sense of the online activities of digital devices (Kruse et al. 2017).

5.1.2 Cyber-Attacks in Recent Days

The word is now nearly solely used to define data-related cybersecurity issues. As it is difficult to see how analog signs through this kind of wire would represent an assault, the visual event was regarded as a physical occurrence (Bloomfield and Moulton 1997). An assault from cyberspace (meaning our digital devices) is an attack against us via cyberspace. Cyberspace, a non-existent cyber database, is now a way to help people grasp the electronic arsenal that is intended to hurt us. But what are real are the goal and the possible impact of the intruder. However, a lot of cyber-attacks are just distractions; few are thoughtful, or perhaps plain serious.

5.1.3 Why Is it Essential to Prevent Cyber-Attacks?

There are tremendous security risks. Electronic blackouts, military tools accidents and leaks of national cybersecurity secrets can be the consequences of cyber-attacks. These can end in important and sensitive data including medical records being stolen. A cyber-attack can interrupt or paralyze mobile and computer networks and data becomes inaccessible. It is not daunting to claim that we recognize the cyber-threats (Carr 2011). There are also more serious threats. "Cybersecurity threats pervade any company and are not always managed by IT explicitly," clarified Gartner. Entrepreneurs pursue their new strategies and those leaders take strategic risk decisions on a day-to-day basis. The U.S. government actively addresses cyber threats, but seems to be reluctant enough to counter them. Of the 96 entities analyzed, 74 were either at 'threatening' or' high risk' in the case among cyber stakes, according to the White House Policy and Budget Office. Improvements to safety are required immediately (Chapple and Seidl 2014).

The U.S. government has undergone several paralyzing data breaches in recent years. Examples include the Federal Office of Personnel Management's monstrous break, and burglary from the U.S. Navy's secret program. Several of these assaults were ascribed to state knowledge organizations in China.

5.1.4 Types of Cybersecurity Attacks

There are three broad categories of challenges to cybersecurity. The attackers are pursuing:

1. Classic economic improvement.
2. Iconic manipulation.
3. Iconic surveillance (including business espionage—patent stealing or state spying).

Almost every cyber-attack falls into one of these three categories. Spiteful performers have a richness of choices regarding attack techniques. Ten types of cyber-attacks are common (Nazli 2011):

1. **Miscellaneous.** Hackers' codes that perform a harmful feature on a goal system or area, such as data destruction or program management.
2. **Phishing.** Phishing is an electronic intrusion using a hyperlink in the text to get the email client to disclose sensitive information or to install malware.
3. **Phishing spear.** A more advanced type of phishing, in which the perpetrator knows about the target and impersonates someone they know and trust.

4. **Attack: "Man in the Middle" (MitM).** A sender and receiver of electronic communications defines and intercepts a role, and can alter the communications in turn. The sender and the receiver say they interact with each other explicitly. The army can use a MitM assault to defeat the opponent.

5. **Trojans.** Named after the Trojan horse from Ancient Greece, a Trojan is a kind of malware which hits an object device and looks as though it is another item, such as a regular piece of software.

6. **Ransomware.** An intrusion that encrypts the target system's data and demands payment in return so that an intruder can access the data again. These threats vary from low level annoyances to extreme events such as the loss of 2018 data from the town of Atlanta as a whole.

7. **Denial-of-service attack or distributed denial-of-service attack (DDoS).** When an attacker takes over many machines (perhaps thousands) and allows them to use the services of the target system, for example, the internet, which causes it to malfunction in the case of an influx of queries.

8. **IoT device attacks.** IoT devices such as automobile sensors are vulnerable to different types of cyber-threats. Hackers take over the computer for a DDoS assault and unlawfully retrieve data from the target system. Due to the numbers, geographic distribution and often out-of-date operating systems, IoT apps are a primary target for malicious actors.

9. **Data infringements.** A misuse of privacy is abuse of the data by a malicious person. Infringements of apps include theft (i.e. identity theft), an effort to reveal a business (e.g., Edward Snowden or the DNC hack) and fear.

10. **Mobile app malware.** Like other computer hardware, mobile devices are susceptible to ransomware threats. In the course of updates of applications, mobile websites, emails, and text messages, attackers may inject malware. Once it has been hacked, the malicious attacker can be granted access to contact personal details, geographical data, commercial accounts and lots more by a mobile device.

5.2 Background

The idea of an assault on a network system utilizing conceptual explosives is not difficult to grasp, and merely having the ability to carry out such attacks on its own does not raise the impact (or relevance) above that of chaos induced by hackers. Every mode of fighting is benefited by being combined with other types. This is an idea already developed in the context of cinematic techniques, whereby the crowds on the crushed step advance after serial attacks have destroyed the opponent's position. The soldiers may request artillery strikes, air support or supplies to aid in their assault. Such "combined combat" is the hallmark of the present battlefield. But what happens when the idea of intelligence falls into action—both as a shield and as an attacking or catching target?

5.2.1 Use of Cyberspace

Use of cyberspace has become part of countries, cultures and individual lives, due to the rapid development and widespread use of IT. Increasing numbers of potential threats and inhibitors have been also increased across cyberspace. Most advanced countries in terms of ICT have established cyberspace policies and tactics in pursuit of supremacy in cyberspace. In order to recognize virtual reality, Choucri proposed the following structured paradigm (Choucri 2015):

- Physical frameworks and infrastructures that permit an environment of cyber-play;
- Logical building blocks to sustain physical architecture and service;
- Collection, delivery and transition in the computational complexity, and individuals, organizations and consumers with a diverse range in this domain.

The state in this new world is under attack, but boundaries within the cyber world are permeable. There is therefore no regard for territories or authority over intelligence, ideas, wishes, and the like. It ensures that common state services do not always extend to cyber domain applications. But the state changes, states develop and implement new control mechanisms, and they actually aim in many situations to be the next main actor in cyberspace. Cyber-war planning has developed as a significant part of military construction in a number of countries. In addition to governments, the vulnerability of cyberspace and its interconnectivity have also been used to cause great damage to countries and societies (Choucri et al. 2006) by non-state actors.

Cyber-attacks have been experienced by states including Lithuania, Georgia, Russia and the United States. The PRISM surveillance fiasco exposed in 2013 has proven that it is extremely hard to maintain peace and stability in cyberspace. Nevertheless, while various countries and individuals have organized and trained in cyber-warfare, there is as yet an absence of global laws administering the internet, specifically, digital weapons security enactment. Since certain nations enjoy a high-profile role in data innovation, PC risk limitations are badly designed. From this unique situation, it has become an earnest need to create worldwide principles, to improve the global law to battle digital dangers, to maintain harmony and wellbeing and to control electronic wrongdoing. The guidelines on internet weapons have become a key part of countries' intelligence on weapons, arms control and demobilization (Lakomy et al. 2013).

From the mid-1970s, the U.S. has been a market leader in IT. It has built up a genuinely wide assortment of internet approaches and strategies and it has increased its development of military powers and monitoring of enemies, concentrated in its invaluable situation with regard to data innovation and sufficient subsidizing. As one of the principle participants in a global arms strategy since World War II, the U.S. holds a fundamental piece of arms control and demobilization around the world. Any single component and intercession it demands on the internet would unavoidably potentially affect the advancement of worldwide internet arms controls (Sofaer et al. 2009).

All through this work into digital attacks, it appeared to be critical to get a handle on the current circumstances on the internet and to address digital attacks. The extent of digital attacks in the worldwide network is constrained by existing global laws as well as the potential provisos in these laws. By the by, the reason for this investigation is to gather the assembled data, which can assist us with explaining the limits of advanced attacks and the internet inaction activated by or adding to worldwide attacks. Albeit frantic powers wished for the China and U.S. to appear to make progress as in another sort of combat, coordinated effort on the internet ought to be an imperative piece of that exertion (Kaplan 2016).

In terms of cyber-warfare, virtual weapons defense and power states, the resulting mode of combat would seem to be whatever industrial policies society adopts. The rise of

IT implies cyberspace is becoming another battleground after ground, sea, air and outdoor space. The internet has become an essential and important part of the economy, culture, and everyday life. Finally, in terms of further development it has gained momentum.

Nevertheless, the web has also carried with it a rising amount of possible issues and obstacles. For starters, in 2011 the amount of cyber-threats grew by 36% relative to 2010, and at the same time the number of malicious codes fell by 41%. "Changes in combat type, from mechanization to intelligence are growing," according to a White Paper (Li and Tian 2013) released in 2013 on national defense in China and around the world. "Major forces are actively developing new and more sophisticated weapons systems to insure that they maintain strategic phenotypic differences in global conflicts in fields such as outer space and cyberspace." An American researcher says the 21st century law of cyberspace was as significant as the regulation of the marine environment in the 19th century and air protection in the 20th century. The internet is growing at an incredible rate globally with just about 50 years of history. In addition to its significant impacts on social stability, national security, sustainable development and social media, cyber-space provides forums for the foreign, legal, protection and cultural exchanges (Madnick et al. 2009).

5.2.2 The Cyber-Battlefield

The growing issue remains the coming of cyber fighting, which is like a type of minor power fight. However, non-mechanized fighting broadens the battlefield too, in a way unheard of since the appearance of the airplane. Worse still, the theatre of war has been extended into organizations that have not historically had any occasion to consider their security against nation-state attackers (Eren 2017). Many global wars are known to take the form of "low intensity," that is to say guerrilla warfare, rebellion, special operations and other such strategies. From the point of view of its critics, only new wars between the U.S. and their opponents can be viewed as not participating in large-scale military operations on set lines. There no longer comes a day when two large armies amass their soldiers on a front of straight battle lines, except in a local battle of only local importance between two smaller powers (Popp and Yen 2006).

In a broader sense it means that the world's dominant forces have the possibility and a roadmap of non-kinetic violence, including in peacetime, against potential opponents. In this community of nation-states, clandestine operations and special strategies usually engage in low-intensity conflicts to avoid being in complete conflict (Herken 2007) with implicit ignorance of the fact that information warfare inevitably results in cyber-warfare becoming a trigger in combat. In reality, America's overwhelming military superiority in terms of traditional combat offers smaller nations a great incentive to participate in cyber-warfare for other purposes. In brief, cyber-warfare provides an economically acceptable form of asymmetric warfare which cannot be caused by a much larger force using a con-ventional military reaction.

The military can lead a digital assault and digital guard at state level, or the individual may execute at an individual level. The push to encroach can be a basic one, or can be a long-haul, broad and state-run activity to destroy the foundation of an adversary nation and accomplish the key motivation, which is incapacitating the working of the administra-tion. The meaning of digital assault is not yet fully clear (Ervural and Ervural 2018), although this generally includes troublesome interruption of a framework or PC organized in regions, for example, hacking, blocking administration, information burglary and dis-turbance of servers. The increase and improvement of politically arranged, hostile-to-state programmers, for example, anonymous associations and other online "hoodlums," further adds to the impact of the digital assault.

All of the world's top 15 countries consider increasing military spending on cyber-offensive and defensive technology. Throughout 2011, there have been cybersecurity initiatives in 68 of the 193 UN member states. In any case, in 2011, the figures increased to 114, with 47 having military digital security programs (Hansel 2018). These 47 nations assess their militarily competent digital security limits and create related military activity plans. In this sense, arms control is becoming an integral part of global military regulation and demilitarization. Nevertheless, throughout cyberspace, in this area, the amount of arms control measures in effect is almost zero and thus underlines the value of universal cyberspace code of conduct agreements being introduced as quickly as possible to establish a framework for controlling global cyber operations. The established U.S.-led countries also formulated relatively complete cyber-war strategies and military programs, utilizing their data innovation and satisfactory subsidizing. In addition, the development of military powers has sped up and sensitive counter-war research has been undertaken (Malin et al. 2008).

As one of the principal building blocks of the global restructuring since the Second World War, the U.S. has a vital position of authority in worldwide military control and demobilization (Dalsen 2009). Any observation on the internet may affect the improvement of universal arms control on the internet. To date, numerous articles have been written explaining the laws of participating in cyberspace and how foreign disputes are prevented. Unfortunately, the way in which states participating in the cyber-war worked was clandestine, meaning the contact laws were not needed.

Nonetheless, Scott J. Shackelford reports that cyber-aggression is separated into the classifications: digital fear mongering, digital war and digital undercover work. Although pretty much every fear-based oppressor has a web presence, genuine digital psychological warfare remains uncommon, and there has not been any huge digital war yet. He guarantees the biggest problems that need to be addressed include digital wrongdoing and corporate fighting. The U.S. military forecaster James Adam states that any sort of digital assault is a sort of digital ambush and that the perils of digital obstruction ought not be thought little of. It was once anticipated that the PC would be a future weapon of war and that, as with physical fighting, there would be no intuitive battleground nor apparatus for holding on to control. The RAND Corporation additionally expressed in one of its investigations (Arquilla and Ronfeldt 1993) the view that "the traditional clash in the mechanical upheaval is atomic war, while the advanced age worldwide fight is basically digital war." Nevertheless, it has long been prepared for electronic combat. Recently, it has accelerated its efforts and intensity to build computer power to fight future cyber-attacks or cyber-warfare. The U.S. has also increased its efforts and has increased its pace, and our infrastructure, policy and governance systems have been fully exposed.

We can no longer ignore electronic weaponry in reference to the modern military arsenal: tactical challenges and cyber-warfare. The problem for everyone is where and when the next assault takes place. The only known thing is that more assaults are going to take place.

5.2.3 Effective Limitations of Cyber-Warfare

"Encounter region" is a term utilized to describe a force brought together to coordinate and incorporate military action with a view to the accomplishment of military missions via air, data, ground, ocean and the environment. In order to effectively exercise fighting power, protect the unit or complete the mission, it will take into account the environment, factors and circumstances. This involves the enemies and cooperative troops, facilities, environment, climate, and the emission spectra within the fields of interest and activities. As we concentrate on the knowledge needed to understand the cyber-warfare operating limits, we need to map out the conventional warfare environment first. Military planners have historically classified capacities to fight battle into four areas. Such areas are used for the creation of tactics and strategies and for the coordination of forces (Tapscott and Williams 2008).

5.2.3.1 Ground Actions

In battle, the oldest area comprises any combat ground forces. Ground forces comprise tanks, cavalry, armored bodies, aircraft, and missile positions. In the U.S., the Army primarily manages the land domain within the U.S. military.

5.2.3.2 Sea Actions

This fighting environment comprises lakes, canals, and deep seas. The deep ocean-domain involves all the naval forces in the world. The U.S. Navy manages the sea domain within the U.S. military.

5.2.3.3 Air Actions

This fighting area involves battles in the sky. The air space involves pilots, helicopters, surveillance aircraft, fuel tanker aircraft and cargo planes. Since World War II, U.S. military air space authority was shifted from the Armed Forces to the Air Force.

5.2.3.4 Space Actions

The military introduced satellite as an area of combat with the invention of space-flight. In this area the key activities include satellite operations and the use of nuclear warheads. The space program is an Air Force project within the U.S. Army.

5.2.3.5 Cyber Actions

In the early days of cyber-attacks, administrators tried to bring the cyber task to these sectors, and each organization took over a role in the effort. In 2010 in the U.S., the Quadrennial Homeland Security Review and the Department of Defense (DoD) were established.

Although the world is human-made, cyber-warfare and the internet are now as critical for DoD operations as the natural fields of property, ocean, mid-air and interstellar. The current field of battle is the least known. For decades of military history, military planners educated in ground and marine operations are depended on when planning for strategic expansion. The battlegrounds of the air and space have only been important since the middle of the last century, and cyber-warfare is even more recent; there was no question that military plans would not fully adjust to this new form of fighting (Salim 2014).

5.3 Development of Cyber-Warfare and Cyber-Conflict

Civilian companies have not been the main battle goals in history and are even omitted as targets. In the early days, there were groups who did not hit practical targets. Such gatherings existed inside the physical limits of the nation-states so they could launch bigger, fundamental attacks on the nation-states or palaces and towns in which they dwelled (Iheagwara 2011). There was clearly no idea of undermining an adversary by concentrating on causing economic damage, without serious loss of life, and even if military efforts were to be concentrated on destroying commercial activity, they necessarily required an emphasis on killing civilians. The only form of fighting in those days was physical combat using arrows, knives, nuclear arms, explosives etc.

Trade was carried out both in nation-states and in the cities using material goods that were brought in by the people themselves. Consequently, even to prevent or stop such commerce, the notion of fighting has necessarily involved transparent attacks against civilians. This reality persisted from the feudal age until the end of the 20th century, when warfare (especially aerial war and bombing) allowed trade institutions to be targeted. Geneva Convention IV (GCIV) (Singer and Friedman 2014) is the fourth Geneva Convention. In August 1949, one of the four Geneva Conventions established humanitarian protection exclusively for the people in war zones. There were anomalies in the extent to which Geneva Conventions were implemented by countries, but those anomalies seemed to stand out as: extraordinary incidents, errors (such as bomber crews hitting the wrong structure because of real manmade faults), or the corruption of countries who by their actions were considered barbaric. Despite these incidental events, nations have, in general, attempted to reach (military) counter-force targets in order to prevent (civil) countervailing targets from being damaged.

This differentiation only improved with the development of the cinematic battle. The advent of LED technology has reduced the death toll of people from bombings to such a low level that was not feasible in previous wars. If once whole neighborhoods were attacked in an assault on a single house of military value, it is now called a tragedy when a mere civil building is destroyed due to confusion or human error. In a sense, industrial sector protection has been a positive side effect of the Geneva Conventions. Regional isolation from battle theatres, as well as a relatively small number of threats, has also decreased organizations' vulnerability. A business owner does not need to wait 1,000 miles away for the failure of his competition (Stiennon 2015).

This had started to change in the late 20th century. Now, with the tools, procedures, and theory emerging around cyber-warfare, the above-mentioned scenario decreased (Swintek 2018). Although the IT networks of the army are often sequestered into enclaves (and with varying success, of course), there is a clear interconnection between private industry and many internet networks and every resident.

In cyber-warfare, "vintage hackers" were exceptionally skilled, but mostly driven by altruism. As long as a hack had been done, it was not uncommon for a hacker to warn a hacked network administrator how to protect it from later situations (Zetter 2014). Their creativity was mainly due to a need for knowledge and greater ability, together with a lack of credible sources. Those people had a clear ethos and never created the circumstances they were able to exploit, although their actions were undeniably immoral.

The advent of the "template kiddie" came later. As internet access was popular, hacker methods became more prevalent, requiring much less ability to get through insecure networks. These people ignored the competence or moral fiber present in their ancestors, usually defacing pages with profane messages simply to gain permission to brag (Ziegler 2011). Most notably, criminal organizations have introduced malware to generate revenue by extortion, embezzlement or stealing identities. This vulnerability has grown in complexity and reach, and appears to present a growing obstacle for individuals and private organizations.

Nonetheless, the retro hacker's complexity and skills and the script kiddie's indiscriminate reach were targeted, hostile efforts to optimize cybercrime's harm. Furthermore, military and intelligence agencies' cyber-warfare divisions have unparalleled equipment. The retro hackers and server admins both did their research on a tight budget and, although better funded by criminal organizations, they still have scarce resources, and a huge need to evade capture and conviction (Melzer 2011). They work inside safe enclaves within which they have no regard for whatever they can do to risk retaliation. Usually the validity of their actions is restricted to that of the nation they represent. Since North Korea and China are two of the more advanced cyber-warfare players, this really is a disturbing thought.

5.4 Emerging Cyber-Attacks

Cyber-attacks never get stagnant: Millions are produced each year. Many assaults adopt the above basic frameworks and are suitable for many effects.

There is a fresh celebration of "zero-day" attacks, for example, that can shock security because they do not bear identifiable digital signatures.

The persistent "improvement" of what analysts call "Advanced Persistent Threats" (APTs) is another worrying phenomenon. As a commercial attacker explains APTs, "It's the simplest way to define the hackers who burrow through networks and retain 'persistence'— a link that cannot easily be prevented by software updates or a device reset."

The very famous Sony Corp. breach is an illustration of an APT, where a nationally famous actor was working for months inside the local network, evading surveillance when exfiltrating huge amounts of data (Barnes et al. 2011).

5.5 Cybersecurity Attacks

Cyber-threats come from a variety of countries, individuals and backgrounds. Mischievous actors include:

- Individuals that assemble assault vectors utilizing their own product apparatus;
- Criminal associations that work like organizations, with an immense number of representatives acting as assault vectors and carrying out assaults (Sechrist 2010);
- Countries;
- Countries acting through terrorists;
- Corporate agents;
- Organized crime gangs;
- Unhappy insiders.

Many of the most genuine assaults are by nation-states. There are a few unique variants of digital dangers inflicted by nation-states. Some are basic surveillance—endeavoring to know the national privileged insights of another administration. Others are focused on turmoil.

For instance, the U.S.'s Chris Painter, in a Brookings Institution report for the State Department, revealed that China and North Korea "have more than once utilized their digital control to achieve their key objectives around the world."

In any case, he observed, "Their aims and objectives vary: while North Korea principally intends to assemble income creating abilities and hostile capacity for potential clashes past North Korea, China, for the most part, utilizes its electronic methods for secret activities and taking of scholarly property" (Case, Defense Use 2016).

"Naming and disgracing" has been a compelling strategy against China on account of the feelings of dread of its legislature about the conceivable blowback on its delicate force. These are the supposed digital arms that could be utilized during a contention to close down vitality in a hostile area. The lines between criminal associations and national insight are foggy in certain countries, with the culprits doing the genuine digital reconnaissance investigation.

On the "dull web," a disrupted yet unavoidable unlawful area of the web, various digital vulnerabilities are purchased and sold. Hopeful programmers will buy ransomware, infections, traded gadget passwords and more in this online bazaar. The dull web acts as a risk generator, with one programmer selling his/her advancement again and again.

5.6 Cyber Defense Best Practices and Protection

Frustration over the magnitude of the threat climate is easy to experience. But a company can be secured from cyber-threats. The user can also protect himself.

5.6.1 Cyber Defense for Industries

Best practice in cyber defense in organizations is the provision of basic but extremely important countermeasures, including patching computers. For example, once an intrusion program has learned it can be used by an attacker to circumvent code and gain root access to the Windows Server, it can issue a workaround and distribute it to all Windows Server owners.

When a software vendor discovers a protection flaw on its computer, it usually writes code to fix or "repair" the problem. Many do this at least once a month. When all the security patches have been enforced on a timely basis by IT departments, further attempts fail (Mavridis et al. 2011).

5.6.2 Cyber Defense for Individuals

For individuals, best practices are modest. The moral summary is that a few very large defense companies like the Verizon SecOps or AT&T stand between the consumer and attacker in most situations. Preventive measures are still required to ensure the privacy of your information (Madnick et al. 2011).

Secret phrase hygiene. Enormous security firms cannot shield clients from phishing or programmers who can break passwords, for example, "1134." User wellbeing against digital dangers is significant with regards to secret key recuperation.

Virus software. Keep antivirus software up to date with normal booked updates.

Be careful about phishing. Be watchful when following links. Lance phishing messages look genuine, yet are most certainly not. If you get an email that says, "last due receipt" with a PDF document, do not open it, unless you are 100% sure who sent it. This most likely originated from an odd source such as xxxXxxxxxxx@gmail.com.

Takeaways

It tends to be an unpleasant time for organizations and customers worried about digital dangers. There are unquestionably dangers and they are changing and increasing. The aggressors are unique, with numerous alarming assailants and objectives.

Regardless of whether an organization is being undermined by an actual nation-state, resources can, in any case, be verified. This requires asset arrangement and a decent security tasks group and a cautious head who will remain working on the most serious digital dangers (Choucri et al. 2016).

5.6.3 Nation-State Cyber-Attacks

Attacks by the nation-state, and their threat, tend to be increasing. The hypothesis that these state-backed cyber criminals are now concentrating on hacking for strategic insight into military or diplomatic data also needs to be expanded to other motivating factors. Nation-state hackers broaden their goals to include not only government institutions but also enterprises and manufacturing facilities (Hudson 2019). Through revealing classified, sometimes important, details, they use more advanced methods to undermine institutions, and their respective countries.

5.6.4 Examples of Cyber-Warfare

Cyber-warfare entails acts by a nation-state or foreign entity directed at disrupting and threatening to destroy the systems or communication networks of another country by, for example, computer viruses or denial-of-service attacks. The RAND Corporation's work gives guidance to military and civilian decision-makers on ways to defend against the harmful effects of cyber-warfare on digital infrastructure in a nation (Dobbing and Cole 2014).

The nature of warfare has changed from traditional to electronic, seeing a deluge of state-sponsored cyber-attacks.

CASE STUDY 1:   OLYMPIC GAMES

Conflict Related:

Iran and the U.S. have no formal or casual conciliatory relations. The Iranian democratically chosen leader was executed following a coup, helped in 1951 by U.S. and British intelligence organizations. U.S. President backed Iran left in the wake of mass protests 26 years later. The former Islamic dictator infiltrated American gatherings and seized the U.S. embassy in Tehran (1979–1981). In 1988, a U.S. warship struck an Iranian airliner. Friendship deteriorated further. In 2002, did they actually suspect Iran of having a secret nuclear weapons program as part of an erroneous system? The U.S. was even blamed by the President of Iran for its 2001 9/11 attacks. The transition in the Iranian government took place in 2013.

CASE STUDY 2:   UKRAINIAN POWER GRID

Conflict Related:

The main East Slavic State, Kievan Rus, has its origins in the Baltic Sea from the 9th century to the middle of the 13th century. Russia and Ukraine originated in this nation. It was additionally part of the administration framed in 1922 in the Soviet Federal Republic and the legislature of Ukraine governed by Moscow. Ukraine is presently a significant flight path for the remainder of the western world, home to around 7.5 million ethnic Russian individuals for the most part from eastern Ukraine and southeast Crimea. Ukraine is now focusing on Russia's biggest petroleum pipeline. Of the 46 million Ukrainian individuals, about 25% consider Russian their first language. It is accepted that Russian chiefs have generally treated the assurance of a territory of impact through nations outside Russia as defensive and it is particularly valuable for Ukraine that Russia considers its younger sibling in light of the fact that Russia does not have features such as waterways and mountains along its western wilderness (Merciai 1984).

CASE STUDY 3:   RUSSIAN HACKERS TRACKING UKRAINIAN ARTILLERY

Conflict Related:

In the case of the Ukrainian power grid (Hollis 2011) the history between these two states is addressed. In favor of Russia-backed rebels in eastern Ukraine, the intelligence purpose could have been used accordingly. The study notes that a hacker affiliated with the Russian government has been credited with mapping and assaulting Ukrainian gun units between late 2014 and 2016 utilizing malware on Android devices.

CASE STUDY 4:   SONY CORP'S HOLLYWOOD STUDIO

Conflict Related:

Albeit pressure between the two countries is to a great extent a result of Cold War strategy, more recent strains and opposition between the U.S. and Korea have arisen. Korea shut its borders to Western exchange in the mid-19th century. In the General Sherman incident, Korean powers assaulted a U.S. gunboat that was sent to arrange an economic agreement and slaughtered its team after the two sides exchanged shots, since it overlooked requests from Korean specialists. In reprisal, there was a U.S. ambush on the Shinmiyangyo.

Long ago, Korea and the U.S. signed a treaty in 1882. Connections rose again when the U.S. agreed a peace treaty at the finish of the R–J battle in 1905. Japan constrained the U.S. to perceive Korea as a feature of Japan's authoritative reach, and when Japan attacked Korea five years after the fact the United States did not question this. Inside Woodrow Wilson's hypothesis of national self-assurance (George and Rishikof 2017), Korean patriots fruitlessly requested help from the U.S. at the gathering of the Treaty of Versailles.

Sony Pictures Entertainment was the object of a distressing digital assault at the end of November and in early December 2014, which included the release of information taken from different movies that presently were not distributed and also from secret staff records, for example, standardized savings numbers and pay rates. U.S. authorities have affirmed that North Korea has sorted out the interruption on the grounds that the North Koreans have not delighted in Sony Pictures' up and coming film "The Interview" (Bunker 2015).

CASE STUDY 5:   ESTONIAN GOVERNMENT ATTACK

Conflict Related:

Estonia is a modest Northern European republic. This lies on the edge of the Baltic Sea, with Latvia and Russia. A previous Soviet satellite state, Estonia ended 50 years of intrusion which transformed the nation from a mobilized fringe area, as the Russian Army took its battle to the West (Heal and Bunker 2014).

The country was exchanged to and fro between the Soviets and Nazis during the 20th century, coming full circle not just with a huge number of Estonian killings but also with a merciless tyrant interfering in their way of life, which inevitably went on for a considerable length of time. Before that Estonia had been represented by different powers, for example, Sweden and Denmark, for quite a long time.

Since the short yet vicious war of freedom that finished when the Soviets attacked the nation in 1944, ethnic Russians in the nation revolted in the most exceedingly terrible savagery Estonia had found in reprisal.

5.7 Impact of the Attacks

5.7.1 Breakdown of Cyber-Tools Used

Digital fighting is frequently depicted in a similar way as atomic fighting: badly damaged telephone networks, electrical grids and national infrastructure. Nonetheless, cyber-battles are more comparable to the separate, much smaller, less tangible, wars of the Cold War. The above outlines the techniques of cyber-warfare and discusses, perhaps most notably, how agile, small-scale cyber-warfare seeks to distinguish cyber-warfare (Schaap 2009a).

5.7.2 Cyber-Illegal

This is a popular way of gathering knowledge about illegal methods of aggression used by state actors. Most of the information collected does not include state secrets and confidential information, but can be used for blackmail purposes. Recent case studies have shown that the U.S. and British intelligence conducted a cyber-espionage campaign in the Middle East to map advanced weapon systems, with a focus on Israel.

5.7.3 Web Damage

A website hacker executes by defacing a website and altering aspects of its malfunctioning layout. This online alternative of vandalism is not a threat and does no harm. The British government hacked the Al Qaeda website and replaced a bomb guide with HTML with cupcake recipes as an amazing illustration of this technique.

5.7.4 Advertising

This is a version of site harm in which the emphasis is not mere agitation but the propagation of political propaganda. Through altering the contents to promote political agendas, the cyber warrior attacks a website. The receiver effectively censors the message of the target with his own in a more extreme form of vandalism. The Sands Corp. case study showing Adelson's strong support for Israeli citizens involved a non-status quo group that invaded and defaced websites operated by third parties and posted a snapshot photo from Sheldon Adelson with Benjamin Netanyahu, along with fire photos on a map of the Sands U.S. casinos (Arquilla and Ronfeldt 1993). In order to advertise and recruit candidates Al Qaeda uses its websites (e.g. Ansar al-Mujahidin).

5.7.5 Confidential Data Acquisition

This is an additional multifaceted and dangerous electronic spy approach requiring knowledge gathering on sensitive subjects. Successful implementation involves maneuvering a company's complex protection system to collect confidential aim data, usually military data and competitive advantages. The contextual investigation for Operation Desert Storm demonstrates that the aggressors separated in the DoD and uncovered military files (Smith et al. 2000), arms frameworks, military and military exercises (particularly for the Desert Storm and Desert Shield Operations) and significantly more; sometimes they also tried nuclear power. The attackers were so aware that they powered their own hard drives on their own computers (Herberman and McIntire 1979).

5.7.6 Distributed Denial-of-Service (DDoS)

This attack mode happens when a variety of devices are targeted by Denial-of-Service (DoS) at different locations on different devices. Consequently, huge groups of people who access a website deliberately overload the system and cause it to avoid attacks. This attack forbids entry by other users to the database and could potentially damage the server hardware if there is adequate protection to deter other users from accessing it (Schaap 2009b). The assault also has a higher frequency, as the novice criminals have a lower entry barrier. Throughout our case studies we can see several cases of DDoS attacks and this seems like a common tool for breaching non-status networks. For example, in the Ukraine grid attack, a non-status quo side used DDoS, a Telephony Denial of Service (TDoS)-style status quo assault to target client call targets by telephone to keep individuals from being brought in to fight the attack. TDoS assaults are indistinguishable from DDoS assaults that incur a deluge of information on web servers. In this example, a huge number of phone calls were made that appeared to have originated from some place in the middle's correspondence systems became survived (Li and Tian 2013).

5.7.7 Equipment Distribution

This usually consists of identifying an online product and/or service request (e.g., supplying combat weapons) and substituting and/or suppressing the command, creating disarray and decreasing the authenticity of the enemy's association. This includes a reasonably high level of system, as these rules, due to their privacy, are profoundly protected from digital assaults. We did not see this kind of assault obliterating the electronic control instrument purposely during our contextual analyses. Yet, it is clear, now and again—for example, the zero-day assaults and Morris-style digital assaults—that this kind of attack was probably conducted from a non-status quo side.

5.7.8 Critical Infrastructure Attacks

This is the negative life of public utilities with viruses designed to impede their operations (power, resources, fuel, communications, commercial or transport systems). In attacks of this degree, it is necessary to understand complex technology and the capacity to overcome cybersecurity barriers. The results of such viruses can be very damaging and concrete, as shown by the Stuxnet assault on the Iranian nuclear project.

5.7.9 Compromised Fake Hardware

This includes the selling of tainted products to consumers by a retailer. These hide the virus in low to standard desktop programs, like the microprocessor code, which is not involved for long years until it is operational. This includes the proper performance of multiple layers of interactions—specifically, communicating with individuals in the production and development phase. The infected computer executes different tasks, from dumping data to destroying the device's power. This kind of backdoor attack is generally called a zero-day assault and was used by Stuxnet in the non-status-quota destruction of the nuclear power plant. The SCADA nuclear reactor operating system has been spread from the OS modules.

5.7.10 Theft or Hardware Destruction

The more "savage power" way to deal with digital fighting—direct contact with a PC—is viewed as the best method for gathering data and devastating a foe. It is accomplished by extracting hardware from the system or by destroying it. The case studies have found that in cyber-war cases such as Stuxnet or the Ukrainian Power Grid, it is a popular weapon.

5.8 Conclusion

The purpose of this chapter was two main concepts. The first goal was to examine previous cyber-attacks from recent days to the present day and collect significant information in a variety of fields such as nation-states, criminals, corporate agents, organized crime groups, disgruntled outsiders, hackers, and industry rivals, and the second objective was to show how these attacks influence people's properties.

References

Arquilla, John, and David Ronfeldt. 1993. "Cyberwar is coming!" *Comparative Strategy 11*(2): 141–165.

Barnes, Christopher R., Mairi MR Best, Fern R. Johnson, Lucie Pautet, and Benoît Pirenne. 2011. "Challenges, benefits, and opportunities in installing and operating cabled ocean observatories: Perspectives from NEPTUNE Canada." *IEEE Journal of Oceanic Engineering 38*(1): 144–157.

Bloomfield, Lincoln Palmer, and Allen Moulton. 1997. *Managing International Conflict: From Theory to Policy: A Teaching Tool Using CASCON*. New York: St. Martin's Press. ISBN: 13:978-0312136758.

Bunker, Robert J. 2015. Fifth Dimensional Battlespace: Terrorism and Counter-Terrorism Implications. url: https://scholarship.claremont.edu/cgu_fac_pub/945/

Carr, Jeffrey. 2011. *Inside Cyber Warfare: Mapping the Cyber Underworld*. O'Reilly Media, Inc.

Carr, Jeff, Billy Rios, Derek Plansky, Greg Walton, Matt Devost, Ned Moran, Rebecca Givner-Forbes, and Shannon Silverstein. 2009. "Project Grey Goose Phase II Report: The Evolving State of Cyber Warfare." Project Grey Goose 20.

Case, Defense Use. 2016. "Analysis of the cyber attack on the Ukrainian power grid." In *Electricity Information Sharing and Analysis Center (E-ISAC)*, 388.

Chapple, Mike and David Seidl. 2014. *Cyberwarfare*. Jones & Bartlett Publishers

Choucri, Nazli. 2015. "Explorations in cyber international relations: A research collaboration of MIT and Harvard University."

Choucri, Nazli, Stuart Madnick, and Priscilla Koepke. 2016. *Institutions for Cyber Security: International Responses and Data Sharing Initiatives*. Cambridge, MA: Massachusetts Institute of Technology.

Choucri, Nazli, Christi Electris, Daniel Goldsmith, Dinsha Mistree, Stuart E. Madnick, J. Bradley Morrison, Michael D. Siegel, and Margaret Sweitzer-Hamilton. 2006. "Understanding & modeling state stability: Exploiting system dynamics." In *2006 IEEE Aerospace Conference*, pp. 1–11. IEEE.

Dalsen, William. 2009. "Civil Remedies for Invasions of Privacy: A Perspective on Software Vendors and Intrusion upon Seclusion." Wis. L. REv: 1059.

Dobbing, Mary and Chris Cole. 2014. *Israel and the Drone Wars: Examining Israel's Production, Use and Proliferation of UAVs*. Oxford, UK: Drone Wars.

Eren, Mehmet. 2017. "Avrupa birliği'nin siber güvenlik stratejisi için kuramsal çerçeve ve strateji belgesi öncesi ab'nin eylemleri." *A Peer Review International E-Journal on Cyberpolitics, Cybersecurity and Human Rights 2*(3): 25.

Ervural, Beyzanur Cayir and Bilal Ervural. 2018. "Overview of Cyber Security in the Industry 4.0 era." In *Industry 4.0: Managing the Digital Transformation*. Cham: Springer, 267–284

Gartner, Digital Business Require Cyber Security", url: https://www.gartner.com/en/information-technology/insights/cybersecurity, accessed on March 28, 2020.

George, Roger Z. and Harvey Rishikof, eds. 2017. *The National Security Enterprise: Navigating the Labyrinth*. Georgetown University Press.

Hansel, Mischa. 2018. "Cyber-attacks and psychological IR perspectives: explaining misperceptions and escalation risks." *Journal of International Relations and Development 21*(3): 523–551.

Heal, Charles, and Robert J. Bunker. 2014. *Fifth Dimensional Operations: Space-Time-Cyber Dimensionality in Conflict and War—A Terrorism Research Center Book*. iUniverse.

Herberman, Ronald B., and Kenneth Robert McIntire, eds. 1979. *Immunodiagnostic of Cancer*. M. Dekker, Vol. 2.

Herken, Gregg. 2007. *Thomas C. Reed, At the Abyss: An Insider's History of the Cold War*. New York: Ballantine Books, *368*, 148–150.

Hollis, David. 2011. "Cyberwar case study: Georgia 2008." 1–10.

Hudson, Valerie M. 2019. *Artificial Intelligence and International Politics*. Routledge.

Iheagwara, Charles M. 2011. "The strategic implications of the current Internet design for cyber security." PhD diss., Massachusetts Institute of Technology.

Kaplan, Fred. 2016. *Dark Territory: The Secret History of Cyber War*. Simon and Schuster.

Kruse, Clemens Scott, Benjamin Frederick, Taylor Jacobson, and D. Kyle Monticone. 2017. "Cybersecurity in healthcare: A systematic review of modern threats and trends." *Technology and Health Care* 25(1): 1–10.

Lakomy, Miron, Richard A. Clarke, and Robert K. Knake. 2013. "Cyber War. The Next Threat to National Security and What to Do About It. New York: Ecco, 2010." *Studia Politicae Universitatis Silesiensis* 11: 316–320.

Li, Xiaobing and Xiansheng Tian, eds. 2013. *Evolution of Power: China's Struggle, Survival, and Success.* Lexington Books.

Malin, Cameron H., Eoghan Casey, and James M. Aquilina. 2008. *Malware Forensics Investigating and Analyzing Malicious Code.* Syngress

Melzer, Nils. 2011. *Cyberwarfare and International Law.* United Nations Institute for Disarmament Research.

Madnick, Stuart, Xitong Li, and Nazli Choucri. 2009. "Experiences and challenges with using CERT data to analyze international cyber security."

Madnick, Stuart, Nazli Choucri, Steven Camiña, and Wei Lee Woon. 2011. "Towards better understanding Cybersecurity: or are 'Cyberspace' and 'Cyber Space' the same?." In *pre-ICIS workshop on Information Security and Privacy (SIGSEC).*

Mavridis, I. P., A-IE Androulakis, A. B. Halkias, and Ph Mylonas. 2011. "Real-life paradigms of wireless network security attacks." In *2011 15th Panhellenic Conference on Informatics*, 112–116. IEEE.

Merciai, Patrizio. 1984. "The Euro-Siberian Gas Pipeline Dispute-A Compelling Case for the Adoption of Jurisdictional Codes of Conduct." *Maryland Journal of International Law & Trade* 8: 1.

Nazli, Choucri. 2011. "Cyber politics in International Relations."

Popp, Robert L. and John Yen, eds. 2006. *Emergent Information Technologies and Enabling Policies for Counter-Terrorism.* Wiley-IEEE Press, Vol. 6.

Salim, Hamid M. 2014. "Cyber safety: A systems thinking and systems theory approach to managing cyber security risks." PhD diss., Massachusetts Institute of Technology.

Schaap, Arie J. 2009a. "Cyber warfare operations: Development and use under international law." *AFL Review* 64: 111.

Schaap, Arie J. 2009b. "Cyber warfare operations: Development and use under international law." *AFL Review* 64: 111.

Sechrist, Michael. 2010. "Cyberspace in deep water: Protecting the arteries of the Internet." *Kennedy School Review* 10: 40–45.

Singer, Peter W. and Allan Friedman. 2014. "Cybersecurity: What everyone needs to know?"

Smith, Pete, David S. Powlson, Jo U. Smith, Pete Falloon, and Kevin Coleman. 2000. "Meeting Europe's climate change commitments: quantitative estimates of the potential for carbon mitigation by agriculture." *Global Change Biology* 6(5): 525–539.

Sofaer, Abraham, David Clark, and Whitfield Diffie. 2009. "Cyber security and international agreements." In *National Research Council, Proceedings of a Workshop on Deterring Cyberattacks.*

Swintek, Philip C. 2018. *Critical Vulnerabilities in the Space Domain: Using Nanosatellites as an Alternative to Traditional Satellite Architectures.* Naval Postgraduate School Monterey United States.

Stiennon, Richard. 2015. *There Will Be Cyberwar: b How the Move to Network-Centric Warfighting Set The Stage For Cyberwar.* IT-Harvest Press.

Tapscott, Don and Anthony D. Williams. 2008. *Wikinomics: How Mass Collaboration Changes Everything.* Penguin.

Zetter, Kim. 2014. *Countdown to Zero Day: Stuxnet and the Launch of the World's First Digital Weapon.* Broadway Books.

Ziegler, Dustin P. 2011. "Foundations of a defense digital platform: business systems governance in the Department of Defense." PhD diss., Massachusetts Institute of Technology.

6

Cryptography and Steganography Techniques

Ninni Singh and Gunjan Chhabra

University of Petroleum & Energy Studies, Dehradun, India

6.1 Introduction

For decades, human beings had two intrinsic needs: (i) to interact and share views or information, and (ii) to interact particularly. Furthermore, these needs act as the foundation of the art of coding techniques. This technique involves coding the messages in such a manner that only the legitimate recipient can access and understand the actual context of the message. Illegitimate recipients are unable to extract the actual meaning/context of the messages even if the coded messages are available to them. There are numerous applications of security ranging from secure business, payment gateways, protecting confidential information such as banking information, healthcare data, etc. One of the vital facets of secure communications is cryptography, but cryptography is not self-sufficient in providing information security (Kahate, 2013; Esslinger, 2016).

> The art of hiding useful information to bring privacy in information security is acknowledged as cryptography.

This chapter illustrates the basic terminologies and concepts of various existing cryptographic techniques.

6.2 History

Cryptography skills were invented along with writing skills. In the times when people recognized and systematized tribes and kingdoms, the idea of battles and politics evolved. With this idea further emerged the notion of sharing information securely with selected people, which acts as a key motivation behind further advancement in this field (NIST, 2001).

6.2.1 The Oldest Cryptographic Technique—Hieroglyphs

Approximately 4000 years ago, the first evidence of utilizing cryptography techniques, that is, "hieroglyphs," was found. "Hieroglyphs" were utilized by Egyptians for communication. "Hieroglyphs" is the coding language known to scribes who were responsible for sending messages as representatives of kings. Figure 6.1 represents one such example of a "hieroglyph."

Researchers discovered that from 600 to 500 BC other cryptographic techniques were utilized, that is, mono-alphabetic substitution. This substitution technique follows some rules defined in an algorithm in which the message symbols (alphabets) are substituted for other symbols (alphabets). The same algorithm acts as a key to recover the actual message from the coded message (refer Figure 6.2).

The cryptography technique utilized by the Romans is recognized as the Caesar Shift Cipher. This substitution technique follows some rules defined in an algorithm in which the message symbols (alphabets) shifted by a number (a shared choice by the communicating parties). The addressee of the message would then reverse shift the symbols (alphabets) by the same number to retrieve the actual message. See Figure 6.3 for an example of this.

FIGURE 6.1
"Hieroglyph" (Source: fr:Image: Egypt Hieroglyphe4.jpg)

Original Alphabet	a	b	c	d	e	f	g	h	i	j	k	l	m	n	o	p	q	r	s	t	u	v	w	x	y	z
Encrypted Alphabet	B	C	D	E	F	G	H	I	J	K	L	M	N	O	P	Q	R	S	T	U	V	W	X	Y	Z	A

FIGURE 6.2
Mono-alphabetic substitution.

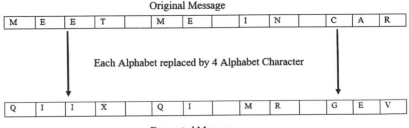

FIGURE 6.3
Caesar Shift Cipher.

6.3 Steganography

Steganography is analogous to cryptography, but it has another dimension. Steganography is a Greek term that means concealed writing. It is the art of interacting in such a manner that no one can sense the existence of a hidden message (Cachin, 1998). This technique has been utilized over hundreds of years; due to advancements in the technology of information sharing (in electronic form) new steganography techniques have been invented. The notion of secrecy further enhanced the requirement for secure communication with particular people, which empowered the evolution of more robust and secure cryptography techniques. As aforementioned, there is evidence of usage of cryptography and steganography techniques initiated by the Egyptian and Roman civilizations (Blanco et al., 1992; Popa, 1998).

The following are the numerous steganography techniques that have been utilized traditionally.

- **Character Marking:** In print documents, selected symbols are overwritten with pencils. These marks are generally not visible until the document (paper) has been kept at a particular angle to the light.
- **Invisible Ink:** A substance is used for writing a message that leaves no perceptible evidence until certain chemicals or heat are put on the paper.
- **Pin Puncher:** Selected symbols are punctured by a small pin. Generally it is not observable until the document put in front of the light.
- **Typewriter Correction Ribbon:** Utilizing the space available between the lines, a confidential message is typed using correction tape. As a result, the confidential message is not visible until strong, bright light is put on the paper (Kour et al., 2014).

Figure 6.4 depicts the various kinds of steganography. As illustrated above, steganography is used to send secret messages for a specific recipient. The aim is to protect the confidential messages against exposure to unauthorized persons. The other research area concerning steganography is copyright marking, which aims to declare exclusive rights over particular documents or messages. This is further segregated into two sub-categories, that is, fingerprinting and watermarking.

Encryption and steganography are used to warrant data confidentiality, though the aim of each of the concepts is different. In encryption, everyone recognizes who is communicating to whom in secret, while steganography hides the presence of a confidential message and no one recognizes who is communicating to whom in secret. Thus, these features make

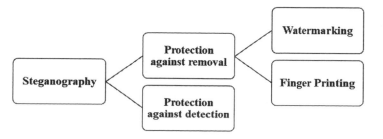

FIGURE 6.4
Types of steganography.

TABLE 6.1

Comparative Study of Various Secure Communication Techniques

Parameters	Confidentiality	Integrity	Un-removability
Encryption	Yes	No	Yes
Digital signature	No	Yes	No
Steganography	Yes/No	Yes/No	Yes

steganography more suitable for some situations where encryption is not appropriate (Popa, 1998; Caldwell, 2003).

Table 6.1 illustrates the comparative study of various encoding techniques used for secure message transmission.

For preserving the data confidentiality using encryption techniques, a key is required to both encrypt and decrypt the same messages. However, attacks are still possible by modifying the coded message, making it unrecoverable for the recipient.

A digital signature enables the sender to embed the author of a message. Although this signature can be detached effortlessly, any modification in the message will invalidate the embedded signature, thus overall integrity is maintained (Ferguson et al., 2003).

As aforementioned, steganography secretly transmits the message which is impossible to remove until the container/holder (in which secret message is embedded) is altered. The embedded message remains confidential unless an attacker finds a way to discover it (Ferguson et al., 2015).

6.3.1 Different Techniques of Steganography

6.3.1.1 Text Steganography

Text-based steganography uses a technique of hiding the data in any text file. This data can further be transmitted over an insecure channel. A few examples of this are mentioned below:

- Source Information Sent: Since Alice can race, encoding text in natural surroundings is deliberately effective.
- Source Information: Since Alice Can Encode source information that he/she wishes to send to the receiver.
- Confidential Message: Confidential information inside.

6.3.1.2 Auditory Steganography

Auditory-based steganography deals with the method of hiding data inside any audio signal media, as illustrated in Figure 6.5. In general, it contains two audio files: the first one acts as a cover file and the other one is the secret message encoded in the cover files.

6.3.1.3 Cinematic Steganography

As shown in Figure 6.6, the secret message, under this methodology, is hidden behind another video file. The benefit of using this method is that one can easily embed a large

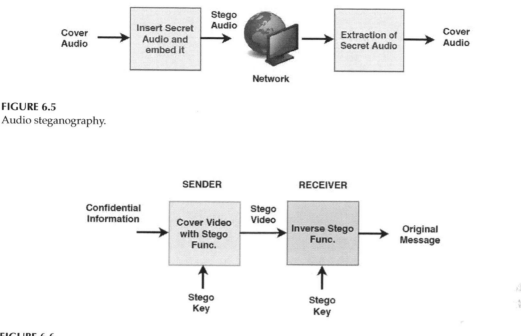

FIGURE 6.5
Audio steganography.

FIGURE 6.6
Cinematic steganography.

amount of data in the cover file, with the sender and receiver using a stego key to encode and decode the secret information.

6.3.1.4 Visual Steganography

Visual or image-based steganography uses images as the cover file to hide the data. Under this process, the secret data can be in any format, that is, textual or image. After the embedding is done by the sender, the stego-image (image with secret information), as illustrated in Figure 6.7, is ready to transfer over an insecure medium of transmission.

Original image

Original image + hidden data

FIGURE 6.7
Image steganography (Source: Vijayakumar, 2016).

Although steganography techniques help in the transmission of secret messages over the unsecured channel, various types of attacks still occur and these are discussed below:

1. **Steganography-Only-Attack:** While this steganographic medium is available for investigation, this attack is effective.
2. **Known-Carrier-Attack:** Under this attack, it is operational when both steganography media and cover are available for the analysis.
3. **Chosen-Steganography-Attack:** In this scenario, the attacker is known or knows the message carrier and the steganography tools.
4. **Known-Message-Attack:** This type of attack happens when the analyst is aware of the secret message(s).
5. **Chosen-Message-Attack:** In this case, the attacker is aware of both the message and the algorithms used to hide the message. It becomes easier for the analyst to decode the secret message.

6.3.2 Applications of Steganography

- To establish secure communication over an insecure channel.
- To protect data from the modification attack.
- To examine the data traffic between the users.
- To offer access to digital information.
- Generally used for video and audio synchronization, broadcasting, etc.

6.4 Cryptography Concepts

Cryptology is the research on techniques that ensure the authenticity and secrecy of information. Furthermore, cryptology is categorized into two sub-categories, that is, cryptanalysis and cryptography (see Figure 6.8).

Cryptography is the research of building such techniques, whereas cryptanalysis is the art of breaching the secrecy of such techniques (Spillman, 2005).

The prime focus of designing and using cryptography techniques is to address the fundamental services of information security (see Figure 6.9 and Table 6.2).

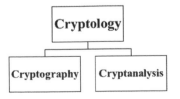

FIGURE 6.8
Cryptology and its types.

FIGURE 6.9
Fundamental services of information security.

TABLE 6.2

Terminologies

Terminologies	Description
Plain text	The actual message that the sender wishes to send to the selected recipient.
Ciphertext	Coded message or message which is hard to interpret.
Encryption	It is the process of hiding the actual content of the message in such a manner that no one can understand and interpret (unreadable format).
Decryption	It is the process of transforming or recovering the actual message from the coded or ciphertext.

Authentication: This service focuses on ensuring that authentic messages are transmitted between the communicating parties. Let us consider a case where the recipient receives a single informational message from any source. This kind of scenario authentication assures the recipient that the messages come from the authentic source and have not been altered by a third party in between.

Confidentiality: The prime focus of this service is to protect the data transmission between two parties from passive attacks. It ensures the communicating parties that the transmitted data remains confidential and no attackers can analyze the traffic flow.

Access Control: This service focuses on ensuring that only the legitimate person can access the assigned facility. Let us consider a case where the individual wants to gain access to any facility. This service first authenticates the individual and then only provides the right access control to the person.

Data Integrity: The prime focus of this service to assure the recipient that the received message is not altered, inserted, duplicated, replayed or rearranged. Thus this service protects the communication from denial of service and modification attacks.

Non-Repudiation: The prime focus of this service is to protect the sender/receiver from repudiation of sent messages.

6.4.1 Types of Cryptography

There are numerous ways to classify cryptography techniques (Stallings, 2006). In this context, based on encryption and decryption techniques employed, cryptography is further classified into two sub-categories.

- Symmetric cryptography.
- Asymmetric cryptography.

6.4.1.1 Symmetric Cryptography

Symmetric cryptography is a traditional encryption or secret key encoding technique. In this encoding system, the sender/receiver utilizes the identical key to encrypt/decrypt the message. Here, the secrecy of the message depends upon the secrecy of the key. Before communication is initiated, both parties must agree on using an identical key (Stallings, 2006; Kahate, 2013).

Figure 6.10 clearly states that the secret key for encrypting/decrypting the information is known to all the receivers. Thus, the message cannot be easily decrypted by knowing the encryption algorithm and ciphertext (Table 6.3).

6.4.1.1.1 Issues in Traditional Cryptography Techniques

An asymmetric cryptosystem is a fast and simple technique. The major issue in this encryption technique is the management of the secret key. As illustrated above, overall secrecy is based on a secret key irrespective of the ciphertext and encryption algorithm being known by the attacker. Here, the major issue is secure exchange of secret keys by the communicating parties. If the secret key is compromised, the whole coding system is in endanger (Stallings, 2006; Kahate, 2013).

6.4.1.1.2 Asymmetric Cryptography

Asymmetric cryptography is termed as public key cryptography. It involves the usage of two dissimilar keys: the private and public keys. The public key is recognized by everyone, while the private key is recognized by the subject itself. Figure 6.11 illustrates that the sender uses the receiver public key to encode the confidential message and the receiver uses its private key to decode the same message (see Table 6.4).

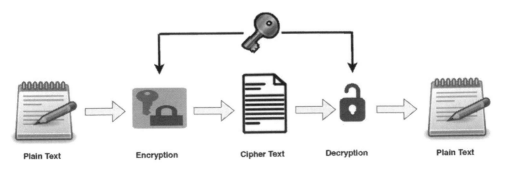

Plain Text   Encryption   Cipher Text   Decryption   Plain Text

FIGURE 6.10
Traditional encryption technique—symmetric cryptography.

TABLE 6.3

Symmetric Cryptography—Examples

Symmetric Cryptography—Examples	Number of Keys	Description
Data Encryption Standards (DES)	56 bits	DES was invented by US Bureau of Standards in 1977. DES considers a 64-bit block size of plain text as input and produces a ciphertext of 64 bits using a 56-bit secret key.
Triple Data Encryption Standards (Triple DES)	$3 \times 56 = 168$ bits	Triple DES overcame the limitations of the DES. This algorithm follows the same algorithm defined in DES, thus it is easy to implement. Although it adds greater security by using large key length, it is susceptible to man in the middle attacks.
Advanced Encryption Standards (AES)	128, 192 and 256 bits	AES overcame the limitations of DES and triple DES. It is built on the principle of permutation and combination. AES accomplishes operations in bytes. It takes 16 bytes of data as input and produces 128 bits of ciphertext.
IDEA	128-bit key	IDEA was established in the year 1991. It takes 64-bit size plain text as input and produces 64-bit size ciphertext using a 128-bit secret key length.

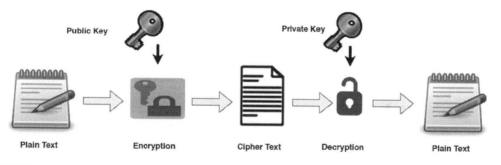

FIGURE 6.11
Asymmetric cryptography technique.

TABLE 6.4

Asymmetric Cryptography—Examples

Asymmetric Cryptography—Examples	Description
Digital Signature Standards (DSS)	DSS utilizes a digital signature algorithm (DSA) established by the National Security Agency (NSA). DSA is used to embed the digital signature in the message sent by the source. The digital signature ensures that this message is sent by the source. It brings authentication and data integrity services.
RSA	RSA is a secure symmetric or public key cryptography technique, developed by the scientists Rivest, Shamir and Adleman. This algorithm incorporates encryption and signing features. RSA is extensively used in commerce protocols and ensures security with long key length.
Elgamal	Elgamal incorporates encryption and signing features. It utilizes discrete logarithm algorithms and is widely used in various applications.

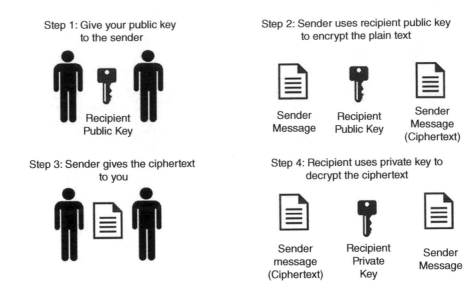

FIGURE 6.12
Process involved in asymmetric cryptography technique.

TABLE 6.5

Comparative Study of Cryptosystems

	Symmetric Cryptography	**Asymmetric Cryptography**
Keys	Single key	Two keys, that is, public and private
Encryption key	Secret key	Public key
Decryption key	Secret key	Private key

Figure 6.12 illustrates the process accomplished in asymmetric cryptography. In step 1, the sender retrieves the recipient public key from the repository. In steps 2 and 3, the sender takes the recipient's public key, encodes the plain text and produces ciphertext, and sends it to the recipient via the secure medium. In step 4, the recipient makes use of its own private key to decode the ciphertext and retrieve the plain text sent by the sender.

A comparative study of cryptosystems is illustrated in Table 6.5.

6.5 Benefits of a Hybrid Approach: Steganography and Cryptography

It has been found that while using steganography and cryptography techniques, individually, the attackers found it easier to decode the secret information. Hence, a hybrid approach, that is, merging both the methodologies, allows a more reliable, strong and highly secure system to be designed (Shukla et al., 2014). Moreover, combining these techniques will also give additional benefits like high security, less use of memory, and robustness of confidential information transmission across the channel. This will enable individuals to communicate with each other without any interference from the third party. Thus it is a more powerful technique for communication on a digital platform (Abdulzahra et al., 2014).

6.6 Recent Trends

Over the digital platform, there has been a continuous rise in information security threats over the past decades and this has become a major bottleneck for security professionals. Steganography and cryptography are considered as best practices to abolish this hazard. In a recent scenario, researchers are coming up with various blended techniques, by hybridization of both techniques. The hybridization of techniques enhances the level of security. In the cryptographic process, data is encrypted by a process known as SCMACS and symmetric key methodology, with both the source and the recipient sharing the identical key in the process of encoding/decoding. On the other hand, the popular and preferred LSB technique has been used for steganography (Dhamija and Dhaka, 2015). Another researcher proposed an extremely secure steganographic technique that combines Hyperelliptic Curve cryptography with a DNA sequence. It provides the advantages of steganography and DNA cryptography and affords an extreme level of secure interaction (Vijayakumar, 2016).

Further research highlights the approach in which a multilevel secret data hiding technique is used. This method uses two kinds of encryption techniques that include visual steganography and cryptography. In the first phase, the half-toning method is used which reduces the pixels and simplifies the process. In the next step, visual cryptography is applied to generate shares and offer the first level of security. Then the steganography LSB technique is applied to hide the shares in various modes of media like images, audio and videos (Patil and Goud, 2016). One of the research articles presented a method that claims to be stronger and more difficult to decode the confidential information. It uses both encryption and steganography techniques to make safe and secure communication. For encryption, the AES encoding technique of 128-bit key size is used to encrypt the information in UTF-8 format and further transform it into a base-64 format and make it appropriate for further processing. The further coded message is again twisted to attain the extreme level of security. Then, finally, the twisted coded messages are inserted in an appropriate cover image. This image is then transmitted securely over a network and carries confidential information. Hence, security is exhibited at four levels and, as a result, a confidential message is sent over an insecure channel (Karthikeyan et al., 2016).

In another approach, the authors used image-based steganography and DES algorithm techniques to send the secret information. In this method, 16 rounds with each block size about 64 bits are used along with the K-means clustering technique to cluster the images. Further, the data is embedded in every segment. In an image, information is available in the form of pixels. Every pixel is made up of three components, that is, RGB. Image segmentation uses these pixels to form a cluster (Pillai et al., 2016).

In another experiment for secure data transmission, the hybrid approach is used. In this method, the TwoFish algorithm is applied for encrypting the data and Adaptive B45 steganography methodology is used for hiding the information. The amalgamation of techniques makes it impossible for others to breach secrecy and to access confidential data

(Hingmire et al., 2016). With recent advancements in digital communication techniques, the authors extend the high-security capability of an encryption algorithm by using Pixel Value Differencing through the steganography AES cryptographic system (Joseph et al., 2015).

A survey on performance analysis of various encryption algorithms is performed, in which analysis is done between RSA, AES, DES, blended with the LSB technique. This helps to draw an implication based on their performances and it has been deduced that the AES technique works well and is incomparable with other methods in terms of time and space utilization (Padmavathi et al., 2013; Almuhammadi et al., 2017). A new encryption strategy is developed by the author in Mishra et al. (2014) in which they used the RSA encryption algorithm (128-byte key size) for coding the confidential message before implanting it into the cover image. This implanting of the confidential message is performed using the F5 steganographic algorithm. The author claims that the proposed algorithm is highly secured against analytical and observed attacks and that it gives high steganographic capacity and faster speed. Another simulation shows the secret information transmission using a combined approach by using the AES and LSB algorithms. A stego-image is generated by using the AES algorithm for encrypting the message and the LSB technique to hide the confidential messages inside an image. The authors claim that this encoding technique is more effective to establish secure and secret communication and attains a strong level of security (Sridevi et al., 2013).

6.7 Conclusion

This chapter describes the need for the secure transmission of confidential information across networks. It is designed to cover the concepts of cryptographic and steganographic techniques from its evolution to the recent trends.

References

Abdulzahra, H. et al. "Combining cryptography and steganography for data hiding in images." *Applied Computational Science*, 128–135, 2014.

Almuhammadi, S. et al. "A survey on recent approaches combining cryptography and steganography." *Computer Science Information Technology*, 7(3): 63–74, 2017.

Blanco, W. et al. *Herodotus, The Histories*. Trans. by Walter Blanco. New York: Norton, 1992.

Cachin, C. "An information-theoretic model for steganography." In *International Workshop on Info Hiding*, Portland, OR, pp. 306–318, 1998.

Caldwell, J., Second Lieutenant, "Steganography, US Air Force," 2003.

Dhamija, A. and Dhaka, V. "A novel cryptographic and steganographic approach for secure cloud data migration." In *ICGCIoT*, Greater Noida, India, pp. 346–351. IEEE, 2015.

Esslinger, B.. "CrypTool–ein E-Learning-Projekt für Kryptographie und Kryptoanalyse." 25th Crypto-Day, 2016.

Ferguson, N. et al. *Practical Cryptography* (Vol. *141*). New York: Wiley, 2003.

Ferguson, N. et al. "Generating randomness." In *Cryptography Engineering: Design Principles and Practical Applications*, pp. 135–161. Indianapolis, IN: Wiley, 2015.

Hingmire, A. et al. "Image steganography using adaptive b45 algorithm combined with pre-processing by twofish encryption." *IESRJ*, 2(4). 2016.

Joseph, F. et al. "Advanced security enhancement of data before distribution." 2015.

Kahate, A. *Cryptography and Network Security*. Tata McGraw Hill Education, 2013.

Karthikeyan, B. et al. "Enhanced security in steganography using encryption and quick response code." In *2016 International Conference on WiSPNET*, Chennai, India, pp. 2308–2312. IEEE, 2016.

Kour, J. et al. "Steganography techniques—A review paper." *IJERMT*, 3(5): 132–135, 2014.

Mishra, M. et al. "Secret communication using public key steganography." *ICRAIE-2014*, Jaipur, India, pp. 1–5. IEEE, 2014.

National Institute of Standards and Technology (NIST). "Security requirements for cryptographic modules." Federal Information Processing Standards Publication (FIPS PUB 140-2), 2001.

Padmavathi, B. et al. "A survey on performance analysis of DES, AES and RSA algorithm along with LSB substitution." *IJSR*, 2(4): 170–174, 2013.

Patil, S. S. and Goud, S. "Enhanced multi-level secret data hiding." *International Journal of Scientific Research in Science, Engineering and Technology (IJSRSET)*, 2(2): 846–850, 2016.

Pillai, B. et al. "Image steganography method using k-means clustering and encryption techniques." In *ICACCI 2016*, Jaipur, India, pp. 1206–1211. IEEE, 2016.

Popa, R. "An analysis of steganographic techniques." Faculty of Automatics and Computers, Computer Science and Software Engineering, University of Timisoara, Timis, Romania, 1998.

Shukla, C. P. et al. "Enhance security in steganography with cryptography." *IJARCCE*, 3(3): 5696–5699. 2014.

Stallings, W. *Cryptography and Network Security*, 4th edn. New Delhi, India: Pearson Education India, 2006.

Spillman, R. *Classical and Contemporary Cryptology*. Upper Saddle River, NJ: Pearson Education, 2005, pp. 144–212.

Sridevi, R. et al. "Image steganography combined with cryptography." *International Journal of Computers & Technology*, 9(1): 976–984, 2013.

Vijayakumar, P., "An improved level of security for dna steganography using hyperelliptic curve cryptography." *Wireless Personal Communications*, 89(4): 1221–1242, 2016.

7

An FPGA-Based Advanced Lightweight Cryptography Architecture for IoT Security and Its Cryptanalysis

Rajdeep Chakraborty[1] and Jyotsna Kumar Mandal[2]

[1] *Netaji Subhash Engineering College, Kolkata, India*

[2] *University of Kalyani, Nadia, India*

7.1 Introduction: Background and Driving Forces

In this era smart era with IoT-based data transfer and communication, digital and information security have become indispensable (Stallings, 2002; Forouzan, 2007; Kaur, 2009). The primary goal of confidentiality is achieved by a proposed cipher (Stallings, 2002; Forouzan, 2007) and lightweight implementation. This is a simple scheme and the result is comparable with the RSA block cipher and TDES block cipher (Stallings, 2002; Forouzan, 2007), which are well known and widely used. Lightweight cryptography is such that its implementation must be within 2000–2500 gates/GEs. Symmetric ciphers or private key block ciphers have the same key for both the encryption scheme/encoding and the scheme for decryption/decoding, if anyhow two keys are used then the first key should be equated from the second key and vice versa. Symmetric ciphers or private key block ciphers have some advantages over asymmetric ciphers or public key block ciphers, which are as follows:

- Symmetric ciphers or private key block ciphers are comparable with asymmetric ciphers or public key block ciphers with respect to cryptographic parameter strength and hardware parameter strength.

- Private key or symmetric ciphers or private key block ciphers generate lesser encryption and decryption scheme throughput time and execution time than those of public key or asymmetric ciphers or public key block ciphers.

- Symmetric scheme ciphers or private key scheme block ciphers, embedded in and for resource-constrained hardware communicating devices like mobile phones and IoT devices, are very easy, which is quite impractical for asymmetric ciphers or public key block ciphers.

The proposed cipher (encryption and decryption) has been designed and implemented in FPGA-based devices (Navabi, 2008; Wolf, 2009) in Spartan 3E Series and for this it has been programmed in IEEE VHDL (Bhasker, 2004; Kaur, 2009). The Spartan 3E series is enough for implementing a lightweight security solution and symmetric scheme key cryptography is widely used for the same purpose. The main reasons for the FPGA-based design and implementation are:

- It helps to create new useful products and lower the cost of useful products by involving a smaller number of working people and used resources in less time.
- It is suitable for and widely accepted as a "green" environment concept.
- Throughput total time and total design area are less.

The above discussion drives the motivation to do research work with this new technology, a Rotational Conical Cipher (RCC), along with SPN and CBC mode, which is proposed and described in this chapter. It is also an FPGA-based lightweight (Stallings, 2002; Forouzan, 2007) symmetric scheme key cryptography or private key block cipher. Figure 7.1 (Chatterjee and Mandal, 2013) gives the formation of the cone from the source block. The method is that we take n-bits and XORED the successive bits to get the next row of (n − 1) bits. This XORING will continue unless we get a single bit. Thus it will form a cone as shown in Figure 7.1, and the source block may be the plaintext or ciphertext. There are four options for encryption and decryption. In Option A, we take all the leftmost bits from top to bottom, Option B involves taking all the leftmost bits from bottom to top, Option C involves taking all the rightmost bits from corner top to corner bottom, and using Option D involves taking all the rightmost bits from corner bottom to corner top. So with every discussed option we will get the output as n-bits. The encryption and decryption is done within the same process and finally circular left rotation of the plaintext is done to achieve the ciphertext.

7.1.1 Literature Review

This proposed block cipher, RCC, is inspired by the NIST (McKay et al., 2017) report about lightweight cryptography published in 2017. In a cryptography project, Kerry A. McKay et al. proposed the working scope of NIST's lightweight cryptography and security project

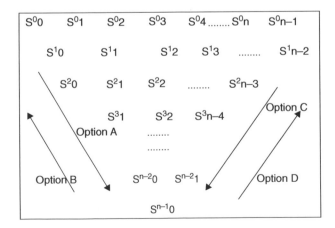

FIGURE 7.1
Formation of cone from source block (SB).

including all cryptographic existing primitives and existing modes which are very much needed in constrained-resource environments. This report's emphasis is on lightweight cryptography, lightweight crypto-hash, lightweight authentication and some protocols. The long-term effective security is very much needed. By using these algorithms, the aim should be implementation in post-quantum security, or these applications should allow all of them to be easily replaceable by those algorithms which are implemented and designed for post-quantum security.

The next survey was carried out in part VI of the Springer book by Peng et al. (2020). In Chapter 19, Dhanda et al. (Dhanda et al., 2020) give a comprehensive security overview of the high perception layer, which is considered the lowermost layer used in IoT architecture and is also used in wireless sensor networks (WSN) and many resource-constrained embedded hardware devices. The discussed devices are very limited in many parameters such as memory, computation, power, and energy. So a large number of attacks are performed against these limited resources devices. Thus a number of solutions, such as lightweight cryptography, and various protocols have been suggested by engineers and researchers. Jha et al. in Chapter 20 (Jha et al., 2020) discuss some security threats for time synchronization lightweight protocols used in IoT architecture that are in the IoT ecosystem. The sensors are generally and eventually located in a remote and unattended environment where there is a high chance of the existence and interference of malicious nodes. Bhanu Chander and Kumaravelan Gopalakrishnan in Chapter 21 (Chander and Gopalakrishnan, 2020) outline the latest vulnerability issues in IoT architecture and security, discussing cyber-attacks in the IoT.

Sebastian Mödersheim and Luca Viganò defined and implemented a cryptography protocol named Alfa–Beta Privacy (Mödersheim and Viganò, 2019), This protocol is based on specifying two formulae α and β in first-order logic with Herbrand universes, where α equates to the intentionally released information and β equates to the actual cryptographic messages the intruder can observe. Therefore (α, β)-privacy means that the attacker cannot derive α knowing the β and vice versa.

Andy Rupp et al. proposed a new lightweight cryptographic ecommerce payment technique for transit systems (Rupp et al., 2015) known as P4R (Privacy-Preserving Pre-Payments with Refunds) that is very suitable for low-cost user IoT devices in resource-constrained environments. This payment solution technique builds on Brands's e-cash technique to calculate the prepayment system and on Boneh–Lynn–Shacham (BLS) signatures used for refund options. Estimation results demonstrate that the data required for 20 rides consume less than 10 kB of memory, and the payment and refund transactions during a ride take less than half a second. This system also protects the privacy of honest users where the transactions are made anonymous (except for deposits) and trips are unlikable. This total system has been implemented through a microprocessor-based system.

The final survey is based on an SCI-indexed publication (Colombier and Bossuet, 2014) involving a survey of crypto-hardware security design with IC that can be used in intellectual property rights. Total cost and total performance are considered to be the main parameters for IC-design; the design and implementation of a secure, efficient, lightweight security protection scheme for a design data set is a serious challenge considering the hardware security community. However, some techniques, schemes and works propose many different ways to protect and provide security to design data that consist of functional locking, hardware obfuscation and IC/IP identification. This study also presents a survey of academic research performed on the protection of design data. It concludes with the need to design and implement an efficient protection technique based on several hardware and security properties.

Section 7.2 describe the lightweight security architecture using RCC and the substitution and permutation technique and CBC, Section 7.3 gives the key generation process, Section 7.4 provides the cryptanalysis, Section 7.5 gives lightweight cryptography analysis through simulation, Section 7.6 gives applications of this proposed cipher, and in Section 7.7 a conclusion is drawn.

7.2 The Lightweight Security Architecture

We have studied many cryptographic algorithms for security but the question is how to implement the security requirement in hardware (Navabi, 2008; Kaur, 2009; Wolf, 2009). As per the definition of lightweight cryptography, one can use only 2500 GEs for implementation. The hardware implementation is also suitable to achieve IoT security. Figure 7.2 gives the micro-architecture (Bhasker, 2004; Navabi, 2008; Kaur, 2009; Wolf, 2009) of lightweight cryptography.

This is proposed working model architecture of actual implementation of lightweight security. This micro-architecture consists of external signals (Navabi, 2008; Kaur, 2009; Wolf, 2009) and internal modules (Navabi, 2008; Kaur, 2009; Wolf, 2009). There are five types of external signals/bus (Bhasker, 2004; Navabi, 2008; Kaur, 2009; Wolf, 2009), 130-bits key bus, 20-bits control bus, 1-bit option bus, 128-bits data bus, power, ground and clock signal buses. Internally there is only 130-bits multiplexed internal bus and this bus is connected with every internal modules. The internal modules are 130-bits key memory register, 21-bits control memory registers, encryption and decryption modules with sub-modules RCC Unit, SPN Network (Stallings, 2002; Forouzan, 2007) and CBC unit, 128-bits data memory register, 64 kB of general purpose memory, Multiplexer and De-multiplexer (MUX–DEMUX) module and control units. The description of each modules and buses are given from Sections 7.2.1 to 7.2.6.

7.2.1 External Signals and Buses

The 130-bits key input bus provides 130 bits of key block to perform encryption and decryption. The 20-bits control bus provides various modes of operation of this micro-architecture which is performed by the control unit. The 1-bit option bus states whether

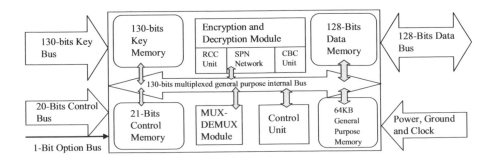

FIGURE 7.2
Micro-architecture of lightweight cryptography model.

encryption is performed or decryption is performed, value "0" for encryption and value "1" for encryption. The 128-bits data bus is bi-directional. When encryption is performed the input is 128-bits plaintext and output is 128-bis ciphertext, and when decryption is performed the input is 128-bits ciphertext and output is 128-bits plaintext. The general power signal and ground signal are provided. The clock signal is also provided so that this micro-architecture may work in both a synchronized and an asynchronized manner when connected to an IoT network.

7.2.2 Internal Bus

The internal bus proposed in this architecture is 130 bits, as it is the maximum limit of data transfer per clock cycle. This bus is multiplexed and controlled by the control unit. All the other internal modules are connected with this bus.

7.2.3 Internal Memory Registers

Four types of internal registers (Bhasker, 2004; Navabi, 2008; Kaur, 2009; Wolf, 2009) are proposed in this micro-architecture:

- A 130-bits key memory registers holds the 130-bits key and is generated by the key generation algorithm as discussed in Section 7.3 and provides to the architecture externally. The key generation module is provided externally to reduce the gate requirements of the proposed micro-architecture. Moreover, the key requirement is pseudo-random number so the user can use other key generation algorithms also.
- The 21-bits control memory has a 1-bit option signal and 20 bits of modes of operation of this micro-architecture which will be illustrated in the discussion of the control unit.
- The 128-bits data memory is basically plaintext or ciphertext to be encrypted or decrypted. This data memory is similar to the accumulator register used in micro-processors. Both the source and destination of one cycle of encryption and one cycle of decryption in unit clock/machine cycle is this 128-bits data register.
- The 64 kB of general purpose register is used here to store 64 kB of plaintext and ciphertext. This register enables this micro-architecture to perform 4096 blocks of encryption or decryption at a time. External buses are generally slower than internal buses, which is why this register will provide 4096 times faster encryption or decryption than that of single block architecture.

7.2.4 Internal Encryption and Decryption Module

This is the main module of this architecture and contains all the logical circuit to perform encryption and decryption. This module has three sub-components:

- RCC Module: RCC performs encryption and decryption of 128-bits blocks at a time. Encryption and decryption are given in Figure 7.1. Here, 128 bits of plaintext are taken and successive bits are XORED to get the next row of 127 bits. This process is repeated to reduce the bits to 1 bit forming a cone. Out of the four options, any option can be taken for resultant ciphertext. The same operation is done for decryption.

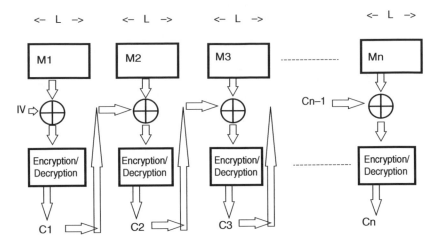

FIGURE 7.3
CBC—Mode of encryption and decryption.

- Option A (00) is taking all the left bits from top to bottom.
- Option B (01) is taking all the left bits from bottom to top.
- Option C (10) is taking all the right bits from top to bottom.
- Option D (11) is taking all the right bits from bottom to top.
- SPN Network: The next phase of encryption is the SPN, where the S-box of AES is used. To get permutation, the shift row and mix column operation of AES is performed.
- CBC Unit: This is a multiple blocks unit encryption mode. The block size is provided in the control bus. Figure 7.3 illustrates the CBC mode of operation. In the CBC mode of operation, during encryption, the plaintext is broken into multiples of 128-bits block sizes, the first block is XORED with initial vector (IV) and fed to the encryption function and the result is the first ciphertext block. In the second round, CBC, the first round ciphertext is XORED with the second plaintext block and generates the second ciphertext block. This process is repeated until all blocks are encrypted. The decryption is the reverse process where the input is ciphertext and the output is plaintext, as shown in Figure 7.3. The IV is same for encryption as well as decryption.

7.2.5 Internal Mux–DeMux Module

This multiplexer and de-multiplexer (Bhasker, 2004; Navabi, 2008; Kaur, 2009; Wolf, 2009) control the internal data bus. When there is encryption or decryption or exchange of plaintext/ciphertext between the 64 kB of general purpose memory and 128-bits data memory through the 128-bits external data bus, it enables the first 128 MSB-bits of internal data bus and the 2 LSB-bits on internal data bus are put in high impedance state. When there is key exchange, this module enables all 130 bits of the internal data bus. When there is control flow, it enables the first 21 MSB-bits of the internal data bus and puts the remaining 109 bits of the internal data bus in high impedance state.

7.2.6 Internal Control Unit

The control unit (Bhasker, 2004; Navabi, 2008; Kaur, 2009; Wolf, 2009) works on the value stored in the 21-bits control memory. Figure 7.4 gives the 21-bits values.

The internal control unit is proposed to work as a 21-bits control memory. The notation CB00 means the first LSB control bit 00 and CB20 means the first MSB control bit 20. The working of the control unit is as follows:

- Option/CB20: This bit contains the 1-bit option external data bus. Value "0" represents encryption and value "1" represents decryption.

- Set–Reset/CB19: This bit contains the reset value of the proposed micro-architecture. When the value is "1" the architecture resets. All the data registers and key registers become zero and encryption/decryption is set to initial vector.

- RCC Option0 and Option1/CB18 and CB17: This is a 2-bits value. It is already seen that RCC encrypts and decrypts in four ways. So, 00 value selects Option A encryption/decryption, 01 value selects Option B encryption/decryption, 10 value selects Option C encryption/decryption, and 11 value selects Option D encryption/decryption as described in Section 7.1. The left circular rotation is done for encryption and right circular rotation is done for decryption. The number of bits rotated is based on block number. The n-times rotation is done for the nth block during both encryption and decryption.

- CBC Enable/CB 16: This bit enables the CBC mode of encryption/decryption if there are multiple blocks to be encrypted/decrypted. All the blocks are transferred from 64 kB general purpose memory and the results are stored in the same location. This continues until the value provided CB00 – CB11.

- Sync/Async/CB15: This bit represents synchronous and asynchronous modes of operation of this micro-architecture.

- Key/Data/Control Transfer/CB14-CB13: This is a 2-bit value, where "00" means 128-bits data transfer, "01" means 130-bits key transfer, "10" means 21-bits control signal transfer through internal data bus, and "11" means memory access.

- Impedance/CB12: This is a flip-flop to put the internal common bus in high impedance state and data/memory/control value transfer state.

Option/ CB20	Set- Reset/ CB19	RCC Option0/ CB18	RCC Option1/ CB17	CBC Enable/ CB16	Sync- Async/ CB15	Key/Data/Con Transfer/ CB14	Key/Data/Con Transfer/ CB13	Impe/ CB12	BS11/ CB11
BS10/ CB10	BS09/ CB09	BS08/ CB08	BS07/ CB07	BS06/ CB06	BS05/ CB05	BS04/ CB04	BS03/ CB03	BS02/ CB02	BS01/ CB01
BS00/ CB00									

FIGURE 7.4
21-bits control memory structure.

- BS10 – BS00/CB10 – CB00: Since 64 kB internal memory is there, 4096 blocks can be encrypted/decrypted using CBC mode of encryption/decryption. Since 2^{12} = 4096, these 12 bits store the address of 4096 blocks of 128 bits each. This is basically the memory address or the 12 bits represent how many blocks are to be encrypted/decrypted.

This section discussed in detail how we can actually realize lightweight cryptography through architecture and how it can be used in IoT security. Section 7.4 gives an idea of cryptanalysis through which we can optimize a block cipher. Section 7.5 gives an idea of some simulation-based results through which we can optimize an FPGA security micro-architecture.

7.3 Key Generation

This section proposes a 130-bits secret key to be used in each session (Stallings, 2002; Forouzan, 2007).

Key generation is considered to be a very important algorithm of block cipher, either symmetric or asymmetric block cipher. In symmetric block cipher or private key block cipher, only a single key is used in encryption of plaintext and in ciphertext decryption. If these two keys are different, that is the encryption key and the decryption key, then knowledge of one key is sufficient to derive the other key.

Table 7.1 (Jha and Mandal, 2011) gives 130-bits key (Stallings, 2002; Forouzan, 2007) generation. The plaintext source file is encrypted by different block sizes with 13 times in

TABLE 7.1

Generation of Secret Key

| | Formation of 130-Bits Secret Key | | | |
| | Decimal | | Binary | |
Iteration Number	Block Size	Option	Block Size	Option
01	128	1st	10000000	00 (A)
02	120	3rd	01111000	10 (C)
03	112	2nd	01110000	01 (B)
04	100	2nd	01100100	01 (B)
05	64	1st	01000000	00 (A)
06	60	4th	00111100	11 (D)
07	32	2nd	00100000	01 (B)
08	30	3rd	00011110	10 (C)
09	16	4th	00010000	11 (D)
10	10	1st	00001010	00 (A)
11	8	3rd	00001000	10 (C)
12	4	2nd	00000100	01 (B)
13	2	1st	00000010	00 (A)

a row of execution. For example, the first iteration or the first round is of 128-bits block size and is encrypted by choosing the first option, for the second iteration or for the second round will be of 112-bits block size and so on. In Table 7.1, block sizes are encoded in 8 bits and options are encoded in 2 bits.

So, in each and every iteration or each round, 10-bits encoded code is obtained. Concatenating these 13 codes of 10-bits each generates 130-bits generated secret key to be used in each session for encryption and decryption. The coded 10-bits values are absolutely pseudo-random. Here, from this table, the 130-bits secret key used for each session is as follows:

$$K = 1000000000011110001001110000010110010001$$
$$0100000000001111001100100000100011110100001$$
$$0000110000101000000010001000001000001000.$$

A new secret key will be generated for another new session.

7.4 Cryptanalysis

The cryptanalysis finds loopholes in the encryption system and is used to optimize any encryption system. This architecture is mainly based on the RCC, SPN and CBC block of encryption. So this security module has been implemented whereby first 128-bits plaintext is fed to the RCC and then to the SPN. Finally, multiple blocks are encrypted using the CBC mode of encryption.

In this section, a Chi-Square test used for cryptanalysis is used to test the NULL hypothesis. This test measures the difference between plaintext and ciphertext.

The Pearson's Chi-Square test was used (Chakraborty and Mandal, 2006, 2011). This is also known as the Chi-Square goodness-of-fit test or the test for independence or non-homogeneity or heterogeneity between source file and target file.

$$\chi^2 = (O - E)^2 \tag{7.1}$$

where
   O is the Observed Frequency ciphertext.
   E is the Expected Frequency plaintext, from where O is taken.
   df is the "degree of freedom" $(n - 1)$ contains variation of characters.
   χ^2 is Chi-Square calculated using Equation 7.1.

The Chi-Square test is calculated by choosing ten different files which are encrypted with RCC first, then with RSA and finally with TDES, respectively. The program using Equation 7.1 finds the Chi-Square values of these ten files.

Table 7.2 gives the Chi-Square values. Figure 7.5 shows a graphical chart calculated using logarithm base ten scales converted to obtain the Chi-Square value of ten different source files. Observing Table 7.2 and Figure 7.5, we can conclude that the Chi-Square values generated for the proposed cipher, RCC, are greater than those of the RSA encrypted source files, but for TDES, the RCC result is 50% better.

TABLE 7.2

Cryptanalysis of Proposed Micro-Architecture (PMA)

File Name	Size in kB	Chi-Square Values		
		PMA	**RSA**	**TDES**
Version.txt	1	1.76	1.74	1.79
Ukraine.txt	5	4.95	4.88	5.08
Content.txt	10	5.68	5.66	5.66
Removdrv.txt	21	5.83	5.82	5.90
PropList.txt	53	5.81	5.80	5.81
Python_25_License.txt	101	6.83	6.83	6.87
Result_analysis.xls	286	5.97	5.78	5.99
Metconv.txt	1156			
Photo0139.jpg	1272	6.45	6.44	6.45
Wildlife.wmv	25631	4.94	4.92	4.93

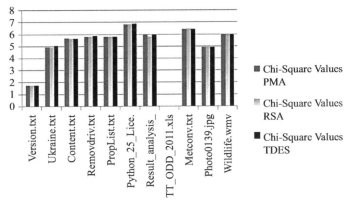

FIGURE 7.5
Chi-Square values in logarithmic (base 10) scale.

7.5 Simulation-Based Results

In this section, the authors have tried to prove and conclude that this proposed cipher, RCC, is indeed a lightweight cryptography in view of its implementation. These analyses may be used to optimize the micro-architecture proposed. These analyses will also helpful for designing any lightweight system for IoT devices. The utilization summary is the list of all the hardware/GE components used in this design and numbers of each of these components used. From the results, it can be stated that this micro-architecture security solution is indeed applicable for IoT security.

Table 7.3 summarizes the synthesis report (Navabi, 2008; Wolf, 2009) which was obtained after successful implementation using IEEE VHDL through simulation in Xilinx ISE 8.1i (Wolf, 2009). The number of four-input Look-Up-Tables (LUTs) of RCC used is 53 and the

TABLE 7.3

Synthesis Summary of Proposed Micro-Architecture

Device Utilization Summary			
Logic Utilization	**Used**	**Available**	**Utilization**
Number of 4 input LUTs	53	1,920	2%
Logic Distribution			
Number of occupied Slices	27	960	2%
Number of Slices containing only related logic	27	27	100%
Number of Slices containing unrelated logic	0	27	0%
Total Number of 4 input LUTs	53	1,920	2%
Number of bonded IOBs	20	66	30%
Total equivalent gate count for design	324		
Additional JTAG gate count for IOBs	960		

number available is 1920, so utilization is 2%. Number of occupied slices of RCC is 27 and available is 960, 2% is the utilization. The number of slices containing related logic of RCC is 100% and it is worth stating that this result is the same for other implementations also. The number of used slices with unrelated logic of RCC is 0%. The number of bonded input–output blocks (IOBs) of RCC is 20 out of 66, so utilization is 30%. The total equivalent gate count is only 324 and the additional JTAG gate count for IOBs is only 960. Therefore, it can be stated that the RCC is indeed a lightweight cryptography with respect to the available resources in Xilinx FPGA.

7.6 Applications

Some of the applications of the proposed RCC–SPN–CBC block cipher/micro-architecture are listed below:

- The proposed cipher, RCC, is well suited for various embedded systems such as mobile phones, smart watches and IoT network devices as it is simple and easy to implement.
- Electronic code books for encoding English alphabets are another application area.
- Virtual Private Networks (known as VPN) and also master-key-based security protocols are both good application areas.
- This technique, RCC, is suitable for hardware applications such as switches, gateways and routers.

7.7 Conclusion

Therefore we can conclude in this chapter that we have successfully proposed and implemented a lightweight cryptographic technique using RCC–SPN–CBC block cipher. The cryptanalysis test done with RSA and TDES using Chi-Square values generates better and also comparable results. Chi-Square based cryptanalysis is a widely used method to test the NULL hypothesis. We can also conclude that RCC is heterogeneous or non-homogeneous in contrast to the widely used RSA and TDES. Moreover, simulation hardware-based results prove that the RCC is indeed a lightweight cryptography. The proposed cipher and micro-architecture can be used in various applications. The lightweight cryptography is widely used today to secure IoT and embedded devices. The RCC–SPN–CBC technique can also be used to develop encryption-based lightweight authentication protocols. The future scope of the author is to develop a lightweight hash function for message authentication and message integrity.

References

Bhasker, J. 2004. *A VHDL Primer*. Thirteen Indian Reprint 2004, Pearson Education Asia, Bengaluru, India, 14–82, ISBN: 81-7808-016-8 .

Chakraborty, R. and J. K. Mandal. 2006. "A microprocessor-based block cipher through rotational addition technique (RAT)," in *9th International Conference on Information Technology (ICIT 2006)*, December 18–21, 2006, Bhubaneswar, India, 155–159, organized and sponsored by IEEE Computer Society, IEEE, ISBN-10: 0-7695-2635-7/06, ISBN-13: 978-0-7695-2635-5.

Chakraborty, R. and J. K. Mandal. 2011. "FPGA based cipher design & implementation of recursive oriented block arithmetic and substitution technique (ROBAST)," *International Journal of Advanced Computer Science and Applications (IJACSA)* 2(4), 54–59.

Chander, B. and K. Gopalakrishnan. 2020. "Chapter 21: Security Vulnerabilities and Issues of Traditional Wireless Sensors Networks in IoT," in *Principles of Internet of Things (IoT) Ecosystem: Insight Paradigm*, 519–549. Cham: Springer. DOI: https://doi.org/10.1007/978-3-030-33596-0_21.

Chatterjee, N. and J. K. Mandal. 2013. "Detection of blackhole behaviour using triangular encryption in NS2," in *1st International Conference on Computational Intelligence: Modeling, Techniques and Applications (CIMTA-2013)*, Kalyani, India, 524–529, http://www.sciencedirect.com/science/journal/22120173/10.

Colombier, B. and L. Bossuet. 2014. "Survey of hardware protection of design data for integrated circuits and intellectual properties," *IET Computers & Digital Techniques* 8(6), 274–287. DOI: 10.1049/iet-cdt.2014.0028.

Dhanda, S. S., B. Singh, and P. Jindal. 2020. "Chapter 19: IoT Security: A Comprehensive View," in *Principles of Internet of Things (IoT) Ecosystem: Insight Paradigm*, 467–494. Cham: Springer. DOI: https://doi.org/10.1007/978-3-030-33596-0_19.

Forouzan, B. A. 2007. *Cryptography and Network Security*, Special Indian Edition 2007. Tata Mc-Graw-Hill India, 61-110: ISBN-13: 978-0-07-066046-5, ISBN-10: 0-07-066046-8.

Jha, P. K. and J. K. Mandal. 2011. *Symmetric Encryption – Algorithm, Analysis and Applications*. LAP - Lambert Academic Publishing, Latvia, European Union, 222–223, ISBN: 978-3-8454-2061-5.

Jha, S. K., N. Panigrahi, and A. Gupta. 2020. "Chapter 20: Security Threats for Time Synchronization Protocols in IoT," in *Principles of Internet of Things (IoT) Ecosystem: Insight Paradigm*, 495–517. Cham: Springer. DOI: https://doi.org/10.1007/978-3-030-33596-0_20.

Kaur, K. 2009. *Digital System Design*. Saarbrücken: Scitech Publications (India) Pvt. Ltd, 21–50, ISBN: 978-81-8371-188-3.

McKay, K. A., L. Bassham, M. S. Turan, and N. Mouha. 2017. "NISTIR 8114, Report on Lightweight Cryptography," 1–10. DOI: https://doi.org/10.6028/NIST.IR.8114.

Mödersheim, S. and L. Viganò. 2019. "Alpha-beta privacy." *ACM Transactions on Privacy and Security* 22(1), 519–549, Article 7. DOI: https://doi.org/10.1145/3289255.

Navabi, Z.. 2008. *Embedded Core Design with FPGA(s)*, Edition 2008. New York: Tata Mc-Graw Hill India, 110–200. ISBN-13: 978-0-07-013978-7, ISBN-10: 0-07-013978-4.

Peng, S.-L., S. Pal, and L. Huang. 2020. *Principles of Internet of Things (IoT) Ecosystem: Insight Paradigm*, Intelligent Systems Reference Library, vol. *174*. Cham: Springer, 467–549. DOI: https://doi.org/10.1007/978-3-030-33596-0.

Rupp, A., F. Baldimtsi, G. H. Lder, and C. Paar. 2015. "Cryptographic theory meets practice: Efficient and privacy-preserving payments for public transport," *ACM Transactions on Information and System Security* 17(3), 10:01–10:31, Article 10. DOI: http://dx.doi.org/10.1145/2699904.

Stallings, W. 2002. *Cryptography and Network Security: Principle and Practice*, 2nd edn. London: Pearson Education Asia, Sixth Indian Reprint, 6–90, ISBN: 81-7808-605-0.

Wolf, W. 2009. *FPGA-Based System Design*. London: Pearson Education Asia, First Impression – 2009, 121–448, ISBN: 978-81-317-2465-1.

8

An Overview of Digital Image Forensics: Image Morphing and Forgery Detection Algorithms

Rahul Chauhan, Preeti Mishra, and R.C. Joshi
Graphic Era Hill University, Dehradun, India

8.1 Introduction

Multimedia data is generating at a much faster rate than ever and thus creating a lot of opportunities in image processing techniques. It is convenient to understand the image content and is an effective natural way of communication compared with text. Proverbs like "seeing believes" create doubt in the mind of the viewer. Tempering and adulteration of images are done on a large scale which is even impossible for the human eye to detect. There are various sophisticated tools and software available on the market which can easily edit the images as per requirements. So it is a challenging task to maintain the authenticity of an image. In digital image forensics, the credibility and authenticity of images is being analyzed by a variety of means. Because of its application in the fields of intelligence, legal service, sports, news reporting and medical imaging, it is fast becoming a popular field. In the past, lots of tampering incidents have occurred in sports. Ball tampering is one such incident, wherein the image extracted from the video frames gets analyzed for possible tampering.

Image forgery is considered to be the main driving force for digital image forensics. It was started in early 1840, when the first fake picture was created by Hippolyte Bayard (Shaid, 2009) in which it seems like he was trying to commit suicide. Later on in history there have been a number of such incidents occurring, and with the advancement in editing tools and software, forgery has become a popular field. As a consequence, the doctored images start appearing everywhere in the world in every application and field. So trust in digital information, especially in visual content, is starting to be lost within society, and the sophisticated tools and software make it even worse.

So the researchers believe that there is a need to understand the history of digital images before making any interpretation and conclusion about any digital visual content. This belief gave rise to two questions among the researchers. Firstly, is the captured image taken by the same sensing device (camera) that is being claimed, and secondly does the information depicted in the image resemble the original scene or not. All these curiosities gave motivation to develop the image forgery detection techniques. Numerous pieces of research work have been carried out on forgery detection algorithms and techniques. Some approaches used trustworthy cameras (Friedman, 1993). During the image acquisition process, digital signatures and watermarks are left by a trustworthy camera. If any modification or tampering has been attempted on an image, one can identify any type of forgery attempted with the calculated value of the digital watermark (Cox, Miller, Bloom et al., 2007; Farid, 2009). However, in practical terms the implementation of digital watermarking is not commonly followed because there are no standard protocols for manufacturing cameras.

8.1.1 A Sequential Processing Cycle of a Digital Image

A digital image needs to go through three steps in its life cycle and it is mainly divided into three important phases starting with image acquisition, then coding, and the last step is editing (Piva, 2013). Irrespective of the type of scene captured and the utility of the captured scene, every image needs to undergo these important steps. As mentioned in Figure 8.1, a digital image needs to undergo all these steps in its life cycle. In the acquisition phase, the reflected light from the highlighted real object or scene is collected by the sensing lens which is generally CMOS based camera technology and it is being focused by the lens, where the digital footprint of the captured scene is generated. Normally the reflected light contains a lot of artifacts and thus is being considered by color filter array (CFA) for filtering before it gets sensed by the sensor. Certain components of light are permitted by CFA because of the presence of a thin film on the sensor (Piva, 2013). Red, green, or blue are generally the main colors generated with respect to corresponding pixels. Thus to obtain a digital color image, all the three primary colors with respect to each pixel of the sensor output are interpolated with the help of a de-mosaicing process. Contrast enhancement, saturation, exposure and white balancing are some tasks related to the camera processing aiming to improve the physical appearance of an image.

Generally the captured 2D-signal is stored in camera memory and due to the limited storage inside camera, lossy compression at the camera end is done in most of the conventional camera sensing technology. Another alternative is JPEG format which is usually followed in commercial sensing devices. There is some post processing that needs to be done on the image to modify its content for better interpretation and recognition of information. A number of geometrical transformations (rotate, crop, resize, translate and

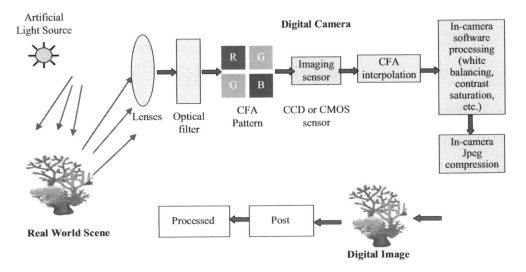

FIGURE 8.1
A schematic representation of the digital image life cycle starting from acquisition to processing.

scaling, etc.) are performed to produce the desired information in an image. Besides that, there are some fundamental operations like saturation, contrast enhancement and white balance that are quite often used to produce a better quality of information in an image. However, after initial editing, very often the image is supposed to be saved in a standard format, like JPEG format, and if required than recompression might occur.

Image forensics is not just limited to forgery and forgery detection algorithms. Morphing is also a type of forgery that is prominently used in the history. Perception of forgery is always negative and there have always been ethical issues associated with it but morphing is considered to be the positive aspect of image forensics. The chapter is mainly focused on highlighting the image morphing process and algorithm. In this chapter, a detailed survey is carried out on the image morphing algorithms like mesh warping, field morphing, radial basis function (RBF) morphing, energy minimization morphing and multilevel free form deformation morphing. In the third section, types of traces are discussed, namely acquisition trace, coding trace and editing trace. The information about the possible forgery can be induced from these traces. In later sections, the detailed classification of forgery detection algorithms has been reviewed and special attention is paid to the copy-move forgery detection.

8.2 Image Morphing

Image morphing is also one of the image processing techniques inspired by the biological term "metamorphosis" which means changing shapes. It is inspired by the fact that some biological species are able to change their shape and color according to the environmental conditions, for example, golden tortoise beetle, cuttlefish, mimic octopus, etc. Similarly for a digital image, when one image is transformed into another image by some technical operation, this process is called image morphing. In morphing an algorithm is responsible for the gradual transformation of a graphical object (i.e., generally the source image) to another graphical image (called a target) (Islam, Inam, and Kaliyaperumal, 2013). In the animation industry it is used to create special effects, while in the advertisement and film industries it is widely used to create various visual effects. The basic idea of morphing is to distort the first image into another image by some predefined set of rules. During this transformation, the middle image generated is the key point of technology. The middle image decides whether the sequence will look good or not. The two fundamental principles of image morphing are image warping and cross dissolving. As morphing is a gradual process of evolution, with the evolution the source image starts degrading and the target image evolves with new features. The early images in the sequence will resemble the source more closely. The middle image has the features of both the source image and the final image and is distorted (Islam, Inam, and Kaliyaperumal, 2013).

Cross dissolves were used for image transition before the development of morphing, for example, linear interpolation. Because of misaligned regions, double exposure effects appeared and hence the results were poor. That problem has been overcome by the use of image warping and it is used before the cross dissolving. For a better image morphing outcome, the two techniques, that is, image warping and cross dissolving, need to be coupled. The correlation between pixels in an image is being controlled and determined by warping. To make warping work, all the important pixels need to be mapped distorted (Islam, Inam, and Kaliyaperumal, 2013).

The very initial object is called a source and the last object is called a target and there are various intermediate images in between source and target. The boundaries (vertices and edges) of images are consider for evaluation. This gradual transformation of the source into the target is being controlled by the blending weights (0.0–0.1), and when one compares the source and target image the weights get swapped, which shows the perfect morphing. For good morphing with respect to an intermediate image, source and target should have the same features.

8.2.1 Processes in Image Morphing

When an image is morphed into another, the new position of the pixels in morphed image must be estimated and also the color transition rate needs to be estimated. There are three main processes in image morphing.

i. *Feature specification*: In a morphing process the most exhaustive aspect is feature specification. The precise placement of primitives requires very careful attention in an environment where the choice of primitives is very diversely distorted (Islam, Inam, and Kaliyaperumal, 2013).

ii. *Warp generation*: This algorithm is responsible for determining and controlling the morphing process and transforming the source into target. For warping in the past, various algorithms have been distorted (Islam, Inam, and Kaliyaperumal, 2013).

iii. *Transition control*: The rate of warping is controlled by transition control and it also controls the color blending throughout the morph sequence.

When the image is morphed, it also creates various artifacts such as the target image may not have the features that are required. This misalignment is common in cross dissolving and this problem is overcome by using warping before cross dissolving. Two images are considered in morphing: the source image (A) and second target image (B). Moreover the source image gradually transforms into an image called the target image, resulting an intermediate image (C) that is distorted through its generation (Singh, Kumar, and Singh, 2014). More interesting intermediate images and animated images are generated if the transition rate is varied. The visual quality can be drastically improved by the use of non-uniform transition functions (Wolberg, 2003).

8.2.2 Image Morphing Algorithms

As mentioned earlier image morphing is achieved by sequential steps and generally cross dissolving is used before morphing to achieve image transitions, that is, the fading from one image to another is achieved by linear interpolation. This results in the misalignment of the regions and double exposure effects and this artifact is dominant in the middle image frames where the contribution of images is equal.

This problem is overcome by image warping which results in the fluidic transformation of images. Here some image morphing algorithms are mentioned like mash warping, energy minimization, and RBF morphing and multilevel free form deformation.

8.2.2.1 Mesh Warping

Mesh warping has been successfully used in various motion pictures like *Willow* (1988) and is still the most popular technique for morphing. Rectangular grid mesh is required for feature specification. For self-intersections among the grids, edges need to coincide with the features in the image. By moving mesh points, mesh resolution can be determined. Mesh points are connected by the Catmull–Rom cubic spline. To have one-to-one correspondence among the grids, meshes should have a topological equivalency for source and target image. Here topological equivalency means that the correspondence between mesh points is one-to-one. Mapping of each pixel is performed and simultaneously the scanning is also done for the auxiliary image by using the Catmull–Rom cubic spline. Generally for the Catmull–Rom cubic spline equation, the coefficients need to be identified and they are substituted for x (Islam, Inam, and Kaliyaperumal, 2013). The generalized equation for the curve is:

$$y(x) = a_1 x^3 + a_2 x^2 + a_3 x + a_4 \tag{8.1}$$

$$y'(x) = 3a_1 x^2 + 2a_2 x + a_3 \tag{8.2}$$

And according to the Catmull–Rom spline,

$$y(0) = a_4 = y_2 \tag{8.3}$$

$$y'(0) = a_3 = \frac{y_3 - y_1}{x_3 - x_1} \tag{8.4}$$

$$s = x_3 - x_2 \tag{8.5}$$

$$y(s) = a_1 s^3 + a_2 s^2 + a_3 s + a_4 = y_3 \tag{8.6}$$

$$y'(s) = 3a_1 s^2 + 2a_2 s + a_3 = \frac{y_4 - y_2}{x_4 - x_2} \tag{8.7}$$

Low computational cost is one of the key advantages of using mesh warping, however it uses a bi-cubic interpolation function for image warping which is very convenient but tedious work.

8.2.2.2 Field Morphing

While mesh features are associated with an ease in specifying the pairs of points, they are sometimes difficult to use. To simplify the user interface for specific data images, Beer and Neely developed the field morphing algorithms, which also deal with the correspondence between pairs. All focus is on the line and the region of interest of a line. This methodology has the advantage of being more expressive than work distorting. This worldwide calculation is quite often slower than work distorting, although it utilizes bi-cubic addition to decide the mapping of all the points. A progressively genuine problem, however, is that surprising relocations might be created as a result of all line sets being chosen at a solitary point (Beier and Neely, 1992). Extra line sets should once in a while be provided to deal with the negative impact of a past set. For illustrators, however, twisting and field trans-forming calculations are utilized to deliver astonishing enhanced visualizations.

8.2.2.3 Radial Basis Function (RBF) Morphing

The broadest type of highlight particularly allows the component descriptor to comprise focuses, straight lines, and twisted lines. Since straight lines and twisted lines can be exam-ined with points, it is adequate to believe that the highlights need to be focused. All things considered, the x- and y-components of a warp can be inferred using the dense surface that adds dissipated focuses (Singh, Kumar, and Singh, 2014). Consider, for instance, M high-light focuses named (uk; vk) in the input image and (xk; yk) in the target image, where inferring curve works guide focuses from the objective image to the source image. Twisting lines by this methodology was broadly overviewed in Ruprecht and Muller (1995). As of late, two comparative techniques were independently proposed utilizing the slender plate surface model. These methods create smooth twists that precisely mirror the element cor-respondence. Besides, they offer the broadest type of highlight, particularly since the curve (e.g., spline bends) might get tested into a lot of focuses.

8.2.2.4 Energy Minimization Morphing

The techniques depicted above do not ensure the coordinated property of the specific warp functions. At the point when a transformation is applied to an image, the balanced prop-erty keeps the distorted image from collapsing back on itself. Energy minimization morph-ing has been proposed by Lee et al. to determine coordinated warp works (Lee, Chwa, Hahn et al., 1996). This technique permits broad element determination natives, for exam-ple, focuses, polylines, and bends. Inside, all natives are tested and decreased to an assort-ment of focuses. These focuses are quite often used to produce a warp, which is inferred as a 2D deformation of a rectangular plate. The necessities for a warp are spoken to by vitality terms and fulfilled by limiting the entirety. The system creates regular warp since it depends on physically significant vitality terms. The implementation of energy minimization deals with high computational costs and expenses.

8.2.3 Multilevel Free Form Deformation (MFFD)

This technique is a lot more straightforward and quicker than the conventional energy minimization technique (Seung, Kyun, and Sung, 1995). Huge performance gains can be accomplished by using this technique (MFFD) over a hierarchy of control grids to produce balanced and C2-constant warp. Specifically, warp was obtained through positional requirements by relating the MFFD as an expansion to free form distortion (FFD). The MFFD generates C2-consistent and coordinated transformation which yields liquid image mutations. The MFFD calculation was integrated through the energy minimization tech-nique in a cross-breed process. Generally it appeared at the center pixel of an image, for all intents and purposes indistinguishable from that delivered utilizing network distorting. The advantage of this methodology, nonetheless, is that the components in particular are progressively expressive and less bulky. They were first embraced in computer vision as a functional shape model (Kass, Witkin, and Terzopoulos, 1988). This process pushes snakes towards striking edges, thereby refining their pixel positions and making it conceivable to catch the precise location of an element effectively and correctly (Wolberg, 2003).

8.3 Traces in Image Forensics

Quite often the digital fingerprint and footprints, which are said to be inherent traces of an image, are left out during the acquisition or post processing phase. This idea creates an opportunity for an image forensics expert to identify a possible forgery. To understand the history of a digital image, these traces are extracted and analyzed. Based on the Figure 8.2, fingerprint traces can be identified during the acquisition, coding, and editing phases.

8.3.1 Acquisition Phase Traces

There has been diversity in sensing technology, optical sensors, camera manufacturing, and software. So the component of an image is modified at a number of stages and thus leaves intrinsic fingerprints. The image acquisition process is almost uniform for every type of commercially available camera, however each manufacturer performs the steps according to their choice. Thus each stage can create imperfections and intrinsic irregularities (Johnson and Farid, 2006; Van, Emmanuel, and Kankanhalli, 2007). It leaves the digital signature of the brand manufacturer and can be considered as the footprint of tampering or forgery. Each sensor is equipped and associated with the individual lens and its properties. These lenses produce several types of artifacts due to their design and manufacturing processes. These unique traces can be used to identify the possible manufacturer and sensing device. Figure 8.2 shows the phenomenon of lateral chromatic aberration. Yerushalmy and Hel-Or (2011) investigate the Purple Fringing Aberration (PFA) artifact based on a camera lens. Instead of camera source identification, the lens shape is used to find the intrinsic radial distortion and further the Gaussian intensity loss model is proposed for modeling the dust patterns by Choi, Lam, and Wong (2006) and Dirik, Senear, and Memon (2008), and thus enables the identification of device. Sensor characteristics also play a significant role in forgery and finding the exact fingerprint trace. As with any electronic component, there is always associated noise with the sensor, thus the captured image is mostly different from the exact scene. Photo response non-uniformity (PRNU) is one of the major reasons for such diffraction. Most of the extensive research is carried out to find the robust PRNU. To affect the high frequency image components, the strong PRNU component has been proposed in a scheme by Li (2009). Some researchers (Goljan, Fridrich,

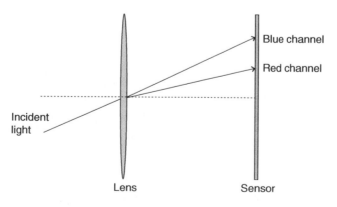

FIGURE 8.2
Phenomenon of lateral chromatic aberration.

and Filler, 2010) developed novel search algorithms like "digests" which allow for fast search within large image databases.

In some cases CFA also creates an artifact that is left out during the acquisition phase.

8.3.2 Coding Phase Traces

Before storing the captured 2D signal, lossy compression is the preferred technique for digital images as it saves transmission time and storage. All conventional cameras have the inherent feature of lossy compression already embedded into them during the manufacturing process. As soon as a camera captures the scene, lossy compression is associated with the image. Thus the coding process always creates some footprints which can be used for detecting possible forgery. In the past a number of algorithms have been proposed for identifying the possible compression techniques. The researchers Fan and Queiroz (Fan and Queiroz, 2000, 2003) proposed a methodology which is capable of revealing artifacts even with a light JPEG compression, that is, wherein the quality factor (QF) is around 95. The proposed calculation depends on the possibility that if the picture has not been packed, the pixel contrasts across 8×8 square limits ought to be like those inside squares. At that point, it is conceivable to construct two capacities, Z' and Z'', considering between and intra square pixel contrasts. The energy of the contrast between the histograms of Z' and Z'' is contrasted with a limit, and on the off-chance that it is higher than this edge, the nearness of the earlier presence is derived.

8.3.3 Editing Phase Traces

Editing in the form of post processing is performed on any image with an objective to enhance the physical appearance and visual quality of an image, to get the specific information or region, and to optimize the space like in compression. Techniques like stenography and watermarking change the schematic information of an image by hiding some text or keywords inside an image. Besides that, there are some geometrical transformation and enhancement operations like crop, resize, contrast stretching, and histogram equalization which create artifacts and thus leave scope for forgery identification and detection. Concerning all these operations, copy-move is the most popular and malicious modification.

8.4 Classification of Forgery Detection (Authentication) Techniques

In the history of forgery detection techniques, several methods have been developed and proposed by the researchers (see Figure 8.3). Here in this survey the methodology is broadly categorized according to whether the technique is active or passive. Active techniques are mainly concerned with hiding information inside the image in the form of digital signatures or watermarks (Luis, Manuel, Mariko et al., 2013); on the other hand, passive techniques are based on investigation of underlying statistics which are altered during image tampering (Luo, Qu, Pan et al., 2007).

(i) *Digital Signature*: This is one of the most basic and fundamental techniques. A mathematical scheme is generally introduced to identify the originality of a document in a digital signature technique. The extraction of some robust bits from the altered image

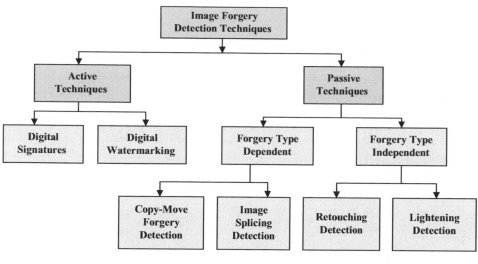

FIGURE 8.3
Detailed classification of forgery detection techniques.

is the key feature and 16*16 pixels block are divided among the image (Shwetha and Sathyanarayana, 2017). In an interval of [0, 1], M random matrices are generated with an "S" secret key and it is uniformly distributed.

(ii) *Digital Watermark*: Digital signatures are embedded into the image at the time of acquisition and these watermarks serve as proof of authenticity of an image. Some digital watermark techniques are based on the check sum method (Zhao, Li, Li et al., 2010) wherein an extra bit is appended to the most significant bit, and some are based on a linear shift register sequence wherein a watermark is identified by the spatial correlation function. However, they have a limitation in terms of human intervention and the requirement for special cameras.

(iii) *Forgery Type Dependent*: In detail, the passive techniques are broadly categorized as forgery type dependent and forgery type independent. The forgery type dependent techniques are mainly concerned with the copy-move forgery detection and image splicing detection. The simplicity associated with the copy-move forgery detection techniques makes it the most popular technique and this technique is explained and discussed in detail in Section 8.5.

(a) *Image Splicing Detection*: Splicing is a process in which a composite image is generated by the combination of two or more different images. Thus artifacts in the form of lines blur and regions are visible at the point of splicing, creating an opportunity to detect any possible forgery. Statistical approaches are used in image splicing detection with the help of some natural statistical models. Dimensional feature vectors are involved in this approach (Moghaddasi, Jalab, and Noor, 2014). Singular value decomposition (SVD), Markov chain, 78-D, and 72-D are some methods used in image splicing detection.

(iv) *Forgery Type Independent*: These are concerned with the techniques that focus on alteration processes occurring during sampling and quantization.

(a) *Retouching Detection*: To satisfy human perception of s beautiful scene, retouching is preferred, and is mainly concerned with the aesthetic appearance of an image.

Detecting any type of blurring, color changes, and enhancements is the key driving force for retouching detection. A classifier has been designed by Murali, Chittapur, and Prabhakara (2012) to detect any possible adulteration in original and forged images. In Basavarajappa and Sathyanarayana (2016), a histogram equalization based approach for detection of retouching is discussed.

(b) *Lightening Detection*: Lightening inconsistencies result in the creation of artifacts and thus opportunities in forgery detection. As the light conditions vary, the hue and saturation are also effected and thus from the forged image it can be easily identified whether the image is doctored or not (Zhao, Li, Li et al., 2010; Moghaddasi, Jalab, and Noor, 2014).

8.5 Copy-Move Forgery Detection Techniques

Because of its simplicity in operation, copy-move forgery is the most popular and common forgery technique (Ghorbani, Firouzmand, and Faraahi, 2011). In this, a specific region of an image is copied and pasted somewhere in the image to hide or to highlight some information. The size, dynamic range, contrasts, and saturation of an image remain the same as those in the copied region belonging to the same image. Thus it is quite difficult to identify possible tampering.

As such, the masked region is chosen from the image itself therefore it is quite impossible to detect the forgery. In the literature several methodologies have been proposed by the researchers.

Among these, the first attempt to detect copy-move forgery was made by Fridrich et al. (Fridrich, Soukal, and Lukas, 2003). To maintain the balance between performance and complexity, they proposed the block matching algorithm, but this method fails to detect the small duplicate region because of the large block size. The model developed by Gopi, Lakshmanan, Gokul et al. (2006) uses auto regressive coefficients for the selection of feature vectors and to detect possible image tampering, an artificial neural network (ANN) classifier is designed. To train the network, 300 feature vectors are chosen. The experiment results showed an accuracy of 77.69% in identifying the correct forgery. The method proposed by Myna, Venkateshmurthy, and Patil (2007) detected copy-move forgery by log polar coordinates and wavelet transformations. It is based on the fundamental feature of wavelet transformation, that is, dimensionality reduction, and in order to identify similar blocks an exhaustive search is carried out by log polar coordinates. Similarly many other researchers have performed exhaustive research work on copy-move forgery detection techniques. If we look towards the classification of such algorithms, then it is clear from Figure 8.3 that the hierarchy is quite high.

Broadly according to the literature the copy-move forgery detection techniques are categorized into two classes (see Figure 8.4). These are block based and brute based techniques which involve exhaustive search. The results of block based techniques are better as compared to exhaustive search and autocorrelation based techniques (Singh and Raman, 2012). In order to extract robust features (RFs), some thresholds can be imposed on mismatching in "approximate block matching" from the suspicious area through comparison (Luo, Huang, and Qiu, 2006). This technique splits the image and in order to extract features a suitable technique is applied on the basis of similarity. For detection of duplicate

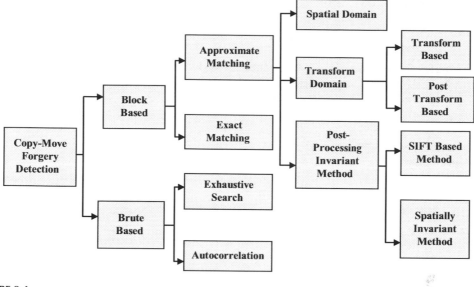

FIGURE 8.4

A detailed categorization of copy-move forgery detection methodology

regions, spatial domain techniques (Ardizzone and Mazzola, 2009) are commonly followed. Seven feature vectors are selected from each block for comparison and the algorithm splits the image into through block overlapping.

Intra component transformations are used generally in approximate block matching techniques like discrete cosine transform (DCT) (Cao, Gao, Fan et al., 2012) and the second most popular technique, that is, discrete wavelet transformation (DWT) (Shih and Yuan, 2010). For computing the local statistical features Huang et al. (Huang, Guo, and Zhang, 2008) have proposed a methodology which is based on the use of SIFT to detect the rotational and scaling changes, however it has shown poor performance. The technique proposed by Pan and Lyu (2010) seems effective as the duplicated regions have shown the distortions as consequences of geometrical transformations. The SIFT algorithm has been proposed for computing the features at key points.

8.6 Antiforensics

Antiforensics is a counter measure to the forensics analysis. On an ethical basis, there is a dilemma among researchers about whether to call it good or bad. Antiforensics or counter forensics has recently struck the research community and researchers have started focusing on its importance. Generally the techniques are classified as universal or target specific. In target specific, the aim is to remove the detectable traces with any particular forensics tool. The type of tool is specified as an attacker (Kirchner and Böhme, 2007). On the contrary, a method is said to be universal if it tries to maintain the multiple image features similar to the features used in the unaltered image.

In a number of places in the literature, compression of images has been explored for antiforensics. For example, Stamm, Tjoa, Lin et al. (2010) proposed a scheme to hide the

JPEG compression history, in which the addition of noise to DCT compression is highlighted, thus making it more difficult to analyze the image for any possible forgery. The PRNU fingerprint is falsified in digital images by sensor imperfections in many other antiforensics operations that have been designed. Based on the application of flat fielding a removal attack is proposed in Gloe, Kirchner, Winkler et al. (2007). In a continuation from it, a fingerprint from a fake camera is estimated from a set of acquired images in a fingerprint copy attack and it is pasted onto an image that is taken from some other camera.

8.7 Conclusion

In the history lots of research work is being carried out by a number of researchers. This chapter aims to provide an extensive survey of the image forensics techniques that are being used in digital image forgery detection. This will provide an opportunity for the researcher to explore new possibilities and ideas to face new challenges that are going to occur as the new forgery techniques evolve. Special attention is paid to the image morphing techniques, as this is the most prominent type of forgery and tampering. A detailed classification of forgery detection techniques is presented based on whether the technique is active or passive. Further more detailed classification of both techniques is given. Upon investigation it has been observed that the copy-move forgery detection technique is the most popular technique because of the simplicity of the way in which it is carried out. In between, a sequential cycle of image tasks is mentioned wherein the possible forgery attack point has been identified. This is one of the key areas which need to be explored more in future. As such it is always better to know the exact reason and location of forgery and tampering in a complete image processing cycle.

Based on the above information, it can be stated that forgery occurs at three different stages, namely, the acquisition phase, sensor level, and coding level. A detailed survey is carried out on all the mentioned phases. In the era in which we are living, information is changing every second and so is visual information in the form of images. Morphing is one such technique, inspired by biology, and a classification of image morphing techniques has been done. It can be concluded that the researchers are developing new algorithms at regular intervals, but there is still a lot of scope for improvement of forgery detection algorithms as all the mentioned algorithms suffer from low accuracy in forgery detection and are very complex in terms of practical implementation. At the end, the development of antiforensics algorithms raises some serious concerns over the ethical acceptability and usability of such algorithms.

References

Ardizzone, E. and Mazzola, G. 2009. "Detection of duplicated regions in tampered digital images by bit-plane analyses." In *Proceedings of the 15th International Conference on Image Analysis and Processing*, Vietri sul Mare, Italy, pp. 893–901.

Basavarajappa, S. B. and Sathyanarayana, S. 2016. "Digital image forgery detection techniques: A survey." *ACCENTS Transactions on Information Security* 2, 22–31. doi:10.19101/TIS.2017.25003.

Cao, Y., Gao, T., Fan, L. et al. 2012. "A robust detection algorithm for copy-move forgery in digital images." *Forensic Science International 214*(1–3), 33–43.

Choi, K. S., Lam, E. Y., and Wong, K. K. Y. 2006. "Automatic source camera identification using the intrinsic lens radial distortion." *Optics Express 14*, 11551–11565.

Dirik, A. E., Senear, H. T., and Memon, N. 2008. "Digital single lens reflex camera identification from traces of sensor dust." *IEEE Transactions on Information Forensics and Security 3*(3), 539–552.

Fan, Z. and Queiroz, R. de 2000. "Maximum likelihood estimation of JPEG quantization table in the identification of bitmap compression history." In *Proceedings of the International Conference on Image Processing (ICIP '00)*, pp. 948–951.

Fan, Z. and Queiroz, R. L. de 2003. "Identification of bitmap compression history: JPEG detection and quantizer estimation." *IEEE Transactions on Image Processing 12*(2), 230–235.

Farid, H. 2009. "Image forgery detection." *IEEE Signal Processing Magazine 26*(2), 16–25.

Fridrich, J., Soukal, D., and Lukas, J. 2003. "Detection of copy-move forgery in digital images." In *Proceedings of the Digital Forensic Research Workshop*, Cleveland, OH, pp. 55–61.

Friedman, G. L. 1993. "The trustworthy digital camera: Restoring credibility to the photographic image." *IEEE Transactions on Consumer Electronics 39*(4), 905–910.

Ghorbani, M., Firouzmand, M., and Faraahi, A. 2011. "DWT-DCT (QCD) based copy-move image forgery detection." In *Proceedings of 18th International Conference on Systems, Signals and Image Processing (IWSSIP)*, Sarajevo, pp. 1–4.

Gloe, T., Kirchner, M., Winkler, A. et al. 2007. "Can we trust digital image forensics?" In *Proceedings of the 15th international Conference on Multimedia*, Augsburg, Germany, pp. 78–86.

Goljan M., Fridrich J., and Filler T. 2010. "Managing a large database of camera Fingerprints," in *Media Forensics and Security II, part of the IS&T-SPIE Electronic Imaging Symposium*, N. D. Memon, J. Dittmann, A. M. Alattar, and E. J. Delp, Eds., vol. *7541* of Proceedings of SPIE, San Jose, CA.

Gopi, E., Lakshmanan, N., Gokul, T. et al. 2006. "Digital image forgery detection using artificial neural network and auto regressive coefficients." In *Proceedings of the Canadian Conference on Electrical and Computer Engineering*, Ontario, Canada, pp. 194–197.

Huang, H., Guo, W., and Zhang, Y. 2008. "Detection of copy-move forgery in digital images using SIFT algorithm." *Pacific-Asia Workshop on Computational Intelligence and Industrial Application*, Wuhan, China, vol. 2, pp. 272–276.

Islam, Md. B., Inam, Md. T., and Kaliyaperumal, B. 2013. "Overview and challenges of different image morphing algorithms." *International Journal of Advanced Research in Computer Science and Electronics Engineering (IJARCSEE) 2*(4).

Johnson, M. K. and Farid, H. 2006. "Exposing digital forgeries through chromatic aberration." In *Proceedings of the 8th workshop on Multimedia & Security*, S. Voloshynovskiy, J. Dittmann, and J. J. Fridrich, Eds., pp. 48–55. ACM, Geneva, Switzerland.

Kass, M., Witkin, A., and Terzopoulos, D. 1988. "Snakes: Active contour models." *International Journal of Computer Vision 1*, 321–331.

Kirchner M. and Böhme R. 2007, "Tamper hiding: defeating image forensics," in Proceedings of the *9th International Conference on Information Hiding*, T. Furon, F. Cayre, G. Doerr, and P. Bas, Eds., pp. 326–341.

Lee, S.-Y., Chwa, K.-Y., Hahn, J. et al. 1996. "Image morphing using deformation techniques." *Journal of Visualization and Computer Animation 7*, 3–23.

Li, C.-T. 2009. "Source camera identification using enhanced sensor pattern noise." In *Proceedings of the IEEE International Conference on Image Processing (ICIP '09)*, Cairo, Egypt, pp. 1509–1512, IEEE.

Luo, W., Huang, J., and Qiu, G. 2006. "Robust detection of region-duplication forgery in digital image." In *18th International Conference on Pattern Recognition*, Hong Kong, China, vol. 4, pp. 746–749.

Luo, W., Qu, Z., Pan, F. et al. 2007. "A survey of passive technology for digital image forensics." *Frontiers of Computer Science in China 1*, 166–179.

Moghaddasi, Z., Jalab, H. A., and Noor, R. M. 2014. "SVD-based image splicing detection." In *IEEE International Conference on Information Technology and Multimedia*, pp. 27–30.

Murali, S., Chittapur, G. B., and Prabhakara, H. S. 2012. "Format based photo forgery image detection." In *Proceedings of the Second International Conference on Computational Science, Engineering and Information Technology (CCSEIT '12)*, Association for Computing Machinery, New York, pp. 452–457.

Myna, A., Venkateshmurthy, M., and Patil, C. 2007. "Detection of region duplication forgery in digital images using wavelets and log-polar mapping." In *Proceedings of the International Conference on Computational Intelligence and Multimedia Applications (ICCIMA)*, Sivakasi, India, pp. 371–377.

Pan, X. and Lyu, S. 2010. "Region duplication detection using image feature matching." *IEEE Transaction on Information Forensics Security*, (4), 857–867.

Piva, A. 2013. "An overview on image forensics." *ISRN Signal Processing 2013*, 1–22.

Ruprecht, D. and Muller, H. 1995. "Image warping with scattered data interpolation." *IEEE Computer Graphics and Applications 15*(2), 37–43.

Shih, F. Y. and Yuan, Y. 2010. "A comparison study on copy-cover image forgery detection." *Open Artificial Intelligence Journal 4*, 49–54.

Shwetha, B. and Sathyanarayana, S. V. 2017. "Digital image forgery detection techniques: A survey." *ACCENTS Transactions on Information Security* 2(5), 658–661. ISSN (Online): 2455-7196, doi:http://dx.doi.org/10.19101/TIS.2017.25003

Singh, J. and Raman, B. 2012. "A high performance copy-move image forgery detection scheme on GPU." In K. Deep, A. Nagar, M. Pant, and J. Bansal, Eds., *Proceedings of the International Conference on Soft Computing for Problem Solving (SocProS 2011) December 20–22, 2011*. Advances in Intelligent and Soft Computing, vol *131*. Springer, New Delhi, India.

Stamm, M. C., Tjoa, S. K., Lin, W. S. et al. 2010. "Anti-forensics of JPEG compression." In *Proceedings of IEEE Conference on ICASSP 2010*, Dellas, TX, pp. 1694–1697.

Van, L. T., Emmanuel, S., and Kankanhalli, M. S. 2007. "Identifying source cell phone using chromatic aberration." In *Proceedings of the IEEE International Conference on Multimedia and Expo (ICME '07)*, Beijing, China, pp. 883–886.

Wolberg, G. 2003. "Recent advances in image morphing." In *Proceedings of Computer Graphics International Conference, CGI*, Hannover, Germany.

Yerushalmy, I. and Hel-Or, H. 2011. "Digital image forgery detection based on lens and sensor aberration." *International Journal of Computer Vision 92*(1), 71–91.

Zhao, X., Li, J., Li, S. et al. 2010. "Detecting digital image splicing in chroma spaces." In *International Workshop on Digital Watermarking*, pp. 12–22. Springer Berlin Heidelberg, Berlin.

9

Analysis of Classification-Based Intrusion-Detection Techniques

S. Sridevi and R. Anandan

Vels Institute of Science, Technology and Advanced Studies [VISTAS], Chennai, India

9.1 Introduction

Wireless Sensor Networks (WSNs) are utilized in a number of areas of science and engineering due to the fact of their handiness and low price of implementation (Akyildiz et al. 2002). Examples include collecting reviews of human activities, army monitoring and identification, transportation; exposing physical and environmental phenomena such as oceans and animals, earthquakes, pollution, woodland fires, and water quality; exposing industrial places, such as building protection, overall performance of equipment manufacturing, etc. On the other hand, protection is a necessary problem in WSNs, particularly if they have mission-critical duties (Chen et al. 2009). In a healthcare framework, a unique affected character fitness file ought to no longer be initiated now at 1/3 celebration events. Securing WSNs is extensively required in tactical (military) functions as safety breaches will result in casualties on the battlefield, as explained in Zhou et al. (2008), Cayirci and Rong (2009) and Wang et al. (2006).

WSN protection assaults are divided into two essential branches: active and passive. Attackers are commonly hidden in passive attacks, and both pay attention to the conversation connection to gather data or break the network's working factors. Passive assaults can be categorized into sorts of eavesdropping, node failure, community manipulation/destruction and site visitor analysis.

In active attacks, the operations in the targeted community are virtually affected with the aid of an attacker. In addition, this has an impact on the goal of the attack, which can be identified. For example, as an end result of these attacks, the network services should be damaged or terminated. You can also prepare aggressive assaults into Denial of Service (DoS), jamming, hole assaults (black hole, wormhole, sinkhole, etc.), flooding and Sybil types. Readers who are greatly involved in security assaults on WSNs can moreover refer to Cayirci and Rong (2009), Wang et al. (2006) and Padmavathi and Shanmugapriya (2009) for further details.

Three procedures can control options for assaults on wired and Wi-Fi networks:

a. **Anticipation (fighting aggression):** This helps to "forestall" any assault before it occurs. Any advised method ought to be protected from the targeted attack.
b. **Detection (detection of attack takes place or not):** When an attacker succeeds in overcoming the steps taken during the "prevention" step, it is probable that in response to the assault there is a tendency to protect. At this time, the safety response will cross over into the attack "detection" area and discover the systems that are being targeted.
c. **Alleviation (after the attack identification):** After an attack is identified in a network, the affected nodes are eliminated or replaced before transmitting the data.

Intrusion is an unapproved network operation that is either done passively (e.g., unknowingly collecting data or listening to the data) or actively (e.g., forwarding the packet unknowingly to legitimate users, erasing the some of the packets, or creating the holes in a network). Within a protection system, "intrusion detection" comes into play when "intrusion prevention" does not prevent intrusions. It is the identification of doubtful activity inside a communication carried out by the user. The Intrusion Detection System (IDS) gives the following details such as proof of the intruder, place of the intruder (e.g., single node or regional), date and time at which the intrusion takes place, what type of attack would take place (e.g., active or passive attack), type of intrusion such as black hole, sink hole, selective forwarding, etc.), and in which layer (physical layer or data link layer) intrusion takes place. Such knowledge will be of great benefit in minimizing attacks, because very detailed data about the attacker is gathered. IDSs are also very critical to network security.

WSNs have specific features including specific energy limitation, less bandwidth, and low memory for storing the information. Because of these restricted computational and power resources of the WSN, the normal security techniques provided in a wireless network are not suitable for WSNs. Designing an efficient and straightforward approach to intrusion detection that is applicable to WSNs is a huge project that has inspired us to focus on this area of study. The first research objective is to carry out an in-depth survey, which has led us to carry out this survey because of the initial results of our study. The chapter is arranged as follows: Section 2 provides an introduction to IDSs, types of IDS and their requirements. Section 3 discusses different intrusion detection techniques in MANET and also describes how they would be applicable to WSNs. Section 4 explains the overall benefits and complications of WSNs compared with conventional wired and wireless networks. In this section the complete literature survey of IDSs in WSNs is discussed. The strengths and weaknesses of each and every method are discussed in Fuchsberger (2005). Further it considers all the strengths and weaknesses of different IDSs and it gives the idea for creating a general model for an IDS that would be applied in all networks (wired/wireless/WSN).

9.2 Intrusion Detection Systems (IDSs)

Any kind of unauthorized operation is referred to as an intrusion in a network. An IDS is a series of software, methods and items to assist in identifying, checking and reporting intrusions. Intrusion detection is generally one part of a regular safety unit constructed around a laptop or machine and is no longer always a standalone feature (Chen et al. 2009).

In Ngadi et al. (2008), encroachment is described as "any set of strikes that strive to compromise the privacy, confidentiality, or availability of a resource" and alleviation methods (including ciphering, setting passwords, manipulation acceptance, comfortable routing and so on) are given as the antecedents of protection against encroachment. The outcome of these methods improves the preventive protection failure. Accordingly, once IDSs have been configured to expose intrusions, those that have occurred up until now on the covered device ought to be disclosed. From a protection point of view, IDSs are regularly taken into account as a second line of protection. IDSs are the online world equal of the burglar alarms that may additionally be used in physical protection these days, according to Zhang et al. (2003).

9.2.1 Requirements of IDSs

The following requirements should be met in the design of IDSs:

- They should not add new interface vulnerabilities.
- They should require few device resources and not limit the usual overall performance of the device by including overheads.
- They should run continuously and be evident on the device and to consumers.
- They should be interdependent and accessible, provide accurate results and prevent false results in detection.

9.2.2 Categorization of the IDS

9.2.2.1 Type of Intruder

The trespassers in a network can be divided into two groups:

Outside intruder: An attacker makes use of a couple of assaults to get right of entry to the network.

    a. **Within trespass:** An attacker gains access to the network via a compromised node which used to be a community member.

Insider assault: In this type of attack, ad hoc networks use two sorts of node, according to Butun et al. (2012):

    a. **Self-centered node:** Uses the strength of the community, however it does not collaborate, saving battery life for its personal contact. It does not have an effect on different nodes straight away.

    b. **Malevolent node:** The aim is to smash different nodes with the aid of partitioning the DoS community whilst saving battery life, which is now not a priority. An IDS can identify exterior and interior intruders, however it needs to be mentioned that it is more challenging to observe interior intruders. This is due to the fact that inside intruders have the requisite keying knowledge to neutralize any measures taken by means of the mechanisms of authentication.

9.2.2.2 Types of Intrusion

Network intrusions can additionally take place in quite a number of ways:

a. **Tried destroy-in:** An effort is made to obtain unauthorized right of entry to the network.
b. **Impersonation:** A false identity is used by an attacker to gain unauthorized entry to the network.
c. **Diffusion:** Unauthorized right of entry to the network is gained.
d. **DoS:** Crew property is blockaded (i.e., bandwidth of conversation) for selected users.
e. **Malicious use:** Deliberate injury is caused to community properties. IDSs may also provide partial methods for detecting this type of assault.

9.2.2.3 Methodologies for Detecting Attacks

IDSs are technically divided into three concerns: detection is primarily based on finding anomalies; detection is primarily based on identifying misuse; and detection is primarily based on specifications.

9.2.2.3.1 Detection Primarily Based on Aberration

This is targeted on modeling statistical behavior. The member's ordinary actions are profiled, and any deviation from the regular activity is marked as an abnormality. The drawback of this approach to detection is that the regular actions may typically change, as the character of the community might also alter unexpectedly. This may increase the weight on sensor nodes that are confined in usable resources. This model for finding trespasses is very dependable and constant, in line with low false eccentric results and false high costs.

In this circumstance, the team of authors identified static patterns of behavior. The downside of this approach to detection is that the detection of unknown or before no longer determined assaults is nicely applicable for miles. Based on Garcia-Teodoro et al., aberration structured specifically on IDSs is in addition split into three groups according to the processing concerned inside the behavior.

(i) **Statistically based**: Completely anomalous statistical IDSs seize crew web page traffic and then produce an index representing their random characteristics. An additional index is generated as the crew operates in everyday stipulations (without any threats). After that, the community is checked and indexes are produced normally and an anomaly ranking is formed by way of the usage of the index profile to take a look at it. If the rating goes above a certain threshold, an incidence of uncertainty will flag the IDS.
   - **Single variation:** Variables are based on totally Gaussian random variables.
   - **Multiple variations:** Differences between or higher metrics are also regarded here.
   - **Time series model:** A language timer used in a tournament brings under consideration the arrangement and recording between the cases and additionally their values.

(i) **Knowledge based:** Initially, knowledge based anomaly IDSs acquire data about a number of community parameters both in standard situations and when under attack.

- **Expert systems:** They are primarily based on a set of classification guidelines.
- **Description languages:** Diagram kinds such as Unified Modeling Language (UML) are created totally on information specification.
- **Finite state machine:** Based on the available records, states and transitions are defined.
- **Data clustering and outlier detection:** Based on the similarity or distance measure, the facts are grouped as clusters. Those values that are not present in any one of the clusters are named as outliers.
- **Machine based learning:** Anomaly based machine learning IDSs describe an express or implicit pattern. This model admits samples to be produced. These are revised normally, primarily based on the previous results.
- **Bayesian networks:** Network variables of this structure are chosen on the basis of probabilistic relations.

(ii) **Machine mastering based**: It is based on two anomalous IDSs and it is classified into a specific or implicit model. This model generates patterns. Based on the preceding effects, these models are updated periodically.

- **Markov models:** These are primarily based on the Markov principle, in which techniques are organized like states interconnected with some chances of change.
- **Fuzzy logic:** This is focused totally on ambiguity and inference.
- **Genetic algorithms:** These are inspired by organic evolutionary theory.
- **Neural networks:** The device is primarily focused on the brain activity.
- **Principal Component Analysis (PCA):** This is primarily related to a methodology for decreasing dimensionality.

9.2.2.3.2 *Misuse Particularly Based on Primarily Signature-Based or Rule Based Detection*

Signatures (profiles) of formerly recognized assaults are created and used as information to uncover assaults. For example, a normal occurrence may be explained as "there are three failed login tries with a brute pressure password assault in 5 minutes". The advantage of this approach to detection is that it can land on common assaults reliably and effectively; consequently, they have a low false positive quality. The drawback is that if the assault is a new shape (which has not been profiled before), it might not be detected with the aid of misuse detection now. Patcha and Park (2007) stated that these structures are very comparable to the anti-virus systems, which can find out most or all of the assault patterns that are considered, but are, however, of little advantage for the unknown strategies of assault. Alternatively, the authors encompass the following tips for monitoring community abnormalities.

- **Law of interval:** Delays between the arrivals of successive messages have to be inside these limits.
- **Retransmission rule:** Intermediate nodes have to ahead transit messages.

- **Law of integrity:** The sender's unique message can no longer deviate till it arrives at the recipient.
- **Delay rule:** The message should be retransmitted after a sensible period.
- **Law of repetition:** The same message can also be transmitted from the identical node in a certain broad range of numbers.
- **Variety of radio transmission:** Messages need to come most handily from adjoining nodes.
- **Jamming rule:** The large range of packet-transmission collisions needs to be below a certain limit.

9.2.2.3.3 *Specification Based on Detection*

A series of specifications and limits is distinctive, which explains the unique function of a software application or rules for communication. The implementation of this device is then checked with attention to the given specifications and constraints. This method was once carried out by Sobh (2006), who adjusted its performance to discover previously unknown assaults, even those displaying a low false outstanding alarm cost. Anantvalee and Wu (2007) described the concept, setting apart many of the anomaly based detection and misuse-based detection models: anomaly detection constructions are trying to discover the impact of attacks, however misuse detection models strive to prevent acknowledged attacks. Completely intrusion based specification detection strategies mix the advantages of both misuse and anomaly based detection strategies with the aid of the use of physically constructed requirements and constraints to exemplify reliable device activities. Specification based intrusion detection strategies are comparable to typical anomaly based detection approaches, in that they each counter assaults as they deviate from the popular profile. Since specification based detection techniques are based on available connections, they have low false alarm costs in contrast to the higher rate of false alarms of detection techniques primarily based on anomalies. On the other hand, the cost of achieving the low rate of false alarms is that enhancing the correct specifications and constraints is likely to be time-consuming.

9.2.2.4 *Audit Statistics Source*

The IDSs can be classified into three groups:

a. **Network based Intrusion Detection System (NIDS):**
NIDS listen, collect and examine community transmission packets. NIDS may additionally look at a complete packet, packet payload, IP addresses or ports.

b. **Host based Intrusion Detection System (HIDS):**
They are restricted to detecting the following instructions and they are successful (but no longer restricted to) at detecting subsequent intrusions: modifications to necessary documents on the server, attempts to access the server persistently failed, recollections of previous allocations of special procedures, unusual CPU operations or I/O behavior. These are performed by means of HIDS either monitoring the host's utilization of the real-time framework, or by reviewing log archives on the server, as explained by Kachirski and Guha (2003).

c. **Hybrid Intrusion Detection System:**
This accommodates the features of NIDS and HIDS and is available with cellular agents. It checks every host and function device log file, whilst a central agent video display measures the network's community traffic.

9.2.2.5 Accumulated Statistics Computing Region

IDSs are divided into four groups by using the role of the amassed statistics:

a. **Centralized IDS:** A centralized laptop computer tracks all community operations and detects intrusions by studying the records about the community operations that are being monitored.

b. **Standalone IDS:** An IDS operates independently on every node, and every choice is primarily based on the documents gathered at its non-public node. Network humans are now not conscious of the intrusions that show up round them due to the fact that stand-by IDS no longer allows each node to collaborate or evaluate information with every other node.

c. **Distributed and Cooperative IDS:** This is proposed for infrastructures in flat society. The node runs an IDS agent that participates in intrusion detection and ordinary community response (cooperatively collaborating in the worldwide intrusion detection selections and movements). Where a node detects an intrusion with inclined or unfinished data, a coordinated world intrusion detection protocol can be implemented. If a node detects a home intrusion with ample evidence, then it can warn the neighborhood independently about an attack.

d. **Hierarchical IDS:** That is advised for multi-layer community infrastructures (clustering). In addition to taking part in worldwide intrusion detection selections, cluster heads (CH) are accountable for monitoring their member nodes.

e. **Mobile IDS based agent:** In Sun et al. (2007), every cell agent is assigned to carry out a unique IDS action on a special node, and intrusion is detected by way of the mutual motion of these node-decided agents. After a reasonable time period or after a selected task, users may additionally migrate to a number of predefined nodes on the way to prolong and/or boost community overall performance of the IDS. Mobile provider requirements are given as follows:

   Mobility: Cellphone sellers convey the code to the records (to be processed) for asynchronous execution on a remote host. This will assist to considerably reduce the quantity of information shared.

   Autonomy: An assignment is provided to cellphone entrepreneurs upon creation of the cellphone: they need to be in a position to accomplish their duties without any exterior assistance.

   Adaptability: Mobile marketers want to adapt their movements in accordance with the know-how they acquire when performing their duties.

9.2.2.6 Infrastructure

Anantvalee et al. (Anantvalee and Wu 2007) subdivided IDSs (for MANETs) into community infrastructure organizations:

a. **Flat:** All nodes are regarded equal in ability and can take part in routing functionality (i.e., this system is best for civilian services, like in-class networking or meeting).

b. **Clustered:** Not all nodes are seen as equal. Nodes are clustered inside the transmission range and pick a node as a CH to centralize routing records for that cluster. CHs generally consist of more powerful machines with backup batteries, resulting in a prolonged range of transmissions. Accordingly, CHs shape a digital community backbone. Intermediate gateways can relay packets in between the CHs, relying on the routing protocol. This kind of infrastructure model is very appropriate for navy purposes which have a command/manipulate hierarchy.

9.2.2.7 Use Frequency

Depending on the frequency of usage, IDSs are classified into two types:

    a. **Uninterrupted:** The IDS always tracks the network.
    b. **Periodic:** The IDS tracks the community all through a specified number of time intervals.

9.2.3 Decision-Making Inside the IDS

The decision-making procedures for IDSs include collective decision-making: all (or some) of the community's individuals work collectively to produce a probability collection. The ultimate choice is taken based on the majority preference: the risk is an intrusion.

Unbiased decision-making: Every participant determines a choice, paying attention to the activities surrounding them in line with Sobh (2006). The IDS determines one of the four selections (with non-zero chances) listed below, based on the choices for an event. Although an intrusion may no longer be anomalous (fake–terrible), the system may still be attacked, however the IDS does now not consider it, as described in Farooqi and Khan (2009).

- No longer invasive, however anomalous (fake–effective): there may not have been an intrusion in the system; however, the IDS erroneously assumes the normal case to be an anomalous one.
- No longer invasive and no longer anomalous (authentic–bad): there has been no intrusion in the system, and the IDS reviews the case as non-anomalous.
- Invasive and anomalous (real–high-quality): the community has had an intrusion, and the IDS concludes the incident to be an anomalous one.

Because of the nature of Wi-Fi communications, the following instances would result in false positives for IDSs in WSNs and are consequently likely to be taken into account in the determination model (Zhou et al. 2010):

- Conflict among the nodes
- Loss of packets
- With the bounded flow
- Vanishing battery electricity

9.2.4 Intrusion Response

If an assault may also happen, the IDS no longer takes preventive measures as the Intrusion Prevention System (IPS) is left with the issue of prevention. Compared to the IPS pre-emptive approach, the IDS functions in a reactive manner, as explained in Elshoush and Osman (2011) and Zhou et al. (2009).The following action(s) should be taken accordingly on the desktop each and every time the intrusion alarm is produced via the IDS.

Requirements of IDS

- All persons in the network, the administrator (if he/she exists) and the base station (if he/she exists) ought to know about the intrusion. Where appropriate, the intruder's proximity and identification ought to be given in the warning message.

- If there is a prevention strategy, the intrusion should be kept out. For example, a computerized corrective action needs to be created via the collective action of the individuals in the community (especially neighboring contributors to the incident), as described in Modi et al. (2013).

9.2.5 Further Literature About WSN

A concise study of IDSs anticipated for WSNs is given in Garcia et al. (2012), which provides an improved survey with in-depth evaluation of the techniques proposed.

- Collaborative structures are given in Cheng et al. (2012). A more precise warning correlation survey is supplied for collaborative smart IDSs (Keung et al. 2012). Different references on a decentralized multi-dimensional warning system for collaborative IDSs is given in Wang et al. (2013).

- Cloud computing IDS surveys are given in Shakshuki et al. (2013), which should be beneficial for future comfy networks.

- Garcia et al. (Kachirski and Guha 2002) provide postmortem intrusion detection data for laptop forensics and cyber safety systems. We provide an approach for classifying log files via the usage of a Hidden Markov Model.

- Escape strategies which threaten IDSs are introduced in the work of Cheng et al. (Rao and Kesidis 2003). They supply data on five distinctive techniques (DoS, packet splitting, replica insertion, payload mutation and shell-code mutation), and examine the efficacy of these strategies on three of the most recent IDSs. It should be noted that the IDS examined in this survey is associated with information safety and PC safety, and is not associated with the problem of "perimeter protection intrusion detection." Readers interested in the latter subject should consult the work in Sun et al. (2003). Our survey does not include the methodologies and ideas proposed to loosen up the IDSs.

9.3 Application of IDS in MANET and WSN

The IDSs for MANETs are very thoroughly researched and evaluated in the literature given here, providing further detail about this cutting-edge work. A summary of the planned usage of IDSs in WSNs is given in Sen and Clark (2011).

9.3.1 Primarily Agent Based Dispensed and Collaborative IDSs

Zhang and Lee posted the first paper on intrusion detection for MANETs. They recommended a primarily agent based dispersed and collaborative IDS that would comply with the working instances of the ad hoc network.

As additionally mentioned in Patcha and Park (2006) and Marti et al. (2000), the IDS agent recognized consists of six blocks established to discover any kind of attack; the real-time statistics are detected by way of the nearby detection engine. When any assault happens in a community it informs neighborhood response, world response or both. If detection requires cooperation among different nodes, then invulnerable conversations can inform cooperative detection and cooperation between neighboring agents. There are two strategies within the "local detection system."

Features: It addresses node routing information, that is, the share of community route changes.

Modeling set of rules: It makes use of properties as an entry to the rule based sample matching set of policies and then determines whether or not the incidence is everyday or no longer in accordance with the already defined method. In this version, the whole system is involved in the decision-making process. At each limit, the nearby IDS triggers the international IDS to make a joint node–neighboring node decision. This choice is taken through a vote by means of plurality. Detection is finished by way of the use of the "entropy" method: as the entropy decreases, the anomaly probability increases. The method proposed is beneficial solely for finding the assaults in opposition to the finding path using communication rules, that is, missing path, updating the incorrect route, losing the packets, and DoS. After irregularities are observed, whether or not a nearby response is created or an overseas (collaborative) reply is created among the adjoining systems relying on the degree of the anomaly. Communications referring to this global reply ought to be evaluated through comfy hyperlinks of numerous of the nodes. In step with the authors, it is a challenging venture to classify the actions that are required to discover anomalies.

Two types of classifiers are used: decision trees and vector machine support. The table maintains the routing information and updates are chosen as hint records in three approaches: share of routes changed, proportion of modifications inside the variety of hops of all routes, and proportion of new routes added. Trace assessment and identification of irregularities are the two key methods which the authors can use for the IDS. Records obtained from normal crew routing operations are fed into the education series of policies for accomplishing classifier reference values. Then deviations (correlate) from popular profile classifications are used to consider the community routing anomalies. The developed method is examined for the following MANET routing protocols at the ns-2 simulator: DSR (Dynamic Source Routing: a reactive, furnish initiated, on-call routing protocol); AODV (Ad Hoc On-Demand Distance Vector: a reactive, supply initiated, on-call routing protocol); and DSDV (Destination Sequenced Distance Vector: a constructive, desk-driven, routing protocol). In line with the results, their algorithm performs greater on-demand protocols than positive protocols seeing that the affiliation between site visitors patterns and routing messages flows into on-demand protocols is much less tough to research.

Butun et al. (2012) proposed the idea of multiple-layer built-in intrusion detection and response as an extension of their preceding research, that is based on the frequently IDS based dispersed and joint agent. The intrusion detection module at-layer must, nevertheless, show up appropriately in the modern-day definition; however, recognition on one layer can be started or supported by means of proof from different layers. Throughout the usage of this approach, the authors say that their IDS can reap greater output in phrases of every perfect greater first-class and raising the nice identification of pretend charges. The scheme should be relevant to WSNs in a way that precise care can be taken: for example, they may want to be included in a hierarchical WSN in which CHs may want to execute the planned schemes in a overseas trip and the tiny nodes in a close by feeling (hard work department).

According to Butun et al. (2012) and Michiardi and Molva (2002), the dispersed IDS structure may be enhanced through the software, such as mobile agents. In contrast to regular processes during which the location information is transmitted in the course of the computation site, mobile sellers transmit the code to the records. Asynchronous implementation of the mediator is carried out on a remote host. This significantly reduces the range of tourist documents (regarding retailers) inside the city. Nevertheless, the character workload of every node is accelerated which is no longer perfect in WSNs. In addition, sending mobile code (an executable element of the IDS is transmitted to the on-site facts processing nodes) will decrease the WSN bandwidth. But, if bandwidth effectively is of great importance, this technique is no longer usually sufficient. Kachirski and Guha discussed the cellular agent's belief with the aid of presenting cell agents an inexperienced distribution with clear IDS duties (network tracking, host control, choice making and taking action) in line with their ability in the Wi-Fi ad hoc culture. In this way, some of the nodes are unfolded to reduce the electrical energy and processing instances related with IDS throughout all nodes and thus the workload of the proposed IDS. The scheme is consequently essential for WSNs. A different approach is to restrict in-depth evaluation of preferred community security to a few available nodes.

9.3.2 Clustering (Hierarchical) Based IDSs

Standard nodes do not interact in the international selection using the method in the Kachirski and Guha strategy. The most beneficial CHs are in charge for the cycle of international decision-making and reaction. This is principally pushed by lowering electricity consumption. We managed to maintain the strength of most nodes by clearly appointing them beneath CHs as subordinates.

Clustering is used to choose a single layer show devices placed in moderation. In Michiardi and Molva (2002), video display structures are used to examine routing wrongdoing by means of statistical anomaly detection. To maintain properties, in this scheme every node is chosen on a time basis to monitor the entire network in order to find the intrusion inside the group of nodes. Under the proposed scheme, a revealing method runs on every monitoring node to uncover nearby intrusions, after which it collaborates with different sellers to check out the source of the intrusion and arrange responses.

In Mishra et al. (2004), the authors advised on a method that would practice a decentralized, supportive approach to detect intrusion into clustered MANETs. A dynamic hierarchy is used as a directorial model that permits better-layer nodes to selectively mix and limit the scope of intrusion, meaning detection can be done from the topmost part to the bottom. So it follows a top-down approach. This infrastructure, which is no longer the most environmentally friendly, permits reviews of intrusion detection to be successfully obtained from the population. However, in addition to inexperienced distribution of intrusion response and manage instructions, gradual aggregation, identification and correlation are included as well. For the following three instances the proposed scheme will be examined:

- Intentional packet loss histories
- Assaults with MANET routing protocol

- Assaults with community and higher-layer protocols

Clustering in the main structured IDSs may also be of gain to WSNs if they should be utilized with unique care. Because of this, CHs would dissipate their sources more quickly than chosen nodes that should purpose segmentations inside the community (node companies that can be separated from each other). Therefore, extra batteries would possibly want to be connected to CHs that will enable them to last longer, or CHs may also be chosen from time to time in a trip so that the node with the best power every time may additionally grow to be the CH.

9.3.3 Statistical Detection Based IDSs

Puttini et al. present an algorithm for intrusion detection notably based totally on Bayesian classification standards. Their structure is primarily based on statistical contrast modeling that performs the use of combination models so that one can cope with an observable traveler composed of a mixture of special traveler profiles due to one form of crew system. It is designed to realize packet flooding, an instance of a DoS attack, and to scan assaults in opposition to MANETs. The proposed model builds a behavioral model that takes into account greater than one person profiles and makes use of an *a posteriori* Bayesian category of knowledge as a section of the guidelines set for detection.

The authors use estimated intermediate node congestion to suggest alternatives about malicious packet loss behavior. They advise that to preserve the statistical regularity from hop to hop, visitor's transmission types have to be used in conjunction with suboptimal medium access control. The proposed strategy for intrusion detection is generalized and ideal for networks. Nevertheless, those that are not restricted with the aid of bandwidth have precise protection standards like tactical networks. Accordingly, they are no longer appropriate for WSNs with restricted bandwidth. Statistical strategies require a lot of processing of records in order to sift statistics that are retained for records.

9.3.4 Misuse Detection-Based IDS

Shin et al. (2010) advised that IDS in reality is based totally on an algorithm for the detection of misuse. Their implementation centered on remote-vector routing protocols like the DSDV protocol. In addition to compromised routers, their implementation centered on detecting DoS and replay assaults. Their simulation results have provided great conclusions based no longer solely on the accuracy and robustness of the scheme but additionally on the average overall performance of the network. However, DSDV calls for regular replacement of routing tables that should not use up the available electricity sources of the nodes but may devour sections of the valuable available bandwidth. Therefore, a software program based on this set of policies for WSNs is not recommended.

9.3.5 Reputation (Trust)-Based IDSs

A trust based IDS encourages node collaboration via collective node observing and appraising the device coupled with collective tracking of outcomes. Garcia-Teodoro and Diaz-Verdejo (2009) used the definition of credibility to measure the contribution a participant makes to the society. The more credible a member, the more chosen members of the family can connect with different community members. As an alternative, crew participants need to refer to that unique node distinguished from the decreased focus nodes. The authors recognized three kinds of reputations:

- Subjective recognition: measured in phases of the direct interface between a concern and its neighbors.
- Indirect recognition: measured with the aid of regional non-neighbors.
- Purposeful acknowledgement: Arbitrary and indirect reputations measured by noting unique aspects (package routing, route discovery, etc.).

Their interactive evaluation system for popularity consists of simple components, including a recognition table, which is a graphical shape that is saved on every node that integrates popularity records that reach a node.

9.3.6 Watchdog Mechanism

A watchdog mechanism measures predefined treasured reputations in conjunction with the records saved on the attention desk and then identifies nodes that are misbehaving. Detection primarily depends completely on an attention limit rate (e.g., 0); if a precise member's credibility drops under the threshold value, then the watchdog mechanism prevents all contact with that member.

Additionally, DoS assaults had been challenging to them. Accordingly, they advised an agreed mechanism primarily based on acknowledgement to put into effect cooperation between nodes. In addition, this identification mechanism avoids DoS assaults ensuing from self-seeking nodes. The CONFIDANT protocol acts as an extension to DSR-composed reactive routing protocols and makes use of a reputation based mechanism that costs nodes based totally on their malevolent behavior. Alarm messages from different nodes are analyzed and the node identification underlying investigation is modified in the easiest way if the messages come from the nodes that are definitely established. A community scheme is used to discover disruptive costs generated in the provided path to the subsequent node. If a particular system senses a spiteful neighbor, it sends a warning message to a variety of nodes according to its list of buddies' dependents. The rule for communication standard can be described as: cooperation between nodes for the sake of fairness in each of the present schemes (Garcia-Teodoro and Diaz-Verdejo 2009). This applies to WSNs with a minor variation: the expiration length for the bandwidth utilization tables will be shortened.

9.3.7 Primarily Sector Based IDS

The crew is divided into non-overlapping zones with photovoltaic sector based IDS (Strikos 2014), and every IDS agent in the vicinity publicizes regionally generated signals. Gateway zones are accountable for aggregating and correlating the regionally produced indicators. The simplest gateway nodes throughout the community can generate massive alarms. Indicators suggest viable assaults and are generated through nearby IDS segments, whilst alarms point out the very final detection and can exceptionally be generated by using gateway nodes. The characteristic of their proposed nearby aggregation and correlation engine is to mix the detection results of the detection engines domestically and examine them, whereas the position of their proposed international aggregation and correlation engine in gateway nodes is to combine and examine nearby node detection effects so that last alternatives can be made. Nearby warning signs are created in accordance with the detection criteria: (1) percentage of exchange in route entries representing the deleted and newly acquired routing entries in a tremendous term; (2) percentage of alternates in a huge range of hops representing a choice of the quantity of hops of all routing entries in a certain word. In line with the simulations of the authors (accomplished on the crew simulator Glo-MoSim), their model responded with far fewer false positives due to the fact that the mobility used to be reduced. In comparison, the aggregation algorithm of gateway nodes ended up notably reducing false positives more than neighborhood node IDS, on the grounds that they can accumulate statistics from a broader location and permit extra correct selections.

The proposed model detects intrusions inside the OSI stack's routing layer, however particular layers are ignored. Since it was once no longer feasible to become aware of assaults in different layers, with the aid of the use of this version, it is a partial IDS. The proposed scheme requires that any node have the surrounding geographical information. Whilst this is viable by means of incorporating an international positioning system (GPS) receiver into MANET nodes, it is no longer possible in WSNs due to the fact most sensor nodes are commonly not equipped with GPS due to cost and electricity regulations.

9.3.8 Game Idea Based IDSs

The authors exhibit a game-theoretical approach in Marti et al. (2000) and Wei and Kim (2012) to look at intrusion detection in MANETs. They use the idea of sport to model the interactions between ad hoc community nodes. As a non-cooperative exercise user, they model the interaction between an intruder and a character node. According to their assumptions, as long as the values are aligned with the facts acquired and the movements are given the principles, the model is technically stable. The proposed schemes require a vital processing machine that will store all the observations gathered about the usage of the monitoring system. In addition to a massive memory area, this requires a significant velocity microprocessor to store the data to be processed. Thus, in an attempt to extend these schemes to WSNs, a centralized WSN ought to be chosen, in a place where there is a base station (BS) equipped with a laptop with high-velocity processing and large memory. The schemes can be modified according to the loading of site visitors in between every node and the BS. A logging machine can be used, for example, and the location of every node may additionally keep records of interactions associated with a number of nodes (and, if possible, attackers). These logs can be submitted to the BS typically based totally on detection for the utility of the game concept.

9.3.9 Genetic Algorithm Based IDS

Sen and Clark investigated the use of evolutionary computing techniques to classify MANET environment friendly detectors (these lack full-size computing unit, have extraordinary cell nodes and limited resources). The authors utilized grammatical evolution and genetic programming strategies to perceive AODV assaults on ad hoc flooding and course destruction. The authors have proven that their constructed applications are carried out immediately on digital networks with particular mobility and site visitor patterns, whilst this methodology is possibly very promising for MANETs, where the location nodes (e.g., PDAs) are sufficiently environmentally friendly to run these electricity-hungry algorithms. That does not extend to WSNs, where the location sensor nodes have minimal information processing and storage capacities.

9.3.10 Other Works

In the watchdog, one characteristic carried out at the pinnacle of the DSR protocol is to make certain that the subsequent node inside the route moreover forwards the packet when a node forwards a packet; in any other case, the following node would be identified as a misbehaving. Watchdogs run on every node, listening in a promiscuous way to transmissions from the neighboring nodes. Due to the packet collisions, watchdogs will not be continuously active. The watchdog mechanism proposed is necessary for WSNs.

Mishra et al. (2004) suggested a hybrid IDS which, in addition to the Wi-Fi ad hoc networks, would permit every device to function on busy networks. All the new model's information and the reviews of the implementation had not been provided, so it is not possible to analyze its overall performance in maintaining the models previously proposed. In addition, the proposed scheme calls for a quit-to-end verbal exchange channel between nodes that typically no longer exist in WSNs. MANETs have been very beneficial for premeditated networks such as command posts, automobile convoys, self-sufficient robotics, and infantry troops as well.

The authors of MITE (MANET Intrusion Detection for Tactical Environments (Sen and Clark (2009)) make it clear why in MANETs, especially in tactical situations, they are developing prototypical options for intrusion detection. Besides the simulation implications, the effects of MITE have been located and examined as real-world implementations. The authors advised an effective and beneficial framework for resource-saving sensor detectors as a beneficial component. The proposed scheme's TOGBAD scheme requires a giant quantity of visitors to the site. It consequently does no longer practice to WSNs the place the bandwidth is an inadequate assist and would like to be carried out resourcefully.

Roman et al. (2006) used the expectation of web page customers to uncover intrusions in Wi-Fi networks. The authors recommended a website traffic prediction model centered normally on the use of time series information targeted on the autoregressive moving average (ARMA). According to their simulations, the version estimated traffic to the net web page without problems and reliably sifted out the attackers. Given the fact that the achievements appear positive, the proposed answer brings a heavy visitor load to the community for monitoring report packets and similarly calls for a centralized processing unit to shop and analyze all site visitor information no longer acquired in WSNs.

9.4 Intrusion Detection System in WSN 212

Intrusion detection in WSNs is turning into a main problem that is being addressed in the literature. Consequently, the research performed so far is summarized at this point. The unique challenging circumstances of modern WSNs that make it challenging to observe conventional IDSs (designed for wired or commonplace Wi-Fi networks) are discussed in Section 9.4.1. WSNs are an individual form of MANETs, with very unique plan constraints. Therefore, the important variations between the two networks will be referred to in Section 9.4.2. Finally, the current WSN literature is provided in Section 9.4.3. After all the tests, we will discuss advantages and dangers of the modern system and provide an evaluation chart.

9.4.1 Restrictions and Research Challenges in WSN

The proliferation of WSNs has led researchers to set up techniques that encompass communications and networking for dispersed community environments, as well as the capability to defend these techniques with restricted resources (Shin et al. 2010). The lack of constant roadmap (i.e., gateways, routers, BSs, etc.) permits models and algorithms applicable to safety layouts and algorithms for WSNs. Bandwidth, capacity and electricity from batteries are the restricted resources that need to be used carefully.

This is accompanied by a brief listing of limitations and the associated issues they pose for WSNs:

- There is no specific structure in WSNs for transferring data, finding the path, real-time vacationer review, hiding of data, and so on.
- Nodes are accountable for the capture, exploitation or hijacking of physical components that have an effect on community operations.
- Compromised nodes can additionally supply the relaxation of the WSN with deceptive routing statistics making the community no longer operational (black hole, wormhole, sinkhole attacks).
- Wireless conversation tends to involve messages that can be heard by other people, which would expose necessary statistics to adversaries and/or jamming/interference, which would be the clarification for DoS in the WSN.
- There is no authority or dependent; selections need to be made in a joint manner. Whilst planning the IDS for WSNs, these are all the properties and difficulties that ought to be considered.

9.4.2 Differences Between MANETs and WSNs

Roman et al. misunderstood the truth that the IDSs that should be configured for MANETs cannot be extended to WSNs. Since they are structured in an identical way to MANETs and IDSs, they would be much less effective in a stationary network that consists of WSNs. The following are predominant one-of-a-kind abilities which distinguish WSNs from MANETs:

- **Mobility:** WSN nodes are generally stationary as opposed to cellular MANET nodes.
- **Computing capacity:** WSN nodes have minimal processing strength in contrast to MANET nodes; regular sensor node like MICAz runs an Atmel ATmega128L processor with a top velocity of 16 MHz, whilst the common MANET node, inclusive of ordinary industrial laptop which may additionally have a CPU, runs with a top speed of 4 GHz (Chen et al. 2009).
- **Communications range:** The verbal exchange range for WSN nodes is roughly 20–30 m (for MICAz), whilst for MANET nodes it is up to 100 meters (for the XBee Wi-Fi module explained in Chen et al. (2009)).
- **Communications bandwidth:** The conversation bandwidth is restricted to 250 kbps (for a state-of-the-art MICAz mote) information cost in WSNs, compared with 65 Mbps information cost in MANETs (for a daily XBee Wi-Fi module (39; Chen et al. 2009)).
- **Power supply:** WSN nodes have a totally limited strength supply, such as 2 AA sized batteries for MICAz motes, whilst MANET nodes commonly have a large battery,

like laptop batteries. This would really have an effect on their lifespan. Assuming their electricity consumption stages are the same, MANETs will have about 15 times the life of WSNs.

- **Autonomy:** In MANETs, every node is managed with the aid of a human operator, whilst in WSNs every node is self-sufficient in terms of the experience that it receives from the BS and the information it sends.

- **Node density:** Node density in WSNs is higher than that in MANETs. As an alternative, WSNs nodes stand a greater chance of hardware disasters (battery constraints, physical damage, and so forth), which should reduce the systems connected in the network. The exceptional abilities ought to be viewed in the past rather than adapting IDS that is designed for a MANET to a WSN.

9.4.3 Proposed Schemes

9.4.3.1 Grouping Based IDSs

A hierarchical form is proposed for intrusion detection and records processing. The price of one-hop clustering was once the focus in the experiments on the proposed structure. The authors believed that their hierarchical framework was advisable for protecting processing functions of WSNs with reference to two lines of defense.

In Strikos (2014), the authors explained a separation desk for correctly discovering intrusions in hierarchical WSNs. Their idea required a two-degree clustering procedure. Their isolation desk intrusion detection methods were successful in detecting assaults in accordance with their study. The trouble with this idea is as follows: the authors announced that every video streaming device can produce the anomalies to the BS. In view of the fact that it is a hierarchical group, any alarm created via the lower-level nodes should bypassed the higher-level nodes inner in case the higher-level node is the intruder. In this way, it does not allow the center node to be privy to its intrusion by way of blockading the warnings collected from the lower-level nodes. In Krontiris et al. (2009), an IDS primarily based on the move towards clustering was proposed. This coverage was additionally established for the safety of CHs. One of the systems in the group displays their leader in the group in a planned manner in their process. In this way power is supplied for all entities in the cluster. On the contrary, members in the cluster are tracked by means of CH, not always via the use of cluster man or woman contributions. This moreover saves cluster individuals' resources. Via simulations, the authors have established that their proposed set of guidelines is a lot greener than different algorithms in the literature. The foremost problem is with this technique. It is a far-reaching section of the IDS, and lets the IDS set pair keys between nodes. The IDS makes use of these keys by using messages authentication. The key administration assumes the nodes are certain desks (fixed) and the new systems cannot be carried till the pairwise keys have been enabled. A disadvantage of the model is also the fact that WSN may also regularly entail the periodic deployment of the latest nodes.

The authors suggested a hierarchical model of IDS in which the team is split into groups and a CH is chosen for every cluster. They supplied centralized routing, which enables data to be sent to the group leader and to the central system. Their suggestion included a method within the CHs to detect intrusion in the neighborhood in order to make the whole network impenetrable with a minimal number of detectors. The authors did not provide any model to generate the results or run any genuine trials. So, it is not yet easy to know whether or not the method would work as proposed.

In Ngai et al. (2006), a set of abnormality-detecting regulations was proposed. They decreased the overhead verbal exchange by way of clustering the measurements of the sensors and first combining clusters then transferring an outline of the clusters to different nodes. The authors applied their anticipated model in an undertaking that is without a doubt international. They have checked that their scheme achieves the same effect in dialog costs when compared with centralized schemes with a large discount.

9.4.3.2 Centralized and Collaborative IDSs

Onat and Miri (2005) advised a centralized WSN IDS targeted on collective management of the network. The authors assessed the usefulness of their IDS scheme for black hole and selective forwarding assaults in a simulation environment. A way to the query the effectiveness of intrusion detection in WSNs developed into an idea about equipping the location nodes with neighboring detector modules to disperse intruder observation. The detector modules precipitated issues about interference inside the internet of the sensor. The authors introduced the prerequisites required to efficaciously expose the intruder and an equivalent algorithm which is proven to act under a commonplace type of threat.

In Agah and Das (2007), the planned IDS used a requirement based on a total detection algorithm. The authors used a decentralized method for finding the fault in which intrusion detectors had been allotted to parts of the community. (Their hole was once one-hop, retaining the entire community.) The accrued information and its transmission had been carried out in an allotted fashion. They believed that this dispersed methodology was more flexible and resilient than a centralized method. Because of the actuality the intrusion detectors had amazing views of the community by way of being assigned to the whole system.

9.4.3.3 Statistical Detection Based IDSs

Rajasegarar et al. (2008) provided a method for the detection of the sinkhole intrusion. The anticipated algorithm first suggests a listing of suspicious nodes after which a community assumes the waft layout, which efficiently determines the intruder inside the network. This method involves stepwise execution of a multiple variation method, primarily based on the chi-rectangular search. Helpfulness and precision of the projected algorithm are established via every arithmetical evaluation and simulation. The authors believed the verbal exchange and computational overheads of their algorithms are cheap for WSNs. In the recommended set of rules, the sensor community adapts to the dynamics norm in its setting in order to notice any uncommon activities. They employ a Hidden Markov Model that helps to achieve this. The authors believed their proposed algorithm was at once easy to use and required minimal processing and storage data. The algorithm's usefulness and practicality are validated by way of experiential circumstances. The advised algorithm makes use of a statistical approach to sift out any uncommon reading. So it is very much a one-of-a-kind IDS that is fully based on the correctness of the accrued data, as a substitute for the safety of the nodes or hyperlinks. In Rajasegarar et al. (2007), the authors recommended a true time based, absolutely anomaly based detection algorithm that uses a sensor node to tune the detection processes. They developed a model for website online content that can be accessed by way of a sensor node and deliberated a scheme to discover irregular modifications at some point in the arrival procedure. The detection series of policies retained the use of a multi-degree sliding window event storage scheme for quick time span statistics. In this way the algorithm will examine the procedures to arrive at a one-of-a-kind time period. The authors believed that their method was beneficial and less complex.

9.4.3.4 IDSs Based on Game Theory

In Bhuse and Gupta (2006), Agahetal considered assault and detection as part of every activity and the techniques devised for each activity. Techniques have been standardized into a non-cooperative, non-zero recreation model in order to amplify the detection rate. Development of the scheme aimed at discovering the network's weakest node and then presenting safety techniques for that system. The trouble with this method was that there may be severe intrusions into the WSN and only one of them will be recognized by the IDS, accordingly allowing others to go undetected.

9.4.3.5 Anomaly Based Detection of IDSs

Anomaly detection methods for WSNs are discussed in Wang et al. (2012). They encouraged researchers not to overlook the intrinsic boundaries of WSNs in their layout, consequently decreasing energy utilization in tiny systems and optimizing the network's lifetime. The same authors recommended a method for decreasing overhead contact inside the network whilst figuring out anomalies happening in group computation. Their answer to this query is based totally on an approach that makes use of allotted area-sphere one-elegance assist vector machines to classify anomalous measurements in statistics. The authors carried out their idea in a real-world venture and stated that their model was power efficient in overhead conversation, even achieving the same precision as a centralized scheme. Bhuse and Gupta proposed light-weight strategies to find intrusions of anomalies in WSNs. Their main notion was once to reuse the available system facts created in unique layers of a neighborhood protocol stack—physical, MAC and routing layers in particular. The authors proposed more than one detector monitoring specific layers of the OSI stack in order to provide a higher detection rate. This is not possible for WSNs due to the truth that monitoring intrusion in distinct layers and retaining the synchronization of these video display units may use up the WSN's scarce sources. Apart from that, the authors proposed their outsider assault schemes to be best, leaving out the insider assaults. This is inadequate due to the fact that tiny systems in a WSN are very prone to insider attacks, which include physical attacks, Sybil assault, and so on. Onat and Miri provided an IDS for WSNs which was once absolutely established on detecting packet level anomalies in electricity. The identification scheme modified into the neighboring nodes of a chosen node centering on transceiver conduction and the rate at which the packet arrived. WSNs are rarely ever cellular and consequently have a healthy sample of dialog relative to MANETs. The unique distinction has been exploited by the authors. The node developed a fundamental statistical model of the moves of its buddies and used this information to identify any suspicious adjustments inside the destination. The planned model worked well in terms of noticing impersonation attacks.

9.4.3.6 Totally IDS Based Watchdog

Roman et al. (2006) have provided hints about static WSN IDS applications (which could be optimized for MANETs). Instead, they suggest the IDS called "impulsive watchdogs" for WSNs in which associates are optimally managed and in which a few nodes choose to watch their region's communications autonomously.

9.4.3.7 Reputation (Trust) Based IDS

Wang et al. (2012) proposed an IDS for WSNs that would use packet markings after which heuristic ranking algorithms would discover maximum nodes inside the network that could be poor. Growing packets are encrypted and sealed so that the place in which the packet arrives can be secured. Some representation of the packet is included in each packet, so that the central node can improve the packet origination using their heuristic ranking algorithm with a small fake fine score; the maximum of bad nodes will be recognized in accordance with their simulations.

9.5 Future Directions in the Selection of IDS for WSN

In system design the energy usage of the IDSs is a significant problem. WSNs absorb power by sensing phenomena, storing the sensed details and transmitting the knowledge that follows. Accordingly, the IDSs need to expend the least amount of energy possible to conserve enough power for critical WSN operations. Because of this low WSN electricity intake requirement, applying a hierarchical version for IDSs is useful. In other words, the network will be split into clusters, each as a way of obtaining a CH. The energy consumption could also be reduced by stopping all nodes from sending data to the BS. The prevention of unnecessary power consumption by IDS algorithms could be most useful at CHs, which could conserve power to relax the nodes and potentially increase the network's lifespan. Different forms of intrusion prevention algorithms are available; the intrusion detection algorithm can be selected based on the requirements of the proposed software, that is, the attacks to be detected, the detection accuracy (percentage of false positive and true positive) and the detection time period. Our rationale for selecting the IDS for WSNs may be similar (different recommendations for specific packages): for mobile packages where sensor nodes are in motion, we suggest using dispersed and cooperative IDS schemes as scalable, efficient and fast.

9.6 Conclusion

In this chapter, IDSs are briefly considered in terms of their classifications, design specifications and amenities. Secondly, IPSs proposed for MANETs are introduced, and their relevance to WSNs is addressed. Thirdly, the IPS planned for WSNs are listed and their specific capabilities are illustrated in a similar way, accompanied by remarks on IDSs which may be appropriate to WSNs. Finally, to assist researchers in the selection of IDSs for WSNs, suggestions for suitable schemes and potential guidance for this research are given.

References

Agah, A., S.K. Das, 2007, "Preventing DoS attacks in wireless sensor networks: A repeated game theory approach," *International Journal of Network Security*, 5(2), 145–153.

Akyildiz, I.F., W. Su, Y. Sankarasubramaniam, E. Cayirci, 2002, "A survey on sensor networks," *IEEE Communication Magazine*, 40(8), 102–114.

Anantvalee, T., J. Wu, 2007, *A Survey on Intrusion Detection in Mobile Ad Hoc Networks*, Chapter 7, 159–180. Springer, Heidelberg.

Bhuse, V., A. Gupta, 2006, "Anomaly intrusion detection in wireless sensor networks," *J. High Speed Networks*, 15(1), 33–51.

Butun, I., Y. Wang, Y. Lee, R. Sankar, 2012, "Intrusion prevention with two-level user authentication in heterogeneous wireless sensor networks," *International Journal of Security and Networks*, 7(2), 107–121.

Cayirci, E., C. Rong, 2009, *Security in Wireless Ad Hoc and Sensor Networks*. Wiley, Chichester, UK.

Chen, R.C., C.F. Hsieh, and Y.F. Huang, 2009a, "A new method for intrusion detection on hierarchical wireless sensor networks," in *Proceedings of the ACM ICUIM-09*, Suwon, Korea.

Chen, X., K. Makki, K. Yen and N. Pissinou, 2009b,"Sensor network security: A survey," *IEEE Journal of Communications Surveys and Tutorials*, 11(2), 52–73.

Cheng, T.S., Y.D. Lin, Y.C. Lai, P.C. Lin, 2012, "Evasion techniques: sneaking through your intrusion detection/prevention systems," *IEEE Communications Surveys and Tutorials*, 14(4), 1011–1020.

Elshoush, H.T., I.M. Osman, 2011, "Alert correlation in collaborative intelligent intrusion detection systems: A survey," *Journal of Applied Soft Computing*, 11(7), 4349–4365.

Farooqi, A.H. ,F.A. Khan, 2009, "Intrusion detection systems for wireless sensor networks: A survey," *Journal of Communication and Networking*, 56, 234–241.

Fuchsberger, A., 2005, "Intrusion detection systems and intrusion prevention systems," *Journal of Information Security Technical Report*, 10(3), 134–139.

Garcia, K.A., R. Monroy, L.A. Trejo, C. Mex-Perera, E. Aguirre, 2012, "Analyzing log files for post-mortem intrusion detection," *IEEE Transactions on System, Man, and Cybernetics*, 42(6), 1690–1704.

Garcia-Teodoro, P., J. Diaz-Verdejo, 2009, "Anomaly-based network intrusion detection: techniques, systems and challenges," *Journal of Computers and Security*, 28(1–2), 18–28.

Kachirski, O., R. Guha, 2002, "Intrusion detection using mobile agents in wireless ad hoc networks," *KMN '02: Proceedings of the IEEE Workshop on Knowledge Media Networking*, Kyoto, Japan. IEEE Computer Society.

Kachirski, O., R. Guha, 2003, "Effective intrusion detection using multiple sensors in wireless ad hoc networks," in *Proceedings 36th Annual Hawaii International Conference on System Sciences (HICSS'03)*, Big Island, HI, 57.1.

Keung, G.Y., B. Li, Q. Zhang, 2012, "The intrusion detection in mobile sensor network," *IEEE/ACM Transactions on Networking (TON)*, 20(4), 1152–1161.

Krontiris, I., Z. Benenson, T. Giannetsos, F. Freiling, T. Dimitriou, 2009, "Cooperative intrusion detection in wireless sensor networks," *Journal of Wireless Sensor Networks*, (5432), 263–278.

Marti, S., T. Giuli, K. Lai, and M. Baker, 2000, "Mitigating routing misbehavior in mobile ad hoc networks," *International Conference on Mobile Computing and Networking (MobiCom)*, London, UK, pp. 255–265.

Michiardi, P., R. Molva, 2002, "A Collaborative Reputation mechanism to enforce node cooperation in Mobile Ad Hoc Networks," in Jerman-Blažič, B., Klobučar, T. (eds) *Advanced Communications and Multimedia Security*. IFIP—The International Federation for Information Processing, vol 100. Springer, Boston, MA.

Mishra, A., K. Nadkarni, A. Patcha, 2004, "Intrusion detection in wireless ad hoc networks," *IEEE Transactions on Wireless Communications*, 11(1), 48–60.

Modi, C., D. Patel, B. Borisaniya, 2013, "A survey of intrusion detection techniques in Cloud," *Journal of Network and Computer Applications*, 36, 42–57.

Ngadi, M., A.H. Abdullah, S. Mandala, 2008, "A survey on MANET intrusion detection," *International Journal of Computer Science and Security*, 2(1), 1–11.

Ngai, E., J. Liu, M. Lyu, 2006, "On the intruder detection for sinkhole attack in wireless sensor networks," *ICC '06*, Istanbul, Turkey.

Onat, I., A. Miri, 2005, "A real-time node-based traffic anomaly detection algorithm for wireless sensor networks," in *Proceedings of the Systems Communications*, Washington, DC.

Padmavathi, G., D. Shanmugapriya, 2009, "A survey of attacks, security mechanisms and challenges in wireless sensor networks," *International Journal of Computer Science*, 4(1), 1–9.

Patcha, A., J.M. Park, 2006, "A game theoretic formulation for intrusion detection in mobile ad hoc networks," *International Journal of Network Security*, 2(2), 131–137.

Patcha, A., J.M. Park, 2007, "An overview of anomaly detection techniques: Existing solutions and latest technological trends," *Journal of Computer Networks*, 51(12), 3448–3470.

Rajasegarar, S., C. Leckie ,M. Palaniswami, 2008,"Anomaly detection in wireless sensor networks." *IEEE Wireless Communications*, 15(4), 34–40.

Rajasegarar, S., C. Leckie, M. Palaniswami, J.C. Bezdek, 2007, "Quarter sphere based distributed anomaly detection in wireless sensor networks," *IEEE ICC '07*, Glasgow, UK.

Rao, R., G. Kesidis, 2003,"Detecting malicious packet dropping using statistically regular traffic patterns in multihop wireless networks that are not bandwidth limited," in *Proceedings of the IEEE GLOBECOM*, San Francisco, CA.

Roman, R., J. Zhou, J. Lopez, 2006, "Applying intrusion detection systems to wireless sensor networks," in *Proceedings IEEE Consumer Communications and Networking Conference*, Las Vegas, NV.

Shakshuki, E., N. Kang, T. Sheltami, 2013, "EAACK—A secure intrusion detection system for MANETs," *IEEE Transactions on Industrial Electronics*, 60(3), 1089–1098.

Sen, S., J.A. Clark, 2009, "Intrusion detection in mobile ad hoc networks," *Guide to Wireless Ad Hoc Networks*, pp. 427–454. Springer, London.

Sen, S., J.A. Clark, 2011, "Evolutionary computation techniques for intrusion detection in mobile ad hoc networks," *Journal of Computer Networks*, 55(15), 3441–3457.

Shin, S., T. Kwon, G.Y. Jo, Y. Park, H. Rhy, 2010, "An experimental study of hierarchical intrusion detection for wireless industrial sensor networks," *IEEE Trans. Ind. Informat.*, 6(4), 744–757.

Sobh, T.S., 2006, "Wired and wireless intrusion detection system: Classifications, good characteristics and state-of-the-art," *Journal of Computer Standards and Interfaces*, 28(6), 670–694.

Strikos, A.A., 2014, "A survey of intrusion detection systems in wireless sensor networks," *IEEE Communications Surveys & Tutorials*, 16(1), 266–282; Strikos, A.A., "A full approach for intrusion detection in wireless sensor networks," In *Wireless and Mobile Network Architectures*, School of Information and Communication Technology, 2008.

Sun, B., L. Osborne, Y. Xiao, S. Guizani, 2007, "Intrusion detection techniques in mobile ad hoc and wireless sensor networks," *IEEE Transactions on Wireless Communications*, 14(5), 56–63.

Sun, B., K. Wu, U.W. Pooch, 2003, "Zone-based intrusion detection for mobile ad hoc networks," *International Journal of Ad Hoc and Sensor Wireless Networks*, 2(3), 297–324.

Wang, Y., G. Attebury, B. Ramamurthy, 2006, "A survey of security issues in wireless sensor networks," *IEEE Communications Surveys and Tutorials*, 8(2), 2–23.

Wang, C., T. Feng, J. Kim, G. Wang, W. Zhang, 2012, "Catching packet droppers and modifiers in wireless sensor networks," *IEEE Trans. Parallel Distrib. Syst.*, 23(5), 835–843.

Wang, Y., W. Fu, D.P. Agrawal, 2013, "Gaussian versus uniform distribution for intrusion detection in wireless sensor networks," *IEEE Transactions on Parallel and Distributed Systems*, 24(2), 342–355.

Wei, M., K. Kim, 2012, "Intrusion detection scheme using traffic prediction for wireless industrial networks," *IEEE Journal of Communications and Networks*, 14(3), 310–318.

Zhang, Y., W. Lee, Y.A. Huang, 2003, "Intrusion detection techniques for mobile wireless networks," *Journal of Wireless Networks*, 9(5), 545–556.

Zhou, Y., Y. Fang, Y. Zhang, 2008,"Securing wireless sensor networks: A survey," *IEEE Communications Surveys & Tutorials*, 10(3), 6–28.

Zhou, C.V., C. Leckie , S. Karunasekera, 2010, "A survey of coordinated attacks and collaborative intrusion detection," *Journal of Computers & Security*, 29(1), 124–140.

Zhou, C.V., C. Leckie, S. Karunasekera, 2009, "Decentralized multidimensional alert correlation for collaborative intrusion detection," *Journal of Network and Computer Applications*, 32(5), 1106–1123.

10

Cryptocurrency and Blockchain

Premkumar Chithaluru[1], Kulvinder Singh[2], and Manish Kumar Sharma[3]

[1] *University of Petroleum & Energy Studies, Dehradun, India*

[2] *University Institute of Engineering and Technology, Kurukshetra University, Kurukshetra, India*

[3] *Chitkara University Institute of Engineering and Technology, Chitkara University, Chandigarh, India*

10.1 Introduction—Definition of Blockchain: A Multiple Faced Technology

Blockchain consists of an important digital technique that is called distributed ledger technology (DLT), in which each has comparable information with everything taken into account and compiled by servers (Houben and Snyers 2016, 2018, Adams, Kewell and Parry 2018), which are stored in a centralized repository. The technique of blockchain utilizes a method of encryption called cryptography. This methodology utilizes cluster algorithms to create and verify data structure and data is embedded with the existing information that cannot be removed. This creates the chain of "transaction blocks" that acts as a fragmented ledger (Bantekas and Nash 2009, De France 2013, Conlon, Vayser, and Schwaba 2019).

- A man/woman joins or departs the framework intentionally, without being (pre-) embraced via any (central) body. The framework trades relied upon system programming. Framework of programming, uncertain reports scattered of middle factors their framework (Walfish and Blumberg 2018). By a lengthy shot the vast majority of advanced sorts of cash proper now on hand for using remember upon permissionless blockchains (for occasion Bitcoin Cash, Litecoin, Bitcoin, etc.) (Bollen 2013, Bovaird 2017, Bianchi, Bovaird and Loeffler 2017).

- The blockchain framework supervisor (who monitors the requirements of the digital cash) can set a preference to be part of the framework. This allows them, among other things (Brito, Shadab, and O'Sullivan 2014, Bratspies 2018), to easily affirm the character of the framework. The manager should select the framework with various digital coins. When doubt arises, permission blockchains are isolated into two subcategories. From the client's point of view, there has been open approval from blockchains (Bryans 2014), which is properly found to everyone, but the place truly encouraged framework used persons is make the trades possibly. Few cryptographic types of cash, like Ripple and NEO, make use of open-permissioned blockchains (Buchko 2017).

10.2 The Basic Working of Blockchain

In the blockchain framework, the supervisor chooses the entire authenticity agreement based on a pre-existing algorithmic authorization system, described as an "understanding instrument." When the factor is affirmed, the new "genuine" technique is deployed in the blockchain (Houben and Snyers 2019), which genuinely realizes an update of the trade record over the Bitcoins framework.

10.2.1 A Distributed Database: Blockchain

The framework of blockchain is very difficult to address the structure, due to blockchain sources being stored in distributed computers.

10.2.2 Bye-Bye Middleman?

Excellent examples of blockchain advancement are licenses revamping an extensive demonstration of trades that would commonly be dispersed (for example, an administrator, a bank, a securities contract system, delegate merchants, and a trade storage facility). On a very basic level, blockchain is connected to decentralization and enabling decentralized approval of trades. Fundamentally, it allows removal of the "specialist" (Chohan 2018).

A great part of the time this will probably result in functionality gains. However, it can also open interfacing social events to particular risks that have previously been supervised via central individuals. More generally, it seems that when an intermediary functions as a buffer against important risks, such as systemic risk, they cannot simply be replaced by blockchain technology (Otsuka and Takehara 2007).

10.3 The Blockchain Agreement Mechanisms

On a crucial level, any middle point inside a blockchain framework can advise the improvement of new statistics in the blockchain. To identify whether or not this development of data (for example, a trade record) is authentic (Data, Statistical 2015), the core points need to land at some kind of comprehension. Here, an "understanding segment" turns into a vital factor. "In the case of cryptocurrencies, such sequencing is required to address the issue of "double-spending" (i.e. the issue that one and the same payment instrument or asset can be transferred more than once if transfers are not registered and controlled centrally) (Nesi 2016, Young 2016, Buttigieg and Sapiano 2020). Understanding sections can be sorted according to distinct habits. A consensus mechanism can be structured in a number of ways. Hereinafter, the two best-known –and in the context of cryptocurrencies also most commonly used – examples of consensus mechanisms will be briefly discussed: the Proof of Work ("POW") mechanism and the Proof of Stake ("POS") mechanism (Directive, Council 2016).

10.3.1 Cryptographic Offers Proof of Work

In a PoW system, network participants have to solve so-called "cryptographic puzzles" to be allowed to add new "blocks" to the blockchain. This puzzle-solving process is commonly referred to as "mining" (Mach 2018). In simple terms, these cryptographic puzzles are made up out of all information previously recorded on the blockchain and a new set of transactions to be added to the next "block" (Yascega and van Thiel 2011). Because the input of each puzzle becomes larger over time (resulting in a more complex calculation), the PoW mechanism requires a vast amount of computing resources, which consume a significant amount of electricity. The cryptographic cash Bitcoin depends upon operation of a PoW agreement.

10.3.2 Proof of Stake

In this structure, a trade (for example, a framework center point) should show obligation related to certain favorable situations or through virtue of superior kinds of cash, a particular in the endorsement of trades. This demonstration of assisting trades is delegated "producing" instead of "mining." For example, with the aid of computerized types of cash, an exchange validator ought to exhibit his "stake" (for example, a magnificent deal) of all coins available to be allowed to verify a trade. Depending on how many coins they hold, they will have a higher chance of being the one to validate the next block (i.e. this all has to do with the fact that they have greater seniority within the network earning them a more trusted position). The alternate validator is paid a trade value for his endorsement benefits via the executing parties (Directive 1991).

10.3.3 Additional Mechanisms

The PoS and PoW mechanisms are a long way from the predominant perception segments now available. Various models include proof of organization, affirmation of destruction, and confirmation of farthest point. Further assessment of these parts falls outside the scope of this examination. Blockchain development can have a number of functions.

While for much of the time blockchain improvement is associated with reducing area or digital money plans, portions, and cash associated organizations, its scope is appreciably broad. Blockchain can be utilized speculatively in a massive range of ways (for instance, trade and business, social protection, and organization). As pointed out previously, this examination will virtually address the difficulty of blockchain development, which is huge for the investigation on cryptographic kinds of cash and can be applied from the perspective of combating illicit price shirking, and fear-based oppressor financing simply as a way to avoid obligation.

10.4 What Are Cryptocurrencies?

Setting up the importance of computerized kinds of cash is no simple endeavor. Much like blockchain, cryptocurrencies have become a "buzzword" to refer to a wide array of technological developments that utilize a technique better known as cryptography. In simple terms, cryptography is the technique of protecting information by transforming it (i.e. encrypting it) into an unreadable format that can only be deciphered (or decrypted) by someone who possesses a secret key. Cryptocurrencies, such as Bitcoin, are secured via this technique using an ingenious system of public and private digital keys.

Hereinafter, we endeavor to outline the importance of cryptographic kinds of cash—dependent on an essential examination of the definitions these days made by various involved methodology makers at European and international levels. Since the emergence of Bitcoin, the subject of cryptocurrencies has been scrutinized by various policy makers, who have each touched upon the subject in a different way. Cryptographic types of cash, for instance, Bitcoin, are virtual fiscal norms of the closing sort: they can be obtained with general cash and sold in opposition to standard money, and they can be used to buy electronics, as well as licensed items and adventures. What is the capability of digital money-related structures? Digital fiscal constructions are described as sold against traditional money. They are not issued by means of a national bank, credit score foundation association, and have specific stipulations that are antagonistic to money. Moreover, cryptographic types of cash, for instance, Bitcoin, contain a decentralized bi-directional (for instance separate) digital cash.

10.4.1 International Monetary Fund (IMF)

In the European Central Bank (ECB), the International Monetary Fund (IMF) has organized cryptographic kinds of money as a subset of digital money-related structures, which it describes as modernized depictions of currency worth, given by personal architects and assigned in their own unit of record. As demonstrated by the IMF, the possibility of digital fiscal constructions covers an increasing number of broad "money associated principles," ranging from clear informal verifications of commitment or "I owe you's" in digital economic models bolstered via assets, for instance, gold, and computerized financial forms, for instance, Bitcoin.

10.4.2 Bank for International Settlements

The Committee on Payments and Market Infrastructures (CPMI) in the form of the Bank for International Settlements (BIS), has certified cryptographic kinds of cash as mechanized fiscal principles or propelled money plans. The key features are as follows:

1. They are assets, the value of which is determined by supply and demand, similar in concept to commodities such as gold, yet with zero intrinsic value;
2. They use digital information to permit the shared exchanges of digital impetus besides trust among events and accept the need for middle individuals; and
3. They are no longer worked with the aid of a particular individual or association.

10.4.3 European Banking Authority (EBA)

The European Banking Authority (EBA) has defined cryptographic sorts of money as digital cash associated models, which it describes as mechanized depictions of massive real worth that are neither given by a national bank or open authority nor in a well-known sense related to fiat money yet are used with the aid of trademark or criminal individuals as an alternate technique and can be moved, taken care of, or traded electronically.

10.4.4 European Securities and Markets Authority (ESMA)

The European Securities and Markets Authority (ESMA) has recently also referred to cryptocurrencies as virtual currencies, in a pan-European warning issued in cooperation with the European Insurance and Occupational Pensions Authority (EIOPA) and the EBA. Fully in line with the EBA's definition, virtual currencies are defined as digital representations of value that are neither issued nor guaranteed by a central bank or public authority and do not have the legal status of currency or money. In line with the EBA's view, digital processes are allowed to represent massive real worth that is neither given nor assured with the aid of a national financial institution and does not have the official reputation of cash or money.

10.4.5 World Bank

The World Bank has assembled cryptographic kinds of cash as a subset of electronic fiscal benchmarks, which it describes as cutting-edge representations of massive real worth that are named in their personal unit of record, indisputable from money, which is essentially a mechanized operation, addressing and naming fiat money. In contrast to most other methodology makers, the World Bank has in addition described cryptographic sorts of money as digital financial measures that be counted upon cryptographic frameworks to achieve understanding.

10.4.6 Financial Action Task Force

Similarly, like other mechanism makers, the Financial Action Task Force (FATF) has pushed towards cryptographic sorts of money as a subset of digital money-related structures.

10.4.7 Framework

The essential point which can be taken from the research findings is that the importance of the time period during which cryptographic types of money are available in the managerial space has not been identified. In reality, progressively, most researchers have avoided describing the term overall.

Most of the groups classify cryptographic kinds of money as a subset or a kind of virtual or progressive financial benchmark. They are intended to constitute a peer-to-peer ("P2P") alternative to government-issued legal tender and are used as a general-purpose medium of exchange (independent of any central bank) that is

(a) secured by a mechanism known as cryptography and
(b) can be converted into legal tender and vice versa.

Hereinafter, we will uncover some understanding of the possibilities of cryptographic types of money (or coins—we will use the two terms separately hereinafter), and more explicitly the dividing line between other closely related ideas, which have to be distinguished from computerized monetary forms.

10.5 Advanced Types of Money—Tokens—Cryptosecurities

The validity period for advanced kinds of money is shorter than for other kinds of money, as it is not permitted to use them in huge transactions. This has to be perceived from two points of view: tokens and crypto protections.

10.5.1 Computerized Monetary Requirements—Tokens

First of all, computerized sorts of money ought to be distinguished from cryptographic "tokens," which provide a different service (for instance, propelled property recorded on an appropriate record, checked through cryptography) and represent a kind of assurance in opposition to an element (or towards its wages, assets, future products or organizations) that emerges from the use of blockchain advancement.

After widespread operation, a couple of tokens represent digital bonds and are typically specified as "security tokens" or "hypothesis tokens." Various tokens permit their owners to gain admission to various types of things with all their benefits and most of the tokens are conventionally "utility tokens." They can be used to acquire certain products or services, yet they do not constitute a general-purpose medium of exchange, simply because they can generally only be used on the token platform itself.

10.5.2 Advanced Kinds of Money—Cryptosecurities

Moreover, computerized sorts of money should in like manner be distinguished from the recent idea that they are "crypto protection." To lay it out simply, it has been argued that blockchain development could be used to select, disrupt, and move conventional items and other corporate assurances, with the goal that an association's capitalization table is always accurate and distinct. Since this mechanism would be checked with cryptography, it has been recommended that these assurances be described as crypto protections. The primary relationship between this recent concept of "crypto protection" and cryptographic kinds of cash is that each of them uses blockchain development.

10.6 Computerized Kinds of Cash—Blockchain

Computerized kinds of money and blockchain have emerged as exciting problems over recent years. The two are every now and again connected in a comparative sentence and are truly associated with every other. They are utilized in a number of ways. It is simple to draw an undeniable line between these functions and cryptographic types of cash, which are, all things considered, one type of utilization of blockchain development. Against this background, regulators need not fear stifling innovation when tackling the subject of cryptocurrencies.

10.6.1 Who Are the Players Being Referred To?

Cryptographic cash adverts are another area where specific on-screen characters are involved in a particular activity. To uncover in more detail the how the market operates and controls the digital transactions, it is necessary to identify the key players in digital payments.

10.6.2 Cryptographic Cash Customers

At first, a huge number of participants are the "cryptographic cash customers," and computerized cash customers are trademark investors making proper transactions by sending and receiving coins:

1. To sell absolute/digital product-based companies (from a lot of unequivocal brokers).
2. To create the peer-to-peer distributions.
3. To store the various digital logs (for instance in a hypothetical way).

Otherwise, advanced digital money transactions can exchange the coins in specific situations:

- Firstly, they can buy their coins in an advanced cash trade using fiat money or some other cryptographic cash;
- Secondly, they can buy coins virtually from every other computerized money consumer (for instance, through a buying and selling platform—this sort of exchange is usually called a "P2P Exchange");
- Thirdly, if they sell products or businesses as a by-product of cryptographic cash, they can in a similar way get cash as an element for those gadgets or organizations.

10.6.3 Excavators

An ensuing participant is the "excavator" who partakes in endorsing trades by disentangling a "cryptographic question." As explained previously, the route towards mining relates to advanced monetary standards that be counted as an agreement operation of PoW. An excavator reinforces the framework by way of harnessing enrolling capability to assist trades and is compensated with recently mined coins (for example, via a modified decentralized new issuance). Excavators can be cryptocurrency users, or, more commonly, parties who have made a new business out of mining coins to sell them for fiat currency or for other cryptocurrencies. At present, the perils recognized with "mining associations" are not a major concern. This will be developed further below.

10.6.4 Computerized Money Exchanges

One-third of the key players are the "computerized money exchanges." Cryptographic cash exchanges are people or components who provide exchange corporations to superior cash customers for a specific fee (for example, a commission). They license computerized money clients to exchange their cash for fiat money or buy new cash with fiat cash. Note that a couple of exchanges (for example, Binance) are unadulterated cryptographic cash exchanges, which suggests that they actually hold various computerized types of cash, frequently Bitcoin, while others (for instance, Coinbase) hold parts in fiat money associated structures, for instance, US dollar or Euro.

Moreover, a range of cryptographic money exchanges in reality license their clients to buy a precise assurance of coins. Thus it can be seen that a range of superior money exchanges (for instance, both standard and unadulterated cryptographic money exchanges) act as guardian wallet providers (for instance, Bitfinex). Taking the whole thing taken into account, cryptographic money exchanges provide their customers with a wide range of component decisions, for instance, wire moves, PayPal moves, Visa transactions, and a number of coins. Some cryptographic money exchanges offer the services on a computerized cash platform.

10.6.5 Trading Tiers

Although cryptographic money exchanges are described as "trading stages," there are superior economic requirements (and, most strikingly, licenses for computerized money customers).

Trading tiers are an element of the time like "P2P exchanges" and "decentralized exchanges." There are many differentiate computerized cash exchanges. However, they do not buy or sell cash themselves. Furthermore, they are not run by an entity or company that oversees and processes all trades, but they are operated exclusively by software (i.e. there is no central point of authority). Trading tiers in fact interface a buyer with a vendor, allowing them to coordinate a path of action, on the web, or even domestically (for example, a frequently closed trade, typically carried out in true cash). A good example of a trading stage for Bitcoins is LocalBitcoins.

10.6.6 Wallet Providers

A wallet provider basically disentangles an advanced cash customer's exchange history into an efficiently intelligible arrangement, which represents a standard record. In fact, there are a couple of sorts of wallet providers:

- Hardware wallet providers that provide cryptocurrency users with specific hardware solutions to privately store their cryptographic keys (e.g. Ledger Wallet1).
- Software wallet providers that provide cryptocurrency users with software applications which allow them to access the network, send and receive coins and locally save their cryptographic keys.
- Companies (on the web) take responsibility for a computerized money customer's cryptographic keys (for instance, Coinbase).

10.7 Orchestrating CRYPTOCURRENCIES—Checking the Crypto-Market

In the wake of tireless development throughout the early years, the market for computerized types of cash took off in 2017, increasing by over 1,200%. At present, there are a few types of cash available for use (with a hard and quick market capitalization of well over EUR 300 billion), and more progress being made continuously.

A few uses of a PoW framework are shown in Table 10.1, while others use any other form of agreement segment. Most are portrayed as pseudo-anonymous, but some are said to strive to be totally perplexing (suggesting that the percentage of cash their

TABLE 10.1

Blockchain Coins Overview

Name	Symbol	Market Cap	Supply Limit
Bitcoin	BTC	$124,969,093,161	21 million
Ethereum	ETH	$57,462,517,858	TBD
Ripple	XRP	$23,790,387,789	100 billion
Bitcoin cash	BCH	$17,159,025,225	21 million
Litecoin	LTC	$6,704,709,572	84 million
Stellar	XLM	$5,128,373,973	100 billion
Cardano	ADA	$5,034,129,651	45 billion
IOTA	MIOTA	$4,038,240,572	2 million
NEO	NEO	$3,386,383	100 million
Monero	XMR	$2,526,586,260	18,4 million
Dash	DASH	$2,592,894,544	17.74–18.92 million

customers guarantee, send, and receive is not always noticeable, perceptible, or linkable via blockchain's trade history). The following examination of the selected advanced financial standards depends solely upon the statistics being accessible on the web.

10.8 Bitcoin and Beyond: Virtual Styles of Money with the Highest Market Capitalization

In reality, the Ethereum coin itself is not a digital forex. Be that as it may, like other open, permissionless blockchains, Ethereum requires an incentive to reinforce exchange approval inside the device (for example, a kind of instalment for the device hubs that execute the tasks). This is the location that Ethereum's local digital foreign money "ether" (ETH) turns into a quintessential factor. Ether would not just allow high-quality agreements to be primarily based on the Ethereum stage (for example, it fills them), and digital operation as a mode of trade (explicitly on the subject of ITOs, the same wide variety of tokens is purchased with ether).

Following Ripple's foundation, Ripple's creators promoted the digital money XRP. XRP turned into a scaffold cash to allow cash-related companies to settle cross-fringe instalments significantly faster and at a lower price than they could utilizing the current global instalment arrangements, which may be sluggish and include numerous mediators (for example, banks). In any case, Ripple's instalment arrangement does not need extension coins to truly work.

Similarly, XRP can deal with in excess of 1,500 exchanges per second. While it was at first created and proposed for huge enterprise use, it has been embraced by a full range of virtual forex clients. Wave (XRP) does not depend on a PoW or a PoS mechanism to approve exchanges, but utilizes its own specific settlement convention.

In contrast to Ethereum's creators, Ripple's innovators did not sell part of XRP by introducing XRP to finance operations. Their business enterprise exchanges are secretly subsidized. At present, it is not absolutely known how XRP (which is for the most part held by Ripple (Labs), Inc.) is or could be dispersed later on.

10.8.1 Wave (XRP) Is Legitimately Adaptable into Fiat Coins

Wave XRP can be legitimately modified into fiat coins on one-of-a-kind cryptographic money trades (for example, to expose the operations on Anycoin Direct, Bitsane, LiteBit175, Kraken, etc.).

10.8.2 Wave (XRP) Is a Vehicle of Trade

Wave (XRP) is being mentioned as a technique for exchange by way of developing a wide variety of (online) dealers for one-of-a-kind merchandise and ventures (for instance, e-cigarettes, nectar, espresso, etc.).

10.8.3 Wave (XRP)

Specifically, since it is clearly still in its early stages, the utilization of the central exchange route requires a great deal of IT information. In addition, both blockchains have to share the same cryptographic function (for example the SHA-256 function) in order for the atomic swap to be possible. While we are not there yet in terms of user friendly cross-chain trading, the emergence of the atomic swap technology brings forth a whole new set of challenges.

10.9 Stellar (XLM)

Like Ripple, Stellar is an open-source, distributed payments infrastructure. Stellar was created in 2014 by one of Ripple's founders. Its goal is to connect people to low-cost financial services to fight poverty and develop individual potential. Stellar can also be used to build smart contracts. It is not based on a PoW or PoS consensus mechanism, but has its own specific consensus protocol.

10.9.1 What Is Stellar?

Stellar is home to the electronic money Lumen (XLM). In short, Lumens are used to pay for transactions on the Stellar network. Lumens merge the capacity to process cash and to arrange exchanges between various monetary standards rapidly and safely.

Stellar's workers contribute code to the structure, yet the system by itself is assumed to be fully free from the connection. Similar to Ripple's cryptocurrency XRP, the total supply of Stellar Lumens is "pre-mined." It is held by Stellar.org, which has been given the task to distribute Lumens for free, in the following manner. The actual distribution is not conducted at once, but over time in a number of rounds.

10.9.2 Stellar Runs on a Permissionless Blockchain

Unlike Ripple, Stellar is well known for its endorsement-less blockchain. Anybody can choose to join the structure and, if certain circumstances have been met, participate in exchanges without being pre-declared or considered by any central authority. While this proves that they are gradually being accepted as a means of payment, they are not a true medium of exchange yet, at least not if you compare them to the coins discussed above.

10.9.3 Lumens Are Pseudo-Processed Coins

Most of the exchanges on the Stellar platform are open, or at any rate they cannot be related to their clients.

10.10 Cardano

Like Ethereum, Cardano is designed and being further developed as a platform on top of which smart contracts and decentralized applications (so-called "Dapps") can be run. The Cardano project began in 2015, and was officially released to the public in September 2017. It is based on what is known as the Ouroboros PoS algorithm.

10.10.1 Cardano's Operations

Cardano operates using decentralized automated cash (ADA). ADA is also utilized to transfer and receive digital money. Transactions are processed by Cardano, much like the money "ether" fortifies Ethereum. Thus, Cardano plans to improve adaptability, security, association, and interoperability with common cash-related frameworks and rules, by extracting from and overhauling practices learned from Ethereum and Bitcoin. What distinguishes Cardano from Ethereum, and from different automated sorts of money, is that it is (one of the first) blockchain activities to be created by a community of scholars and designers. Another notable difference at present is the cryptographic money (ADA).

10.11 NEO

Similar to Ethereum and Cardano, NEO is an open-source blockchain platform on top of which smart contracts and decentralized applications (so-called "Dapps") can be run. NEO, sometimes referred to as the "Chinese Ethereum," was originally launched under the name "Antshares" in February 2014.

10.11.1 What Is NEO?

In short, the NEO project is aimed at digitising assets and automating the management of digital assets, in order to create a so-called "smart economy" (i.e., an economy where parties can agree on a contract without the need to trust each other).

10.11.2 NEO's GAS Offers Digital Coins

NEO's coins are similar to the coins discussed already. In any case, NEO's originators are presently suitably dealing with an idea that would permit coders to tie a specified "modernized character" to a bona fide character. It is not entirely inconceivable—yet at this time still highly unclear—that this technology will also impact GAS's pseudo-anonymous character.

10.12 Monero

Monero is also open-source peer-to-peer cryptographic money "with thought on private and oversight safe exchanges."

10.12.1 Monero's Operations

Monero was launched in April 2014 and depends upon CryptoNote. It proposes that two units of XMR can generally be regularly subbed and there can be no boycotting of express units by XMR merchants or trades by virtue of their relationship in past exchanges. Non-fungible cryptographic sorts of money, such as Bitcoin and Litecoin, are hypothetically vulnerable to boycotting by various operations of blockchain until the end of time, in the event that they have been utilized for an unlawful action. Unlike some different coins, Monero (XMR) is not pre-mined.

10.12.2 Monero Is a Permissionless Blockchain

Much like Bitcoin, Monero (XMR) runs on various blockchain permissions. Anybody may join the system, without previously being guaranteed or considered by an executive.

10.12.3 Monero Is Obviously Convertible into Fiat Cash

Monero (XMR) is obviously exchanged into fiat cash on various cryptographic money exchanges (for example, Anycoin Direct, Kraken, LiteBit, etc.).

10.12.4 Monero Is a Digital Trade

It is perceived as a new methodology for making a number of online transactions fairly. Like Bitcoin, it fittingly sets up a trade operation.

10.12.5 Monero Is an Exchange Coin

On an absolutely immediate blockchain, for example, the Bitcoin or Ethereum blockchain, exchanges for every circumstance are unquestionable and not directly detectable by anybody. In the long run—regardless, this will be no essential undertaking—the sending and enduring regions for such exchanges could similarly be related to an individual's genuine identity.

10.12.5.1 Ring Secret Transactions

Legitimately, Monero utilizes inferred ring secret transactions. RingST joins the procedure of ring identity and is hinted at in the crypto-ideology for probability in the arranged exchange:

- Ring marks join or "blend" a client's record keys with open keys picked up from various blockchain techniques, and known as a RingST of potential lenders, which infers outside onlookers cannot relate an imprint to a particular client. Taken together with stealth addresses (see below) they combine to obscure the two sources and beneficiaries of the ring;

- Secret exchanges combine another hierarchy of protection to conceal the extent of every exchange. Without revealing the actual numbers, they include acryptographic proof that the sum of the input amounts is the same as the sum of the output amounts.

10.12.5.2 Stealth Addresses

Additionally, and in spite of RingST, Monero similarly utilizes stealth addresses. Stealth addresses for each exchange are usually made by the sender in the light of a real concern for the beneficiary.

10.12.5.3 The Project—Kovri

It should be noted that the community of (core) developers and cryptography experts behind Monero is currently working on a project to add yet another layer of privacy to the Monero ecosystem by routing and encrypting XMR transactions via I2P Invisible Internet Project nodes. The use of I2P will obfuscate a transactor's IP address and provide further protection against network monitoring.

10.13 Dash

Dash is open-source peer-to-peer security-driven money. This process was previously known as Darkcoin. Dash's blockchain is affirmed by techniques for accepted "expert center points" in spite of the PoW done by excavators.

10.13.1 Dash's Operations

Dash (DASH), formerly known as Darkcoin, is an open source P2P privacy-centric cryptocurrency. It was first launched in January 2014 and is based on what is known as the X11 PoW algorithm. What is specific to Dash, and makes it different from most other coins, is that it has a two-tier network. Dash's blockchain is secured via so-called "masternodes" in addition to the PoW done by miners. In short, a masternode is a server connected to the Dash network which guarantees a certain minimum level of performance and functionality to perform certain tasks related to PrivateSend and InstantSend (Dash's anonymity and instant transaction features). Exchanges with standard cryptographic kinds of money can be repetitive (for example, they can take anywhere between a few minutes and over 60 minutes). This is due to the fact that enough squares need to go to guarantee that an exchange endeavor to twofold experience cash that has as of late been spent. Dash handles this issue using its ruler center approach. Masternodes can be called upon to form voting quorums to check whether or not a submitted transaction is valid. The masternodes 'lock' the inputs for the transaction and broadcast this information to the network, effectively promising that the transaction will be included in subsequently mined blocks and not allowing any other spending of these inputs during the confirmation time period. Thus, Dash is said to be in a position to push for rapid exchange frameworks like those, for example, of MasterCard.

10.13.2 Dash Is Unmistakably Convertible into Fiat Cash

Dash can be unmistakably exchanged into fiat cash through different money exchanges (for example, Anycoin Direct, Kraken).

10.13.3 Dash Is a Vehicle of Trade

Much like Monero, Dash is perceived as a methodology for partition by consistently making a number of online merchants. In this manner Dash similarly sets up trade.

10.13.4 Dash Is a (Discretionary) Confusing Coin

Like Bitcoin's blockchain, Dash's blockchain is transparent by default, which means that generally speaking transactions are always openly verifiable and traceable on the blockchain. To give its clients genuine budgetary security, Dash offers the decision to utilize a part called PrivateSend. This PrivateSend obscures the starting phases of a client's actions through a strategy known as "blending."

10.14 Conclusion: A Taxonomy and Time Frame of Cryptocurrencies

Based on the research analysis and information, a taxonomy has been set for cryptocurrencies which allows more accurate regular analysis and also allows issues concerning the framework to be raised. Bitcoin's taxonomy is considered first.

What is obvious from the chart is that the promoted cash is non-existent. However, there are agreements with respect to issues such as how the cryptocurrencies are formed, on which process they run, the level of privacy offered, and so forth.

Table 10.2 addresses these groupings. The selected cryptographic kinds of money are analyzed according to different parameters: whether they run on permissioned or permissionless technology; their decentralized nature; whether they were initially offered by an identifiable person or entity; whether they are electronically exchanged; whether they are genuinely convertible into fiat cash; whether they are a vehicle of trade; and whether they are pseudo-anonymous or thoroughly dark. These parameters are not picked carelessly.

The table reflects our understanding of the selected cryptocurrencies. It should be read mindful of the fact that making clear-cut distinctions between cryptocurrencies is not easy. Complicating factors are inter alia the scarcity of the information available and the often highly technical nature thereof. Moreover, cryptocurrencies are a moving target. For example, the mechanized money that is not really a vehicle of trade at present may be one tomorrow. Accordingly, the review does not profess to be the major methodology for outi

10.14.1 Conclusion

To obtain a precise scenario in the context of cryptocurrencies and to provide simple policy advice for the different features of the topic, there is a scope for more work and also deep research is required. Table 10.2 presents the options which can be considered as a workable area and draws several conclusions on the basis of the analysis done.

TABLE 10.2

Taxonomy of Coins

Name	Permissionless/ Permissioned	Decentralized	Initial Offering by an Identifiable Person or Entity	Electronically Traded	Directly Convertible Into Flat Currency	Medium of Exchange	Pseudo-anonymous/ Anonymous
Bitcoin	Permissionless	✓	×	✓	✓	✓	Pseudo-anonymous
Ethereum	Permissionless	✓	✓	✓	✓	✓	Pseudo-anonymous
Ripple	Permissioned	✓	✓	✓	✓	✓	Pseudo-anonymous
Bitcoin cash	Permissionless	✓	×	✓	✓	✓	Pseudo-anonymous
Litecoin	Permissionless	✓	×	✓	✓	✓	Pseudo-anonymous
Stellar	Permissionless	✓	✓	✓	✓	✓	Pseudo-anonymous
Cardano	Permissionless / Permissioned	✓	✓	✓	✓	✓	Pseudo-anonymous
IOTA	Permissionless	✓	✓	✓	✓	×	Pseudo-anonymous
NEO	Permissioned	✓	✓	✓	✓	×	Pseudo-anonymous
Monero	Permissionless	✓	×	✓	✓	✓	Anonymous
Dash	Permissionless	✓	×	✓	✓	✓	Anonymous

References

Adams, R., Kewell, B. and Parry, G., 2018. Blockchain for good? Digital ledger technology and sustainable development goals. In *Handbook of sustainability and social science research* (pp. 127–140). Springer, Cham

Bantekas, I., and S. Nash. 2009. *International Criminal Law*. Routledge.

Bianchi, C., Bovaird, T. and Loeffler, E., 2017. Applying a dynamic performance management framework to wicked issues: how coproduction helps to transform young people's services in Surrey County Council, UK. *International Journal of Public Administration*, 40(10), pp. 833–846.

Bollen, R. 2013. "The legal status of online currencies: Are bitcoins the future." *Journal of Banking and Finance Law and Practice*.

Bovaird, C. 2017. "Why the crypto market has appreciated more than 1,200% this year." *Forbes Magazine*.

Bratspies, R.M., 2018. Cryptocurrency and the Myth of the Trustless Transaction. *Mich. Tech. L. Rev.*, 25, 1.

Brito, J., H. B. Shadab, and A. C. O'Sullivan. 2014. "Bitcoin financial regulation: Securities, derivatives, prediction markets, and gambling." *Columbia Science and Technology Law Review*.

Bryans, D. 2014. "Bitcoin and money laundering: Mining for an effective solution." *Ind. Law J 89*: 441.

Buchko, S. 2017. "How long do bitcoin transactions take?" *Coin Central 1*.

Buttigieg, C. P. and G. Sapiano. 2020. "A critical examination of the VFA framework—The VFA agent and beyond." *Law and Financial Markets Review* 14(1): 48–58.

Chohan, U. W. 2018. "International law enforcement responses to cryptocurrency accountability: Interpol working group." Available at SSRN 315653.

Conlon, S. D., A. Vayser, and R. Schwaba. 2019. "Valuation of cryptocurrencies and ICO tokens for tax purposes." *Est. Plan. & Cmty. Prop. LJ* 12: 25.

De France, B. 2013. "Les dangers liés au développement des monnaies virtuelles: l'exemple du bitcoin." *Focus*, 10–15.

Directive, Council. 2016. "1164 of 12 July 2016 laying down rules against tax avoidance practices that directly affect the functioning of the internal market." *OJ l 193*(19):7.

Directive, E. C. 1991. "Council directive 91/356/EEC 1. Laying down the principles and guidelines of good manufacturing practice for medicinal products for human use." *Official Journal of the European Communities l 193*: 30–33.

Data, Statistical. 2015. "Commission staff working document accompanying the document communication from the commission to the European parliament, the council, the European economic and social committee and the committee of regions the marco polo programme-results and outlook."

Houben, R., and A. Snyers. 2016. *Cryptocurrencies and Blockchain*. Policy Department for Economic, Scientific and Quality of Life Policies.

Houben, R., and A. Snyers. 2018. *Cryptocurrencies and Blockchain: Legal Context and Implications for Financial Crime, Money Laundering and Tax Evasion*. European Parliament, Brussels.

Houben, R. and A. Snyers. 2019. "Address2vec: Generating vector embeddings for blockchain analytics."

Mach, J. 2018. "Automatic exchange of information on the issued tax interpretations in the context of a taxpayer's rights." *Studia Iuridica Lublinensia* 27(2): 117–125.

Nesi, G., ed. 2016. *International Cooperation in Counter-Terrorism: The United Nations and Regional Organizations in the Fight against Terrorism*. Routledge, London.

Otsuka, T. and M. Takehara. 2007. "Proposal for a directive of the European parliament and of the council amending directive 2002/96/EC on waste electrical and electronic equipment." *Environmental Research Quarterly* 14: 33.

Walfish, M. and Blumberg, A., 2018. *Realizing the Promise of Proof-based Verifiable Computation*. New York Univ., New York.

Yascega, M., and S. van Thiel. 2011. "Assessment of taxes in cross-border situations: The new EU directive on administrative cooperation in the field of taxation." *EC Tax Rev.* 20: 148.

Young, M. A. 2016. "Financial transparency in Britain's secrecy jurisdictions has just got a whole lot murkier following the UK's decision to leave the EU." *Journal of International Banking Law and Regulation* 31(11): 583–586.

11

Cyber Security in Cloud Platforms

Shiv Dutta Mishra[1], Bhupesh Kumar Dewangan[2], and Tanupriya Choudhury[2]

[1] *Bhilai Institute of Technology, Durg, India*

[2] *University of Petroleum and Energy Studies, Dehradun, India*

11.1 Introduction to Cloud Infrastructure

Cloud computing is nothing but sharing computable resources over the internet as desired by users and service providers (Pal 2020). Cloud infrastructure is related to its architecture and the integration of many loosely coupled cloud components. The cloud computing architecture is classified in two parts: one is the front end and another is the back end. Both of the ends are joined to each other through the internet connection.

Figure 11.1 shows a diagram of the cloud computing architecture. The front end is cloud clients using computing devices. These are servers, normal PCs and nowadays these computing devices include laptops, mobile phones and sensing devices. The cloud client consists of the Application Program Interface (API) and applications required to access the cloud computing platform (Dewangan et al. 2016). This internet API makes a lot of decisions that the sending program must follow with the goal that the internet can convey the information to the goal program. The back end is the cloud, which represents all the resources required to provide cloud computing services and it consists of a database, operating system, application, services models (Dewangan et al. 2019a), deployment models, network servers, storage (Dewangan et al. 2019), and so on. Through the programming interface, the cloud determines the code running towards one side of the framework and requests that the internet foundation conveys information to a particular goal program running on another end framework (Dewangan et al. 2018). The back end is represented in 3D architecture because all these services are to be managed and secure. The back end is also responsible for providing security of data along with the management of traffic flow.

11.2 Cloud Deployment and Services Models

Cloud computing is used by almost all organizations because of the use and pay feature. Different types of clouds are used to solve different issues (Dewangan et al. 2020). Because no one cloud can fulfill the requirements of all different organizations, there are three cloud deployment models.

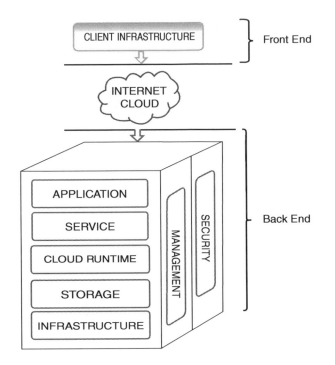

FIGURE 11.1
Cloud computing architecture.

11.2.1 Public Cloud

The services are provided for common users, where the resources are provided by third-party service providers.

11.2.2 Private Cloud

In the private cloud, a personal cloud may either be set up physically at any organization's onsite data center or it may be hosted by the third-party service supplier. The service and infrastructure are completely under the control of the non-public network. It may be used by an organization because of the sensitivity of their data and other privacy concerns.

11.2.3 Hybrid Cloud

The resources are provided by a combination of the two models previously mentioned by permitting the data and programs to be shared between them.

These clouds offer different types of services:

11.2.4 Infrastructure as a Service (IaaS)

IaaS is mainly focused on providing hardware and network resources over the internet. In this model, a third party owns all the resources and other peripherals which are requested by the user. It also provides many applications and frameworks to supports the user's requirements. The user can use infrastructure like servers to service networks, storage to store information and operating systems to supervise resources. For example, IBM Smart Cloud Enterprise, Windows Azure and Amazon Web Services (AWS) are major service providers.

11.2.5 Platform as a Service (PaaS)

PaaS is a distributed computing framework which carries applications over the Web. In a PaaS model, a cloud supplier sends equipment and programming tolls, usually those which are needed for application improvement, to its clients as assistance. A PaaS supplier has the equipment and the programming without the foundation of anyone else. Accordingly, PaaS liberates clients from introducing in-house equipment and programming in order to make or run another application. PaaS do not supplant a business' whole framework, however, a business depends on PaaS suppliers for key administration, for example, Java advancement or application facilitation. Be that as it may, a PaaS supplier supports all the basic registering and programming; clients just have to sign in and then initiate the utilization of the stage for the most part through the interface of a Web program. PaaS suppliers at that point charge on the basis of every entry per client or on a month by month basis.

11.2.6 Software as a Service (SaaS)

SaaS is mainly focused on applications-based service, in which a client does not need to install any software or applications to run any complex computing problem. The computing problem executes in servers through the Web browser and provides the desired report to the user. SaaS has become an indisputably pervasive conveyance model as fundamental advancements and new enhancements that aid in Web administration and administration arranged engineering (SOA) have been developed and become renowned, for example, Ajax. SaaS is strictly identified with the ASP (application specialist organization) and on-request processing of the programming conveyance models. The International Data Corporation (IDC) identifies two conveyance models for SaaS, specifically the facilitated application model and the product improvement model.

11.3 Benefits of Cloud Computing

- **Accessibility:** Cloud resources and services can be accessed anytime from anywhere using an internet connection.
- **Low cost:** The organization has to pay only for the computing resource and services used.
- **Cost reduction:** The organization removes the cost of purchasing infrastructure and computing requirements.
- **Scalability:** Dynamic resources are supplied by the provider according to the resources demanded by the client.
- **Reduced task:** The organization's tasks are reduced as infrastructure and its management are not required.
- **Backup and recovery:** In cloud computing, backup and recovery of the organization's data are easy.
- **Flexibility:** The organization can customize resources and services to fulfill its requirements.

162	Information Security and Optimization

- **Security:** Security of the organization's data depends on the service provider and deployment model.
- **Less maintenance:** It does not require much maintenance as no infrastructure is required.

11.4 Literature Review

Chadwick (2020) proposed a structure and organization model for supporting the private cloud and security ensuring sharing of data about digital threats. Stergiou (2020) reviewed IoT and cloud computing innovations with a focus on security issues that the two advances confronted. Especially, these two previously mentioned innovations have been considered with the intention of analyzing the well-known qualities and looking at and finding the advantages of combining them to provide assurances about their utilization. In all, the engagement of the cloud with IoT improves the activity of Big Data framework. Gai (2016) addresses cyber incident (CI) execution concentrating on cloud-based assistance contributions and proposes a protected digital episode examination system utilizing Big Data. Their methodology is intended for coordinating diverse digital threat situations, which utilizes vault information. Their reconstruction has provided hypothetical confirmation of adoptability and attainability. Elnagdy (2016) centers on this issue and audits an expansive range of materials to increase profound comprehension of the scientific classification of digital security threats for protection. Takahashi et al. (2010) presented an ontological system to resolve the cyber security threats in the cloud and Jouini et al. (2012) observed the quantitative measurement of information security. In 2020, Jouini et al. (2020) again presented quantitative security analysis system for the cloud. Stergiou (2020) presented a Machine Learning based secured system for Big Data under the cloud and IoT operations. Dewangan et al. (2020) presented the comparative analysis of different cloud scheduling algorithms with security and other measures.

The comparative study of cyber security in cloud techniques is shown in Table 11.1.

TABLE 11.1

Comparative Study of Cyber Security in Cloud Techniques

Techniques	Over Cloud	Over IoT	Over Big Data
Chadwick (2020)	√		
Stergiou (2020)	√	√	
Gai (2016)	√		√
Elnagdy (2016)	√		
Takahashi et al. (2010)	√		
Jouini et al. (2012)	√		
Jouini et al. (2020)	√	√	√
Stergiou et al. (2020)	√		
Dewangan et al. (2020)	√	√	√

11.5 Issues and Challenges

The following issues are observed in cyber security in the cloud (Cawthra et al. 2019):

11.5.1 Exfiltration of Encrypted Data

An organization unconsciously has an undermined machine that is being utilized by a malevolent on-screen character to exfiltrate information. The malignant character is encoding the information to prevent location. The information security arrangement will provide observation functionality to help identify the breach. The arrangement will likewise tell the security group of the movement and react according to the method that will stop the exfiltration of information.

11.5.2 Lance Phishing Campaign

Because of a lance phishing effort, a pernicious on-screen character can see and control a database. Restricted information stored in the database is uncovered. The information security arrangement will check with the security group to ascertain that information has been obtained or potentially exfiltrated (Blum et al. 2010). The arrangement will likewise react with activities that promptly end access for the malevolent on-screen character.

11.5.3 Ransomware

A user takes ransomware casually and is this indicating the substance to restrictive documents from the representative's organization's record server and interest for cash to quit getting to and sharing documents (O'Gorman et al. 2012). The information classification arrangement will observe and log actions to decide the degree and seriousness of an information breach. The outcomes from the checking arrangement will inform the appropriate reaction to cease the information leak.

11.5.4 Accidental Email

Sometimes a user accidentally copies an email to someone who ought not to have access to the email connection, as it contains restricted data. There is a chance of the user misusing the data they received accidentally is a major security threat.

11.5.5 Lost Laptop

A client loses their laptop which contains their organization's restricted data. The information may become public and confidentiality may be breached.

11.5.6 Privilege Misuse

A worker, utilizing director authorizations, accesses information for individual gain. The representative prints a few sensitive records and afterwards exfiltrates the rest of the information. The security arrangement will likewise react with appropriate activities to quickly prevent the record from being accessed. The time and procedure required to reestablish the record will be dictated by the arrangement.

11.5.7 Eavesdropping

An external on-screen character bargains with an organization's system and commandeers correspondence by means of a man-in-the-middle assault, bringing about a data breach. The information classification arrangement will identify the unapproved access and react appropriately to prevent further access.

11.6 Cyber Security Mechanism

In cloud platform security and privacy there have always been serious concerns because data are stored on a remote server and can be accessed via wired or wireless networks over the internet by various devices like PCs, laptops and smart phones (Barrett et al. 2018). The security frameworks are:

Identify—Need to find the systems assets to be checked. There are five important categories:

- **Asset management**: The enterprise must identify the devices, users, data sets and processes and these must be managed according to their importance so they are protected from cyber attack.
- **Business environment**: The enterprise must identify the enterprise mission, goal and stakeholder. On the basis of these roles, responsibility and security decisions are made.
- **Governance**: The enterprise must identify policies and procedures for managing and monitoring operations and legal requirements.
- **Risk assessment**: The enterprise must identify cyber security risks that impact the enterprise, its users and devices used daily for its operation.
- **Risk management strategy**: The enterprise must identify the functions related to risk toleration to make security decisions.

Protect—The enterprise must reduce the impact of cyber security risks by implementing practices to protect data. The protect function limits and controls secure access to systems and assets and prevents unauthorized access. The protect function has the following important categories:

- **Identity management and access control**: The enterprise must create secure access so that unauthorized users cannot access the enterprise data and assets and credentials related to unauthorized users must be managed.
- **Awareness and training**: The enterprise must create awareness and provide training to their employees so that they protect the enterprise data and assets.
- **Data security**: The enterprise must create a policy to protect confidential data, preserve integrity of data and control access to data by authorized users.
- **Information protection processes and procedures**: The enterprise must create security policies, processes and procedures to protect enterprise data and assets.

- **Maintenance**: The enterprise must ensure that maintenance is performed properly and regularly.
- **Protective technology**: The enterprise must create documentation and review audits, log records and protection of networks and Universal Series Bus (USB) drives.

Detect—It has following important categories:

- **Anomalies and events**: The enterprise must detect events and activities that are anomalous.
- **Security observation**: The enterprise must observe users' identities and security measures.
- **Detection method**: The enterprise must maintain and test all the processes and procedures used to detect events and activities that are anomalous.

Respond—It has following important categories:

- **Response planning**: The enterprise must maintain and execute processes and procedures to ensure it responds during or after a detected cyber security event.
- **Communications**: The enterprise must communicate with internal and external stakeholders to coordinate response activity.
- **Analysis**: The enterprise must investigate notifications from detection systems and analyze the impact of cyber security events to ensure it responds and help recovery activity.
- **Mitigation**: The enterprise must perform mitigation activities to prevent the effects of cyber security events.
- **Improvements**: The enterprise must improve response activity.

Recover—It has following important categories:

- **Recovery planning**: The enterprise must maintain and execute recovery processes and procedures to ensure recovery of systems and assets during or after cyber security events.
- **Improvements**: The enterprise must improve recovery activities after learning from cyber security events.
- **Communications**: The enterprise must communicate with internal and external stakeholders to coordinate recovery activities.

11.7 Solution: Proposed Framework for Security in Cloud Platform

A proposed framework for security in the cloud platform is shown in Figure 11.2. The framework includes the five criteria mentioned previously: Identify, protect, detect, respond, and recover.

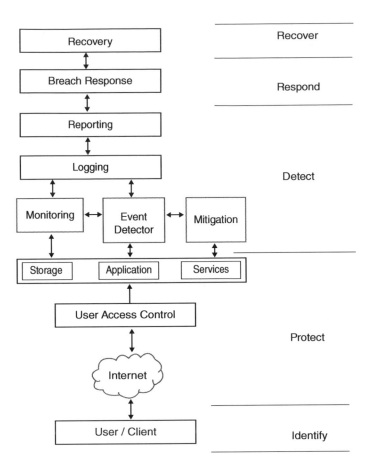

FIGURE 11.2
Proposed framework for security in the cloud platform.

11.7.1 Identify

Organizations should identify the weaknesses in the identify function of the frameworks making them vulnerable to cyber security threats, for example, individuals, resources, information, and functionality. Likewise they need to recognize unapproved information streams, client conduct, and access to information and recognize resources that may become the focus of information integrity assaults.

11.7.2 Protect

Insider dangers that threaten information integrity, regardless of whether they are unintentional or deliberate, are hard to forestall. Pre-emptive measures can be taken to guarantee that the effect of a malevolent insider is recorded, and this guide will set out those measures through review logs and document integrity systems. Secure storage and protection act as an additional safeguard against insider dangers. Access controls, which are essential for forestalling insider dangers, are beyond the remit of this task, which will concentrate on information, not clients.

11.7.2.1 User Access Control

Access rights management (ARM) identifies the following threats:

- Insiders gaining entrance through access creep and undocumented records
- Standard clients unexpectedly accessing unapproved information or frameworks
- Outsiders gaining entrance by utilizing malware strategies

These points additionally allow us to understand the vulnerabilities that outsiders can abuse because of the absence of automated ARM abilities. We also recognized the accompanying vulnerabilities:

- Undocumented accounts
- Accounts with unnecessarily enhanced benefits
- Dependence on individuals to uphold client access strategies

These threat variables can likewise be seen from a business activities risk viewpoint:

- Restricted access—guaranteeing that individuals only access the frameworks necessary for them to perform their duties decreases the danger of inappropriate or unapproved utilization of access that could then affect accessibility of other people.
- Cost of execution—carrying out ARM once and utilizing it over all frameworks may diminish both framework advancement costs and operational expenses.
- Consistency with existing industry measures—the Federal Financial Institutions Examination Council (FFIEC) requires consideration and control of legitimate access to corporate assets.
- Maintenance of esteem and prestige in public.

11.7.3 Detection Systems

It is responsible for the identification of unauthorized pieces of information and client's behavior. Although it is a very tough job to identify the insider threats, it is possible by incorporating the following points.

11.7.3.1 Monitoring

System activities are monitored continuously and data are analyzed to detect any suspicious activity by authorized users or unauthorized access from users outside the enterprise. The logged data are reported so that action may be taken as needed in response to alerts.

11.7.3.2 Event Detection

Ransomware for monetary gain involves a malevolent users setting up an apparently genuine space with dangerous malware masked as a real infection checking program. Once introduced, it encodes the organization's record framework and requests payment in order to unscramble the documents. Left unmitigated, the malware on one framework is intended to move horizontally inside the system to other customer and server frameworks inside an organization's system, scrambling those frameworks and requesting payment in return for their documents. Information destruction malware involves a malevolent user wishing to affect an organization's tasks and generally leaves a few contaminated USB drives in the structure's parking garage. At the point when an unknowing representative plugs in the drive, it promptly alters record contents and erases media documents on the client's machine. Virtual machine data loss occurs when a favored client running programmed support on the organization's virtual machines (VMs) inadvertently erases one of the VMs. The client does not immediately notice the accidental deletion. Server permissions change occurs when an attacker wishing to access an organization's tasks launches a lance phishing effort against particular people in the target organization using a contaminated email link. At the point when one of the clients opens the link, the malware promptly starts making secondary inroads for the attacker to use at a later point. The changes occur in the file when any insider is authorized by the manager to access or update the file. Utilizing these accreditations, the insider looks for their name in the organization's records and backup records, endeavoring to increase the number of benefits they receive as part of their yearly compensation. Traded off server updates occur when, during routine machine updates, an update is downloaded and introduced that allows indirect access. A malevolent outsider at that point utilizes this indirect access to increase unauthorized access to the machine.

11.7.3.3 Mitigation

This involves identifying the potential occasions and groups when there is a threat. Threats or risks may be posed by the structure or existing lack of protection in the organization. The probability of all incoming and repeating threats and their effects should be identified. When the appraisal is completed, protection systems should be initiated, and if a risk requires changes, follow the above steps to reflect updates in mitigation techniques.

11.7.3.4 Logging

As a proactive step towards internal security, the organization needs to monitor each and every framework action that is recorded in an event log. A data framework should director deal with the huge volume of the event logs and in turn arrange security logs.

11.7.3.5 Reporting

Identifying and reporting unauthorized actions by clients and data should incorporate checking and revealing programming.

11.7.4 Breach Response

An organization's information breach reaction group will preferably contain nontechnical individuals who center around lawful, regulatory, and advertising, among other important issues. While essential for legitimate breach response, these functions will not be canvassed in the venture. They will accept that the organization can comprehend and execute its nontechnical duties in the consequence of an information breach.

11.7.5 Recovery

Organizations must have the option to rapidly recover from an information integrity assault and trust that any recouped information is exact, complete, and free of malware. Information integrity assaults brought about by unauthorized inclusion, erasure, or alteration of information have undermined corporate data including messages, worker records, money-related records, and client information. A few organizations that have encountered fundamental assaults that caused a brief discontinuance of activities recommend the recovery effort following information breaches includes giving point by point data with regards to the degree and seriousness of the rupture like:

- Virtual machine reinforcements are utilized to remediate the harm.
- System state reinforcements are utilized to reestablish the record structure.
- Database reinforcements are utilized to reestablish the database structure.
- Backups are utilized to reestablish the records.
- Backups are utilized to remediate the harm.

11.8 Conclusion

This chapter is concerned all about the security issues and challenges of the cyber cloud. First of all, cloud security and cyber security are elaborated, followed by the service and deployment models offered by the cloud worldwide. The security issues are discussed in brief and the major challenges are also identified. The proposed framework is discussed step by step and covers all the issues presented. A new framework is introduced based on identification, detection, different security measures, and observations. This framework assists in securing all the resources which are used in the cloud.

References

Barrett, M. P. et al. 2018. "Framework for improving critical infrastructure cybersecurity version 1.1." NIST Cybersecurity Framework.

Blum, A. W. et al. 2010. "Lexical feature based phishing URL detection using online learning." In *3rd ACM Workshop on AIS*, Chicago, IL, 54–60.

Cawthra, J. et al. 2019. "Data confidentiality: Detect, respond to, and recover from data breaches." NIST.

Chadwick, D. W. et al. 2020. "A cloud-edge based data security architecture for sharing and analysing cyber threat information." *Future Generation Computer Systems*, 710–725.

Dewangan, B. K. et al. 2016. "Credential and security issues of cloud service models." In *2nd International Conference on NGCT*, Dehradun, India, 888–892.

Dewangan, B. K. et al. 2018. "Autonomic cloud resource management." In *Fifth International Conference on PDGC*, Himachal Pradesh, India, 138–143.

Dewangan, B. K. et al. 2019a. "Design of self-management aware autonomic resource scheduling scheme in cloud." *IJCISIM 11*: 170–177.

Dewangan, B. K. et al. 2019b. "Self-characteristics based energy-efficient resource scheduling for cloud." *PCS 152*: 204–211.

Dewangan, B. K. et al. 2020. "Extensive review of cloud resource-management-techniques in industry-4.0: Issue and challenges." *Software: Practice and Experience.* https://onlinelibrary.wiley.com/doi/abs/10.1002/spe.2810

Elnagdy, S. A. 2016. "Understanding taxonomy of cyber-risks for cybersecurity-insurance of financial industry in cloud-computing." In *IEEE 3rd International Conference on CS Cloud*, Beijing, China, 295–300.

Gai, K. Q. 2016. "A novel secure big-data cyber-incident analytics framework for cloud-based cybersecurity insurance." In *2nd International Conference on Big-Data-Security*, New York City, 171–176.

Jouini, M. et al. 2020. "Towards new quantitative cybersecurity-risk-analysis models for information systems: A cloud computing case-study." In Brij B. Gupta, Gregorio Martinez Perez, Dharma P. Agrawal, Deepak Gupta (eds.), *Handbook of CNCS*. Springer, Cham, 63–90.

Jouini, M. et al. 2012. "Towards quantitative measures of Information-Security: A Cloud Computing case-study." *IJCSDF 1*(3): 265–279.

O'Gorman, G. et al. 2012. *Ransomware: A Growing Menace.* Symantec-Corporation, Mountain View, CA.

Pal, M. 2020. "Homomorphic-encryption method for business data-security in cloud." *Our Heritage, 68*(8): 175–183.

Stergiou, C. L. 2020. "Secure machine-learning scenario from BigData in Cloud Computing via Internet-of-Things network." In Brij B. Gupta, Gregorio Martinez Perez, Dharma P. Agrawal, Deepak Gupta (eds.), *CNCS*. Springer, Cham, 525–554.

Takahashi, T. et al. 2010. "Ontological approach toward cybersecurity in cloud-computing." In *Proceedings of the 3rd International Conference on SIN*, Rostov-on-Don, Russia, 100–109.

12

Biometrics–Unique Identity Verification System

Gunjan Chhabra, Varun Sapra, and Ninni Singh

University of Petroleum & Energy Studies (UPES), Dehradun, India

12.1 Introduction to Biometrics

Today's world is working under the umbrella of digitization. Everyone is nowadays predominantly performing his/her major and minor activities on the digital platform. People are surrounded by computing devices such as smartphones, iPads, wearable devices, home automation and many others. With the advancement of technologies, every individual is now storing his/her data, whether personal or professional, in digital format, which can easily be accessed anytime and anywhere. With the increase in popularity of the digital platform, it has also opened up the gateway to modern ways to commit crimes, known as cyber-crimes. Thus, to overcome this issue one has to identify modern methods to provide security. Here, security does not mean to secure only digital data but also means to provide security to protect digital devices from damage, attack or unauthorized access.

Major crimes on the digital platform happen due to the loss of identity, that is by gaining unauthorized access. In previous decades, a lot of research has been done to develop strong authorization methods like strong password systems, secure ID card systems, two-way authentication systems, 3D secure systems and many more. Every system has its limitations and flaws like stealing secret passwords/IDs, brute-force attacks, remembering strong and long passwords and many others. Further research on security comes up with a more reliable and better solution: biometrics (Narayanan and Chhabra 2013).

Biometrics is a process of measuring biological characteristics of an individual for recognition, authentication and verification. These biological characteristics carry some unique features that may help anyone to recognize the right person and then provide access controls to them. Every human being has various biological characteristics that are unique, distinct and are measurable, and in addition that higher uniqueness provides high security (Narayanan and Chhabra 2013). This will help in developing highly reliable systems in comparison to the traditional methods used for authentication. At present, a large amount of data and information is available which should be kept secure; hence, biometrics is widely used for securing them as it provides a high degree of accuracy in terms of recognizing an individual. In terms of physical and behavioral characteristics, humans are all different from one another. With the help of these characteristics, one can analyze a person's attributes, which will help an individual to stand out from the rest (Jain et al. 2004).

In simple language, one can say that biometrics is an autonomous recognition method for an individual based on his/her physical or behavioral eccentricities. On the other hand, biometric systems is a modern technology, which helps in recognizing a person's physiological and/or behavioral characteristics, verifies them, identifies an individual and distinguishes them from others. In a human body, there are several biological characteristics available that can be measured easily, but not every characteristic can be used as a biometric feature. Any biological trait falling under the category of biometrics must satisfy the following properties (Jain et al. 2004):

- **Robustness**: This property indicates that the characteristic should not change over time, that is, it should be permanent. This is because if it changes with time, it will be difficult for a system to recognize the unique property of an individual. Along with that, for the matching criteria, it should be adequately invariant. The reason behind this is that if there is high intra-class variability, there will be difficulty in distinguishing between individuals.
- **Availability**: Secondly, the characteristic should be universal, in other words every individual should possess that characteristic. Until and unless availability or universality of the property are not followed, one cannot include that characteristic as a biometric.
- **Collectability**: Another important property is that the characteristic should be easy to acquire and able to be measured quantitatively.
- **Distinctiveness**: This property concerns the uniqueness of the characteristics. In the broad population, there must be large variation in the characteristics among the people. In simple words, one can say that two or more people must carry such characteristics that make them sufficiently different from each other.

While working with these properties, one has to consider some other issues also related to biometrics. These issues are related to the computational point of view: circumvention deals with how the system can easily be bypassed (spoofed) by falsified approaches; performance deals with accuracy and speed of the system for recognition; and acceptability deals with the number of people who accept the use of a particular biometric identifier in their day-to-day life. Hence, for biometrics systems, the above-mentioned properties must be satisfied by the biometric characteristic chosen (Jain et al. 2004).

12.2 Authentication vs Verification

In terms of security, the very first step is concerned with *verification*, followed by *authentication* of the user. With the advancement of technology and the initiation of biometrics, security has been enhanced a lot. However, people generally use the terms authentication and verification interchangeably; actually, both words have different meanings. The difference between the two is revealed in Table 12.1 below.

12.3 Types of Biometrics: Physical and Behavioral Biometrics

Based on the various characteristics of human beings, biometrics are divided into two categories, namely *physical biometrics*, which are those that need physical contact

TABLE 12.1

Difference Between Verification and Authentication.

Verification	Authentication
Verification means ensuring that the data is associated with a particular individual.	Authentication refers to a process of determining that an individual is only who they claim to be.
For verification, the given data, which is entered by an individual, is matched with the previously stored information available in the database.	For authentication, the individual has to answer specific questions to find out whether that person or individual is eligible to have certain rights to access this resource or not.
Verification alone is required by some businesses and is merely an extra layer of security for others.	Authentication takes confirmation to the next level and is especially important when individuals are dealing with online transactions.
Verification ensures the match/association of certain elements/identifiers about an individual in question. From an identity perspective, that refers to the real-world identifiers of name, date of birth and address matching the individual undergoing a verification procedure.	Authentication is the process or action of proving something to be true or genuine/valid. From an identity perspective, it would mean determining that the person is who they say they are.

between sensors and the human body to capture the features for identification and verification. They focus on the physical characteristics of an individual. Secondly, *behavioral biometrics* are those in which no physical contact is required to capture the features for identification and verification. They focus on the behavioral characteristics of an individual.

Biometrics uses a sensor, which behaves as a transducer that is used to convert the user's biometric traits, such as iris, face, fingerprint and so on, into an electrical signal. These sensors come in two different types: physiological and behavioral. Figure 12.1 below illustrates the basic working of the biometrics system. These systems are used in various applications in this digital world.

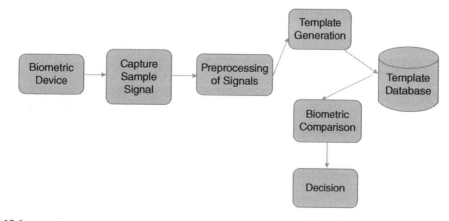

FIGURE 12.1

Block diagram of a biometrics system. (Based on Hernández Álvarez et al. 2009)

12.3.1 Physical Biometrics

Physiological biometrics works with humans to identify physical characteristics. It measures the unique patterns of the body for identification. Different types of physiological biometrics commonly used nowadays are:

- **Fingerprint recognition**: Fingerprint biometrics have been considered the most popular and effective authentication technique for the identification of human identity as they work based on a natural truth that no two individuals have common fingerprints (Eng and Wahsheh 2013, Alsaadi 2015). It is also one of the oldest ways of confirming one's identity. Previously, ink and paper were used to take a thumb impression and to verify the human being; however, fingerprint biometrics is an inkless method, which senses the ridges and valleys on a surface tip of the finger.

- **Face recognition**: This is a passive technique that depends on a unique shape like the position of eyes, chin and lips, and the distance between features, cuts and so on (Koong et al. 2014). It is widely accepted and used to identify a person from a digital image or a video source. Face recognition can be done in two ways: static recognition based on a static camera photograph, and real-time recognition based on video camera (Satone and Kharate 2012). The accuracy of the face detection system depends on various factors such as makeup, aging effects, motion estimation and low-quality videos.

- **Iris recognition**: This is a method for confirming a person's identity from a random pattern of the iris. The iris is a muscle in the human eye that controls the amount of light entering the eye. Infrared light is used to take a high-precision photograph of the iris and this is then compared with the existing templates (Kak et al. 2010). It is highly accurate and really hard to spoof but it is very expensive to set up.

- **Hand geometry**: It is one of the oldest techniques which was first mentioned in the 1970s. The concept uses the measurement of different traits of human hands like palm thickness, length of the hand, measurement of fingers and so on. The advantage of the system is that it is widely accepted and easy to implement but it has a disadvantage as well in that it is not highly unique.

12.3.2 Behavioral Biometrics

Behavioral biometrics is a branch of science that utilizes human behavior (like habits and movements) to recognize a human being. Some of the popular behavioral biometric techniques are:

- **Voice recognition**: This is also known as speaker identification where the voice template is matched with different stored voice templates to identify a human being.

    It first gained attention in 1952 with the development of a system capable of identifying spoken figures. In the last decade, the voice recognition hardware devices gained a new boost with the introduction of devices like Alexa and Google home. According to one of the surveys conducted by Strategy Analytics, the sales of voice-enabled devices will exceed 15 million by 2020.

- **Keystroke dynamics**: Keystroke dynamics depend on the style in which one writes with a pen or types with a keyboard. The rhythm in which the individual performs the said actions is measured to identify the human being. It is based on the earlier concept of the telegraph.

12.4 Types of Biometric Systems

Broadly, biometric systems can be categorized into two divisions:

- Unimodal biometric systems
- Multimodal biometric systems

Biometric systems that utilize a single biometric trait or a single source of information for the confirmation of human identity are called unimodal biometric systems. Although unimodal biometrics are good, they are not sufficient for handling complex security systems because of non-universal biometric traits and their susceptibility to noise in the sensed data, such as a scar on a finger. Hence, multimodal biometric systems are required to handle such data complications. Multimodal biometric systems provide a hybrid way of using two or more biometric traits for the identification of an individual (Oloyede and Hancke 2016, Ammour et al. 2020). This simply increases the accuracy of identifying a person by reducing the problem of non-universality. From a business point of view, these multimodal biometric systems have certain advantages, such as security, because they minimize the risk of spoofing. Universality as a system is capable of reading multiple types of traits in order to identify a person.

12.5 Biometrics System Performance: False Acceptance and False Rejection

Numerous performance evaluation methodologies are available for biometric authentication systems. The most commonly accepted performance evaluation methods are listed in Table 12.2.

In non-biometric systems, no complex pattern recognition techniques are required. In contrast, in biometric systems, data representation depends on various factors, such as the method of acquisition, the environment of acquisition, user–machine interaction and various other phenomena.

The overall performance of the system depends on the **presentation** of data acquired (user–machine interaction), on the **imperfection in data acquisition** (conditions and environmental effects during data acquisition), and on **accuracy**. In terms of the accuracy of the machine, for biometric systems, two types of errors have been classified: **false acceptance** and **false rejection**.

The performance of a biometric system depends on two measures, namely the False Acceptance Rate (FAR or Type I Error) and the False Rejection Rate (FRR or Type II Error), shown in Figure 12.2. The FAR is the measure, as a percentage, of unauthorized entries that are wrongly accepted. The FRR refers to the percentage of instances where correct entries are wrongly identified or marked. The two error rates have a proportional effect on one another in a way that if the FAR goes down, the FRR will go up (Recogtech 2020).

The Equal Error Rate (EER) is the threshold point and also the midpoint between the FRR and the FAR when measuring the system's accuracy in rejecting an invalid entry.

TABLE 12.2

Brief Description of Performance Evaluation Methods.

S. No	Method	Definition
1	Genuine Accept Rate (GAR)	It is the ratio of the number of input samples appropriately classified as authentic to the total number of positive input samples. A higher value of GAR indicates better performance.
2	Genuine Reject Rate (GRR)	It is the ratio of the number of input samples correctly classified as an impostor to the total number of impostor input samples. A higher value of GRR indicates better performance.
3	False Accept Rate (FAR)	It is the proportion of impostor input samples falsely classified as positive samples. A lower value of FAR indicates better performance of a system.
4	False Reject Rate (FRR)	It is the proportion of many actual input samples falsely classified as impostor samples. A lower value of FRR indicates better performance of a biometric authentication system.
5	Equal Error Rate (ERR)	When FRR becomes similar to FAR, the ratio is called the same error rate. A lower value of ERR indicates better performance.
6	Failure To Capture (FTC) or Failure To Acquire (FTA)	It is the ratio of the number of times. A biometric system fails to capture the biometric sample presented to it. A lower value of FTA indicates better acquisition performance.
7	Failure To Enroll (FTE)	It is the ratio of the number of users that cannot be successfully enrolled in a biometric system and a total number of users presented to the biometric system. A lower value of FTE indicates better population coverage.

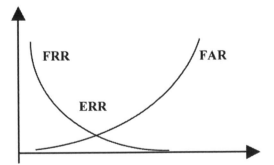

FIGURE 12.2
False Rejection Rate vs False Acceptance Rate (Recogtech 2020).

12.6 Issues and Concerns

Biometrics is undoubtedly a technology for the future as it provides a higher level of spoofing proof technology and user accountability.

In one of its surveys, the American analysis company Tractica estimates that the turnover of biometric companies will exceed $69.8 billion by 2025 (IQUII 2020).

Even with such popularity and success of biometrics systems, it has some limitations.

1. **Robustness**: The biometric systems are generally tested in a controlled environment in ideal setups but in a real-world scenario, this is not possible.

2. **Social acceptance**: Privacy concerns are related to data collection. Someone can record the user's voice to gain unauthorized access to the system without his/her knowledge.

3. **Consistency**: The biometrics traits are inconsistent, for example, in facial recognition the aging effect produces a change in the face's image, and some types of scars affect fingerprints.

4. **Liveness detection**: It is important to discover whether an original, genuine living user has submitted the given biometrics or if it is a fake entry. For example, in the case of 2D image biometrics, it is easy to capture a 2D photograph of the face and the machine can be easily fooled.

5. **Template protection**: The entire security of the biometrics system depends on the security of stored biometric information. Such requirements need extra security features to be implemented.

12.7 Performance Enhancement of Biometrics Systems

With the advancement in techniques and technologies, the performance of biometric systems can be improved. Artificial intelligence methods have provided a gateway for solving various issues and concerns while dealing with biometrics. Machine learning has gained a lot of attention in the last decade because of its capability to mine and find complex relationships between huge datasets. Machine learning can learn from human behavior and can be implemented successfully on large datasets, which makes it suitable for biometric systems. In the past, machine learning has been applied successfully in many domains such as medicine, image processing, agriculture and so on. Now researchers are extensively using machine learning to improve the performance of biometric devices. In their research, Taigman et al. proposed a DeepFace one-shot face recognition method. They illustrated the method with the Siamese network and support vector machine (SVM). The authors used three different image datasets. The features were extracted using the Siamese network and the differences between features were computed and then fed to the SVM classifier for the classification process. They were able to achieve 97.35% accuracy (Taigman et al. 2014). Sarfaraz et al. proposed a model for cross-modal face matching between the thermal and visible spectrum. They used a deep neural network approach for capturing the non-linear relationship between the two modalities. Their model achieved an accuracy improvement of 10% and was able to reach 86% accuracy (Sarfraz and Stiefelhagen 2017, Phillips and Przybocki 2020).

With time and aging, human behavior changes and a person uses more and more devices. These devices or machines with embedded machine learning will then be able to diagnose human behavior and can adapt to the changes and hence eliminate confusion or inconsistency in the behavioral patterns over time.

12.8 Applications of Biometrics

Today everything is running on digital platform and security is the major concern and challenge for everyone. Hence, biometrics is one of the best methods that will help in making transactions and operations safer and convenient. Here are a few areas of deployment of biometric systems to provide identity solutions.

- **Security using biometrics**:
  Nowadays biometric systems are used for security purposes in homes and offices as security locks. Biometric security systems are more secure than the conventional key and lock systems used previously. Various types of smart locking systems have been developed by using biometrics and are now widely in use.

- **Attendance system**:
  Employee attendance systems are now based on biometrics. This helps an organization to maintain logs, track scheduling and helps in avoiding false attendance markings, which is a very common practice with manual attendance systems.

- **Access control**:
  Biometric systems provide a stronger and safer access control solution than traditional locks, smart cards or Personal Identification Number (PIN)-based systems. Issues related to traditional locking systems include keys being stolen or lost, forgetting PINs and so on, whereas by using biometric systems such issues are resolved.

- **Gadget access control**:
  The whole world is using various types of smart gadgets to carry critical information, hence proper security and safeguards against unauthorized access are required for those portable devices. Biometric systems have given a convenient solution to control access to those gadgets and the information available in them.

- **Other applications**:
  Biometrics are not only limited to the above-mentioned applications but are also widespread in every domain where authentic access is required. More areas of application include healthcare informatics, banking transactions, home automation, airport security, border security systems, personal identification cards (e.g., Aadhar and passports) and many others.
  Biometric systems are widely in use for various applications wherever security is concerned. To date, huge market demand and acceptance have been seen in society but a lot more research is required to overcome the issues related to biometric systems. More and more information is being generated by every individual and so everyone is concerned about its security. Due to the high demand for secure locks and access control devices in the market, biometric systems have acquired millions of dollars of financial investment and are going to acquire more in the near future.

12.9 Conclusion

Conventional systems including password-based systems, ID card-based systems, conventional locks and others used for identification and recognition of individuals have been the cause of various frauds in past decades. Hence, new technologies have come up with a solution in the form of the use of biometrics. Biometric systems are now widely accepted in every mode (physical as well as digital) of access control. Due to their ease of use and high-security mechanisms, biometric systems are being applied to various applications. The performance of biometric systems is still an issue, therefore hybrid AI-based mechanisms have been used to enhance and solve the related concerns. In the future, a huge scope of research under this umbrella can be visualized, which may generate high revenue for the industries. Moreover, to enhance the functionality of biometric systems, it is advisable to adopt multimodal systems that will reduce biometric attacks such as fake biometrics, replay attacks, template tempering and so on.

References

Alsaadi, I. M. 2015. "Physiological biometric authentication systems, advantages, disadvantages and future development: A review." *International Journal of Scientific & Technology Research*, 4(12), 285–289.

Ammour, B., Boubchir, L., Bouden, T., and Ramdani, M. 2020. "Face–iris multimodal biometric identification system." *Electronics*, 9(1), 85.

Eng, A. and Wahsheh, L. A. 2013. "Look into my eyes: A survey of biometric security." In *2013 10th International Conference on Information Technology: New Generations*, pp. 422–427. IEEE, Piscataway, NJ.

Hernández Álvarez, F., Encinas, L. H., and Ávila, C. S. 2009. "Biometric fuzzy extractor scheme for iris templates." https://digital.csic.es/bitstream/10261/15966/1/SAM3262.pdf.

IQUII, "Biometric recognition: Definition, challenges and opportunities of biometric recognition systems." https://medium.com/iquii/biometric-recognition-definition-challenge-and-opportunities-of-biometric-recognition-systems-d063c7b58209 (accessed January 20, 2020).

Jain, A. K., Ross, A., and Prabhakar, S. 2004. "An introduction to biometric recognition." *IEEE Transactions on Circuits and Systems for Video Technology*, 14(1): 4–20.

Kak, N., Gupta, R., and Mahajan, S. 2010. "Iris recognition system." *International Journal of Advanced Computer Science and Applications*, 1, 34–40.

Koong, C. S., Yang, T. I., and Tseng, C. C. 2014. "A user authentication scheme using physiological and behavioral biometrics for multitouch devices." *The Scientific World Journal*, 2014, 781234.

Narayanan, A. and Chhabra, G. 2013. "Reducing cyber threats: Via a multimodal biometric system." *International Journal of Artificial Intelligence and Neural Networks –IJAINN*, 3, 10–14.

Oloyede, M. O. and Hancke, G. P. 2016. "Unimodal and multimodal biometric sensing systems: A review." *IEEE Access*, 4, 7532–7555.

Phillips, P. J. and Przybocki, M. 2020. "Four principles of explainable AI as applied to biometrics and facial forensic algorithms." arXiv preprint arXiv:2002.01014.

Recogtech. "FAR and FRR: Security level versus user convenience." https://www.recogtech.com/en/knowledge-base/security-level-versus-user-convenience, last accessed on January 17, 2020 (accessed January 17, 2020).

Sarfraz, M. S. and Stiefelhagen, R. 2017. "Deep perceptual mapping for cross-modal face recognition." *International Journal of Computer Vision*, 122(3), 426–438.

Satone, M. P. and Kharate, G. K. 2012. "Face recognition based on PCA on wavelet subband of average-half-face." *Journal of Information Processing Systems*, 8(3): 483–494.

Taigman, Y., Yang, M., Ranzato, M., and Wolf, L. 2014. "Deepface: Closing the gap to human-level performance in face verification." *IEEE Computer Vision and Pattern Recognition (CVPR)*, 5, 6.

13

Security Tools

Keshav Kaushik[1], Rohit Tanwar[1], and A. K. Awasthi[2]
[1] *University of Petroleum & Energy Studies (UPES), Dehradun, India*
[2] *Lovely Professional University, Phagwara, India*

13.1 Introduction: Background and Driving Forces

The world is changing at a very rapid rate in terms of computer technology. With the advancements in technology, people are being connected with each other in a much more efficient way than in the past. Today, the internet is crossing all the barriers and it has changed the lifestyle of people to a significant extent. Now, there is the easy availability of information of any sort through the internet via our smartphones and laptops. The "cyber-space" comprises a virtual environment created on a global level that facilitates online communication through the electronic medium. Cyberspace allows users to interact with each other and share digital media and ideas on various social platforms. The entire cyber-space is based on an information system, which is responsible for adding intelligence to various domains and services. The general public, defense personnel, governments, NGOs, the business sector, media and everything else that is connected to the internet come under cyberspace. Therefore, the information under cyberspace needs to be secured for the smooth functioning of the information system. Actually, cyberspace is expanding its boundaries with the advent of new technologies and the number of "things" being connected to the internet. Therefore, today cybersecurity is the need of the hour, whose importance is becoming more significant. Cybersecurity or information security involves ensuring the confidentiality, integrity and availability of information. It also means detection of cyberattacks, providing solutions for cyberattacks and placing the entire information system in a "safe" environment. Cybersecurity is crucial to the general public in also providing confidentiality, integrity and availability of users' information. Cyberattacks are increasing day by day as hackers (people with malicious intentions) find loopholes or vulnerabilities in the system and then exploit the system to extract critical information.

13.2 Cybersecurity Tools and Methods

Due to the vast boundaries of cyberspace, there are several possible methods of cyberattack. Therefore, cybersecurity experts should be able to secure and protect cyberspace from attackers and malicious persons. Cyberattackers perform cyberattacks to steal confidential information from users, governments and private organizations. Cyberattacks can cause huge financial loss and can affect the reputation of organizations. In this part, the two most significant cybersecurity and forensics tools—Wireshark and Autopsy—will be explained.

13.2.1 Wireshark—A Packet Sniffing and Packet Capturing Tool

Wireshark is a packet sniffer application, which captures packets and lets you analyze them. It works promiscuously on the network interface card and reads all the traffic passing through it. Figure 13.1 (Macfarlane, n.d.) shows the position of Wireshark sniffing the packets passing through the set network adapter.

There are various reasons why cybersecurity experts use it:

- Network administrators use it to troubleshoot networks.
- Network security engineers use it to examine the security problems.
- Quality assurance engineers use it to verify network applications.
- Developers use it for debugging purposes.
- People use it to learn network protocols.

It is a very important tool, which is helpful in various situations as follows:

- It can be used on Windows and UNIX.
- Various packet capturing programs may open the network packets captured by Windump/tcpdump.
- Text files with a hex dump of packet data can be imported.
- The packet is displayed with detailed information related to protocols.
- The packets are exported in captured file formats.
- Packets are filtered based on criteria and conditions.
- Saved packet data are captured.
- Searching of packets is based on criteria.

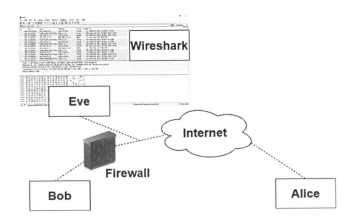

FIGURE 13.1
Locating Wireshark.

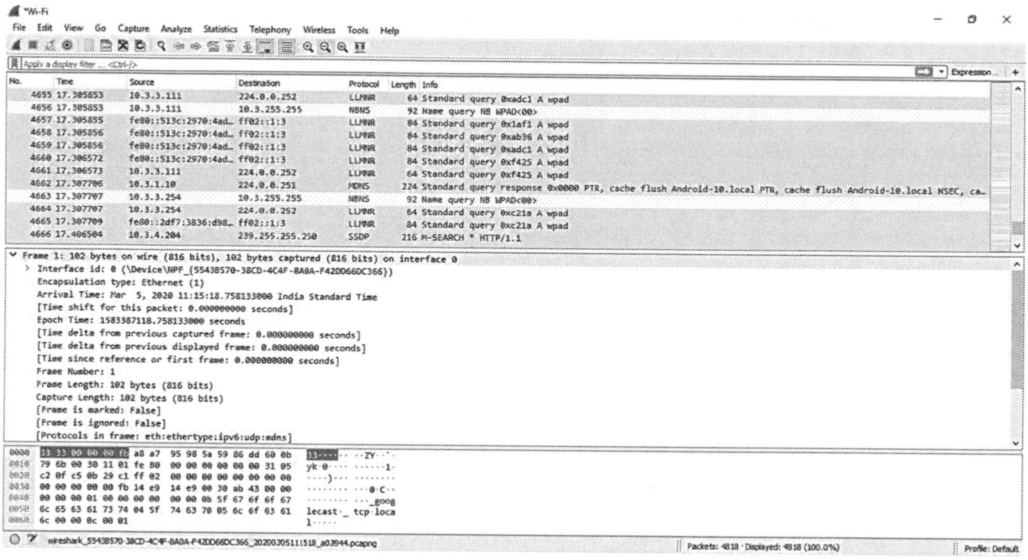

FIGURE 13.2
Wireshark capturing packets and analyzing their content.

- Packets are colored according to filters.
- Statistics are created.

Packets captured by Wireshark can be examined, as shown in Figure 13.2.

Wireshark enables you to capture live network traffic from many different network adapters and media including Wireless LAN, Ethernet, USB, Bluetooth and more. Such examples are available on https://wiki.wireshark.org/CaptureSetup/NetworkMedia. These are related to daily-life examples and may be easily understood.

You can also import files from many other programs. There are several myths also about Wireshark, which include:

- Wireshark is not an Intrusion Detection System (IDS). It is used for network traffic capturing and analysis. It will not warn you about any malicious activities on a network. However, it will help in finding out what is really going on.
- Wireshark is not used for "manipulation" purposes. It is used for "measuring" the network traffic.

The entire packet sniffing structure of Wireshark is shown in Figure 13.3. It consists of a packet capturing library and packet analyzer. Every data link layer is a frame, which is received or sent from a computer and is also received by a packet capturing library. Higher-layer protocols like TCP, UDP, FTP, HTTP and IP encapsulate messages that are exchanged before being transmitted over an Ethernet cable and physical medium. Figure 13.3 shows that all upper-layer protocols are encapsulated within the Ethernet frame by assuming Ethernet as the physical medium. All data link layer frames are captured to get the detailed information about all received and sent messages by all applications and protocols running on the computer.

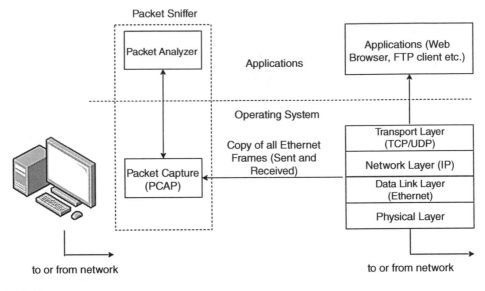

FIGURE 13.3
Structure of packet sniffer (Wireshark Tutorial, n.d.).

The packet analyzer is the second component of a packet sniffer, which shows all fields of the message. This can be done only when the packet analyzer understands the format and structure of all messages exchanged by communication protocols. In Figure 13.3, various fields of messages exchanged by the HTTP protocol are displayed. The packet analyzer understands the Ethernet frames format and identifies the internet protocol datagram. Finally, the packet analyzer understands the segment structure of TCP and extracts the HTTP message in the segment of TCP.

There are five major components in the Wireshark interface:

- There are some standard pulldown menus, which are located at the top of the window and are known as **command menus**. They contain file and capture menus, which are used to capture packet data and save that packet data in a file. The file menu also allows opening of the previously captured packet data and exiting the Wireshark application.

- The second component is a **packet details window**, which displays the summary of the captured packet. The summary comprises various entities, which include a timestamp of captured packets, packet number, types of protocols, source and destination address of packets, and other information related to protocols. This packet list can be sorted by various categories based on names available in a column.

- The details about the selected packet are displayed in the **packet header details window**. The selected packet includes details like the IP datagram and Ethernet frame information. These details can be expanded or minimized by right-clicking on the packet details window. The packets are carried over UDP or TCP protocols and the details can be minimized or expanded. Final details about the received or sent packet are also available in the packet details.

- The contents of the captured frame are displayed in hexadecimal and ASCII format under a **packet contents window**.

- The packet display filter field is positioned at the top of Wireshark. GUI, Protocol detail name and other information can be applied to filter the information in the packet details window. For example, the packet display filter field may be used on those packets that are HTTP messages, not on a Wireshark header.

A structured attack, comprising various stages, was carried out by an ethical hacker. It involved network scanning, which is done at the initial stage known as reconnaissance. Wireshark plays a crucial part in the network-scanning phase. A network scanner tool is capable of providing critical information about the remote machine and can identify open and closed ports on a remote machine. The entire reconnaissance phase includes OS scans, hot sweeps and ping sweep scans. There are various endpoints on which Wireshark scans the network. These include: fiber channel, Bluetooth, Ethernet, UDP, USB, IPv4, IPv6, TCP and so on. Another feature of Wireshark that makes it an exceptional tool in its domain is Wireshark statistics. The statistics give the percentage of TCP or UDP captured packets. Since Wireshark is a live network capture tool, maintaining the correct time zone and time is crucial for further analysis of captured packets. The captured packets can also be used for digital forensics purposes to investigate cybercrime. Therefore, we can conclude that Wireshark is a versatile open-source tool with a wide variety of features and properties which is widely used in various domains of network security.

13.2.2 Autopsy—A Packet Sniffing and Packet Capturing Tool

Two of the most famous and widely used open-source digital inspection tools which are available with multiple platforms—Unix, Linux, Windows, and OS X—are Autopsy and Sleuth Kit. Sleuth Kit and Autopsy can be used to analyze disk images as well as performance during in-depth analysis of the file systems (such as Ext3, FAT, and NTFS) and several volume system types (Information Security Team, n.d.).

For an investigation, examiners and analysts can use Autopsy graphically or the Sleuth Kit command-line tools. In this case, they must firstly apply the graphical interface of Autopsy using the command line built into Sleuth Kit. Sleuth Kit and Autopsy provide .dd or some disk image files of other types to the examiner and hash the files. They search the files and information which are available in files and subfiles. In HTML and Excel formats, it is possible to generate reports of searches, results, comments, and notes.

13.2.2.1 Download and Installation

An official website is a proper channel to download Autopsy. Autopsy and Sleuth Kit files can be downloaded easily and quickly. Some wizards are available which facilitate smooth installation. After the Sleuth Kit installation is complete, users can write and add their own models in Python and Java. To install Autopsy, use the following steps:

1. Run required Autopsy msi file.
2. If Windows prompts about User Account Control are shown, click yes.
3. Click on dialog box prompts until the finish prompts appear.
4. Autopsy should be completely installed.

It most cases it recommends disabling and removing any type of antivirus software from the computers where it will be processing or reviewing cases. This is because these may clash with forensics software and can remove some files or results before they can be inspected by you.

13.2.2.2 *Features and Working*

Autopsy and Sleuth Kit have the following features (Information Security Team, n.d.):

1. The timeline analysis feature supported by Autopsy provides a graphical interface for viewing events (Basis Technology, n.d.).
2. Hash filtering ignores known good files and marks known bad files.
3. It is capable of recovering files in general formats using file system forensic analysis.
4. It is easy to find files containing relevant terms through the keyword search feature.
5. It is able to import and extract data related to history, cookies and bookmarks from popular web browsers.
6. Multimedia support is provided by extracting EXIF from pictures along with being able to watch videos.
7. It can analyze the email messages in MBOX formats, such as Thunderbird.

Hashing and write-blocking are used for the changes in the disk file after the creation of the disk image, but here it becomes necessary to analyze the disk image. During the analysis process, the investigator also must search for information suited to the case being compiled.

This means not only looking for current content on the drive, but also looking for deleted files, missing or hidden information, and hidden partitions that may not appear at first glance. Often a suspect will attempt to hide and delete the information as a precaution. We can see this information inside the Autopsy/Sleuth Kit. Autopsy/Sleuth Kit is known as a free tool, so it is a good option for analysis of disk images in Linux as well as in Windows systems.

When Autopsy is used for the first time, a wizard provides guidance on the process of creating a case and adding a disk image to the case. Following configuration, it starts the automated disk analysis, which Autopsy calls ingest. This process is shown in Figure 13.4. After the creation of the case, you can add extra images. You can also reconfigure ingest and restart the automated disk analysis (Keffer, 2013). The steps to be followed while working on Autopsy are shown in Figure 13.5.

Following these steps, you can choose to continue the further analysis of the image contents.

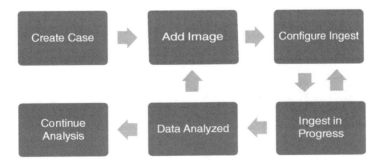

FIGURE 13.4
Autopsy process flow.

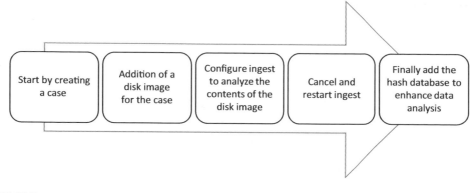

FIGURE 13.5
Working process on Autopsy.

13.2.2.3 Advantages of Using Autopsy

Use of Autopsy for forensic activities is supported by certain advantages which are listed below:

- It provides a GUI interface that enables a user to extract files, search keywords, and generate a report.
- It supports both raw and E01 formats of an image, while its rival software supports only E01 types of image format.
- It is supported on a variety of platforms including Linux, Windows, and Mac.
- It is issued and released under a free software license instead of a commercial one.
- It has been designed with a modular architecture and it can incorporate third-party modules that are written in Python or Java.
- A detailed insight and the updated document are available for users as well as developers.

13.3 Conclusion

Cybersecurity is becoming the most important aspect in the area of critical capacities like financial applications, nuclear domains and so on. In a pool of available cybersecurity and forensic tools, Wireshark and Autopsy are suitable for educational as well as organizational use. Distribution under a free license and support on a large number of platforms make them suitable for use with real-time problems. With features ranging from recovering data from memory cards to analyzing network packets, these tools are used for practical research and demonstration as well. However, other tools exist that perform similar tasks but with certain limitations, such as distribution under a commercial license or support for limited formats, which inhibit their use on such a wide scale.

References

Basis Technology, n.d. Autopsy: Training document. http://www.sleuthkit.org//autopsy//, accessed on March 30, 2020 at 9:00 pm.

Information Security Management and Analytics Research Team, n.d. Kali Linux Sleuthkit. https://ismart.unm.edu/files/8813/9252/1107/Tutorial_6_-_Kali:Linux_-_Sleuthkit.pdf, accessed on March 12, 2020 at 9:40 am.

Keffer, J., December 2013. Autopsy forensic browser user guide. https://juliakeffer.files.wordpress.com/2013/06/autopsy_user_guide.pdf, accessed on March 14, 2020 at 10:24 am.

Macfarlane, R., n.d. Lecture notes. http://www.soc.napier.ac.uk//~40001507/CSN11102//Lab5.pdf, accessed on April 5, 2020 at 11:37 am.

Wireshark Tutorial, n.d. https://cs.gmu.edu//~astavrou/courses//ISA_674_F12//Wireshark-Tutorial.pdf, accessed on April 5, 2020 at 11:40 am.

14

Introduction to Optimization Algorithms–Bio Inspired

Rakesh Kumar Saini[1], Shailee L. Choudhary[2], Anupam Singh[3], and Amit Verma[3]

[1] *DIT University, Dehradun, India*

[2] *NDIM, New Delhi, India*

[3] *University of Petroleum & Energy Studies (UPES), Dehradun, India*

14.1 Introduction

The optimization process (Løvbjerg, 2002) refers to deriving the most suitable solution from a set of possible alternate solutions or resources. Currently, bio inspired optimization techniques are widely used in diverse fields from biological biomolecule structure prediction in the medical domain to predicting the customer behavior patterns in business organizations. Today's world talks about BigData, which involves the information derived from multiple locations being effectively used for decision making by business organizations and researchers. The dynamic data fetched by automated models based on statistical techniques and data mining algorithms are used to interpret the information. In order to achieve the best results among numerous possibilities and strict constraints, we need optimization techniques. There is no standard definition of the word optimization: for an engineer or technician it refers to "hit and trial" methodology, whereas for a manager it may refer to "selecting the best option". A simplified definition for optimization could be: "Under a given set of circumstances and constraints, the action of deriving the best solution with the aim to minimize the efforts and maximize the expected output." Evolutionary Algorithms (EAs) and swarm intelligence are best at facilitating optimized solutions. Figure 14.1 depicts the family of bio inspired algorithms.

14.2 Evolutionary Algorithms (EA)

EAs are a type of machine learning algorithm (Holland, 1988; Coello and Lamont, 2004) that are based on the biological process of evolution. As nature involves the survival of the fittest, that is, the higher the fitness of the creature the better, similarly EAs aim to discover

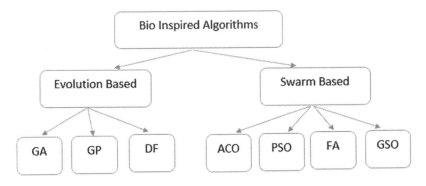

FIGURE 14.1
Family of bio inspired algorithms.

the behavior having the highest fitness score. Thus, algorithms that imitate the behaviors of nature to solve complicated problems are called EAs. All EAs are conceptualized on the basis of Darwin's concepts of evolution. All living organisms follow elementary functions like selection, mutation, reproduction and recombination, and during all these processes fitness acts as the catalyst to derive the best possible solution. However, EAs also have their darker side. Firstly, EAs offer effective optimization but not always the optimal solution. Mostly EAs are used in the background to keep measuring the efficiency of the solutions against each other. Secondly, the computational requirements of EAs are slightly elevated due to the complexity of fitness computations.

EAs are widely used to solve optimization problems (Kachitvichyanukul, 2012), specifically complex computational problems in engineering and business. Engineering based computational problems refer to fields such as automotive or engineering design, robotics, routing optimization in telecommunication, traffic and shipping. In the business domain, from finance and investment strategies to marketing and merchandising, EAs are used to yield efficient timely outputs with fewer difficulties in understanding problem-specific properties. Mostly, parameters are to be adjusted to derive a generic solution.

14.3 EA in Practice

EAs (Kachitvichyanukul, 2012) are problem-solving methods based on the natural evolution theories (Nowak et al., 1990; Ursem, 2002), where the selection process derives the optimal solution for a given problem, and reaches the optimal solution by adjusting the measurement parameters to minimum or maximum. For example, in financial trading markets, EAs like the GA are used to derive the best combination of the parameters in trading rules. Once derived, the optimal combination can be used for an Artificial Neural Network (ANN) model for stock market strategies and trading optimization. Although EAs are random in nature, that is, they do not guarantee the solution as optimal for any specific problem, they will definitely offer a good solution if it exists.

Another real-life optimization area where EAs hold stronger grounds for finding the optimal solution is timetabling. Timetabling is one of the core process in schools and colleges which refers to the arrangement of both rooms and faculty/teacher allocations as per the requirements of the academic guidelines. The entire process has large numbers of constraints, such as the number/type of rooms; faculty can only be allocated to one class at a time and to their specialist subject(s); one student cannot be allocated to two classes simultaneously, and so on. Timetabling is a combinatorial problem and is referred to as NP-hard. It involves substantial numbers of computations, thus searching for the optimal solution may not be feasible option, so we can look for heuristic approaches instead. EAs have provided satisfactory solutions to such scheduling problems. Mathematical optimization techniques (Lhotská, 2008) applied to engineering problems which are mostly large-scale often fail to deliver the optimal solution due to the complexity involved. For example, linear encoding and dynamic encoding methods generally fail to resolve NP-hard problems optimally as they have a large number of variables and non-linear impartial utilities (Krink and Løvbjerg, 2002). One of the beneficial points with EAs is that they are free from human bias. They focus on generation of fitness function as the most important step, and once derived, the effective fitness function helps the algorithm reach the optimal solution. This chapter focuses on three types of EA namely: Genetic Algorithm (GA), Genetic Programming (GP) and Particle Swarm Optimization (PSO), with the emphasis on differentiating each on the basis of their working principles, strengths and weaknesses. The outcome expected after reading the chapter is that the reader will be able to understand the application of a particular algorithm in the specific domain or problem.

Before implementing an EA (Lobo et al., 2007) for a specific problem, two pre-requisites need to be met, namely:

1. On the basis of the specific problem we need to encode the candidate solution; in GA it is bit string, whereas in GP it is represented by a syntax tree. This encoding makes mutation and crossover simpler. Thus each candidate comprises a sequence of zeros and ones.

2. EAs are not measured as right or wrong, or black or white, thus before applying EAs we need to derive the fitness function (Pytela, 2012) which can return a scale of 1–100 rather than just 1 or 0 as it guides the algorithm to move towards better solutions.

Figure 14.2 depicts the basic working of EAs.

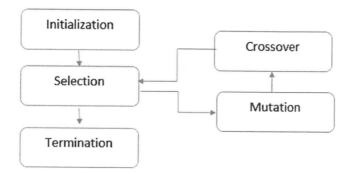

FIGURE 14.2
Evolutionary algorithms.

14.4 Genetic Algorithm

Genetic Algorithms (Dasgupta and Michalewicz, 2013) fall under the umbrella of Probabilistic Search Algorithms which transform the population of objects (a fixed binary string) iteratively. A fitness value is assigned to each, resulting in generation of a new population of objects. GAs are centered on Darwin's theory of survival of the fittest and aim to imitate the heritable operative's similar crossover and mutation. GAs follow a process of natural selection which works on the principle of choosing the fittest individuals for reproduction of the next generation's offspring. The entire search process uses random choice to discover the scope of exploration. The working of the GA is summarized below (Figure 14.3):

1. The generation of the initial population is based on random choice.
2. The next step aims at selecting the fittest individuals from the present population in order to generate a new generation of the population.
3. The major functions performed to create the new population are crossover and mutation among the chosen representatives from step 2.
4. In order to create the new generation, replacement is performed among the current generation.
5. New generation offspring are checked for their fitness value and the fittest are chosen.
6. If the stopping criteria are met, the algorithm stops.

The probability of selection is dependent on the fitness value. As more fit chromosomes are chosen to be parents each time, a situation may come when the new solution produced is very similar to the previous generation causing declined diversity of the population.

The pseudo code of the inherent algorithm is as follows:

Pseudo-Code : Genetic Algorithm (Goldberg & Holland, 1988)

```
initialize random population
        evaluate each chromosome  for its fitness
        while (Stopping criteria achieved) do
            select parent
            perform crossover with probability pc
            perform mutation with probability pm
            calculate fitness of offspring
            survivor selection
            find best
    return best
```

FIGURE 14.3
Genetic algorithms.

This situation is called population stagnation. Mutation is the process that induces diversity in the population by injecting random small changes (Goldberg and Holland, 1988; Alba and Tomassini, 2002).

Like biological organisms that are made up of cells consisting of a nucleus enclosing the genetic material "genes" in a unit called a "Chromosome," our problem also consists of chromosomes, which are input variables in the problem. The input variables' container may be signified as an order of fixed measurement binary string where each bit corresponds to biological nucleotide. The sequence of bits performing or representing an input variable is called a gene and a collection of genes is called a chromosome. The total sum of the entire chromosome represents the genotype of the system and its actual interpretation corresponds to is its phenotype, that is which solution it actually leads to.

The various terminologies used in the context of GA can be defined as follows:

- **Initial population:** The initial population for the problem is created randomly at the beginning of the algorithm (see Figure 14.4). The initial set of chromosomes (candidate solutions) is usually generated randomly. According to the chosen scheme of representation of chromosomes, the way of generating chromosomes may differ. Some chromosomes in the population are also previously decided and usually depend on the type of application. In a genetic procedure, the established genetic factor of a separate population is characterized by means of a sequence, usually a string of ones and zeros.

- **Fitness function:** Respectively genetic material is evaluated for its suitability to the problem using some pre-specified appropriateness criterion. Again, the fitness function is also application dependent and varies from case to case. Following this evaluation, an individual can now be ranked according to its suitability.

- **Selection:** It involves the extraction of a subset of better-quality chromosomes from the given population. The quality is measured through their fitness values.

- **Crossover:** Crossover is the process by which child chromosomes are generated to make a new population (Figure 14.5). The selected parents undergo an exchange of some of their genes which are inherited by their child. The factors affecting this process are crossover rate and crossover type. The result of crossover is a population which is double the size of the original population as each pair of parents produces two children. Each chromosome or binary string of input variables undergoes a crossover.

- **Mutation:** Mutation, unlike crossover, occurs in any one individual within the population. Mutation occurs when a randomly generated number is greater than a

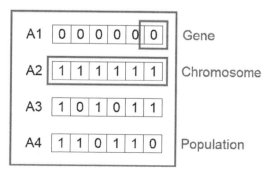

FIGURE 14.4
Initial population.

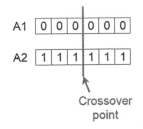

Crossover
point

FIGURE 14.5
Crossover.

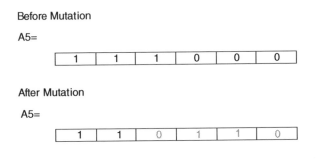

FIGURE 14.6
Mutation.

mutation probability provided. A mutation is a flip of a bit at a randomly selected mutation point within the chromosome. For example, an individual is 001100110 and has a mutation at the fifth point from the right then it becomes 001000110. Mutation may or may not produce a fitter individual and does not add a single individual to the population (Figure 14.6).

Although GA has been widely applied in diversified fields to solve complex problems and is one of the most popular optimization techniques, the major limitations faced by GA are the fixed length chromosomes and syntax free approach which makes it unsuitable for a program generation approach. As an additional influence, regression methodology used by GP works on the principle of reaching the concluding parse tree by maintaining the relationships among variables.

14.5 Genetic Programming

Genetic Programming (Wolfgang et al., 2009; Pytela, 2012) is an extension of GAs. Although inspired by biological evolution, GP is a machine learning technique used to derive the optimal solution on the basis of fitness score. It aims to achieve automatic programming by using natural selection principles and operations that are biologically inspired, namely crossover and mutation (as used in GA). Being a domain independent method, in order to derive solutions to specific problems it genetically breeds a population of computer programs.

Both GA and GP are special optimization methods of EAs. Both approaches start with initialization of some random population (input variables set in the case of GA (Zhang and Cheng, 2009) or a tree with operator and variables in the case of GP). The population

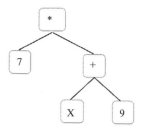

FIGURE 14.7
Genetic programming—basic representation.

initialized is then evaluated based on a fitness function (function to be optimized) and selection is made for the fittest individual (those with the solution nearest to the required solution). The individuals selected are then paired up for crossover. There is a chance of mutation occurring within any member of the population with a certain probabilistic value. The above operations are based on Darwin's theory of survival of fittest whereby if the population is evaluated at any given time on a fitness test—for example, climatic conditions or level in food chain—the one that survives this fitness test will reproduce to produce a new generation. The new generation is again evaluated on the same or a different fitness test and the process continues until all the individuals in the population are fit. The population set which does not lead to a fit offspring moves towards extinction with the passage of time. There is also a probability of mutation, for example, the organism modifies its parts to adapt to given circumstances; however, since it is a chance modification, mutation may not always lead to a fit individual.

Like biological organisms that are made up of cells consisting of a nucleus enclosing the genetic material "genes" in a unit called a "Chromosome," our problem also involves chromosomes, which are input variables in the problem represented in the form of a parse tree. Input variables can be represented as nodes of terminals and operators where each node corresponds to a biological nucleotide. The sub tree of the main parse tree having a tendency to alter the objective is called a gene and a collection of genes is called a chromosome. The total sum of the entire chromosome represents the genotype of the system and its actual interpretation corresponds to is its phenotype, which is the solution it actually leads to.

In GP, the genes are the elementary elements of an individual which are grouped together to form code. A separate platform is of a similar construction to a tree. Genes are of two kinds, namely utilities and stations. In sapling language, nodes with branches are called functions, whereas nodes without branches are called terminals (leaves). An example of an equation is **7(x + 9)**, where the functions are + and *, whereas 7, x and 9 are the terminals. Selection or creation of genes within a GP system is decided by the user. It is an important decision as poor selection may result in an insignificant solution (Figure 14.7).

14.5.1 Genetic Programming Algorithm

Step 1. The initial population is created based on random choice from the available primitives.

Step 2. Repeating loop.

Step 3. Each individual program is executed and checked for its fitness.

Step 4. On the basis of fitness probability, one or two programs are selected.

Step 5. Genetic operations with specific probability are applied to create new programs.

Step 6. Until condition (an acceptable solution/stop criteria have been reached).

Step 7. The best solution so far is returned.

14.5.2 Basic Terminology Used in Genetic Programming

1. Terminal set—This mainly consists of the program's external inputs as independent variables and constants.

2. Operator set—This mainly consists of arithmetic functions like add, multiply, subtract, divide and related branching operators.

3. Fitness function—The fitness function specifies what needs to be done. It is a numeric value attached to each individual population. It is a primary method to check the appropriateness of the solution.

4. Control parameter [m]—Specification of the control parameter is an administrative task to control the entire run process. The major control parameters are:

   a. Inhabitants scope—This is a significant restriction as it affects the solution to a large extent. As a rule, we can say that "the higher the complexity of a problem, the greater the population size required".

   b. Supreme number of compeers—Time is an important factor in evolutionary processes, thus a higher number of generations may result in higher probability of reaching an optimal solution. On the contrary, no guaranteed solution can be reached even if the generations evolve further.

   c. Probability of crossover and reproduction.

14.5.3 Advantages of Genetic Programming over Genetic Algorithms

The following are the criteria which prove that GP is better than GAs:

1. **Chromosomal Representation:** GAs follow a string of characters, which is generally a binary string representing its chromosome, while GP uses a tree to do the same. For example, 0101010110 may be a chromosome structure for GAs, while a tree such as that shown in Figure 14.7 may be an example of a chromosome in GP. It is very noticeable that trees are really easy to parse as each node has a meaning and algorithms can be applied easily to manipulate trees, while it is difficult to mark the start and end of the string if multiple chromosomes are represented together.

2. **Chromosome Length:** GAs deal with fixed length chromosomes in contrast to the variable length in GP. The fixed length representation makes it really difficult to apply their structure dynamically. Moreover, variability in chromosomal length increases the application domain and removes the coding restrictions.

3. **Domain Syntax:** Generally the domain specific symbols are encoded to a binary string or any other character string in GAs, which is not the case with GP. This leads to a reduction in time required for encoding and decoding domain input variables in GP.

4. **Executables:** Since GAs have an intermediate encoding format, executables which can be fed directly to the interpreter are very rarely found except in a few situations where input variables are actually binary. On the other hand, when we talk about GP, the nodes in the tree structure have a defined meaning as they are either a terminal or an operator, and an interpreter is available for tree manipulation, so it is easy to have executables of GP code.

5. **Basic Domain:** GA is a search optimization process, while GP is an extension of GA which not only provides a search functions but also helps in the generation of new programs. These programs may be actual programs where blocks of code are

terminals while conditional, branching or looping statements act as operators. When dealing with mathematical expressions, the operators are actual mathematical operators, while the terminals are functions or constants. This makes GP applicable to a wide range of domains.

14.6 Particle Swarm Optimization (PSO)

PSO is a swarm intelligence based procedure (Lhotská, 2008) inspired by the social behavior of birds flocking. PSO shares many similarities with GAs and GP, specifically random initialization of the population and updating generations when searching for an optimal solution. In comparison with GAs and GP, PSO does not use evolutionary operators, namely mutation and crossover. Potential solutions in PSO are called subdivisions which aim to explore the search space by imitating the optimal particles. Unlike GAs, implementation of PSO is easier because few parameters require adjustment.

PSO works by simulating the flocking behavior of birds. In simple terms, imagine a scenario where the aim is for a group of birds (swarm) to search for food in a given area.

Constraints:

1. All birds are hungry and simultaneously searching for food.
2. The area has only one piece of food.
3. The location of the food is not known to any bird.

Problem: Finding the best strategy to discover the food.

Solution: Imitating the bird who is nearest to the food and evaluating the distance from the food in an iterative manner.

The behavior of the birds mentioned in the scenario, where the tasks are multiple but the resources are limited, is simulated in the computation domain and the algorithm is called PSO. By learning from the above scenario, diverse real-time problems are solved using PSO where in a given search space each solitary resolution is referred to as a "bird" (particle). A fitness value is assigned to each particle according to the value derived on the basis of the fitness function to be optimized. The particles are directed for movement (flying) by their velocity (inertia). The direction of overall movement can change whenever a particle's best movement is better than the overall swarm's best. The entire operation makes the movement disordered and maximizes the probability of closeness to global minima of the cost function.

The algorithm begins with initialization involving the with collection of random particles (solutions) and updating generations to search for optima. Each iteration results in updating the following "best" values:

1. Fitness (best solution) achieved so far by particle is referred to as p_{best} (personal best).
2. Fitness (best solution) evaluated by PSO among particles in the population is referred to as g_{best} (global best).
3. Best value achieved by a particle in its topological neighborhood is referred to as l_{best} (local best).

Once the two best values, namely p_{best} and g_{best}, have been evaluated, the velocity and position of the particle are simplified through the following two equations:

$$p_y[\ ] = p_y[\ ] + l_{f1} \times rand(\ ) \times \left(p_{best}[\ ] - present[\ ]\right) + l_{f2} \times rand(\ ) \times \left(g_{best}[\ ] - present[\ ]\right) \quad (14.1)$$

$$present[\ ] = present[\ ] + p_y[\ ] \quad\quad\quad\quad\quad\quad (14.2)$$

where

p_y refers to particle velocity

l_f refers to learning factor

rand() represents the random number between 0 and 1

The first equation updates velocity for each particle, whereas the second equation identifies the location of each particle. In the algorithm the information is shared with others using g_{best} and l_{best} only, which makes it a one-way statistical distribution instrument, whereas in GAs chromosomes share all information with each other. Thus the statistical distribution instruments are different in GA and PSO.

PSO offers one more advantage over GA, namely assigning real numbers as particles rather than genetic operators or binary encoding.

The pseudo code of the PSO is shown in Figure 14.8.

Pseudo-Code 3.2: Particle Swarm Optimization (Kachitvichyanukul, 2012)

```
For each particle
    Initialize position and velocity
End
Do
    For each particle
        Evaluate for fitness value
        If fitness > pBest
            pBest=fitness
    End
    Choose the particle with the best fitness value of all the particles as the
    gBest
    For each particle
        Update velocity using equation
```

$$v[] = v[] + c_1 \times rand() \times (pBest[] - present[]) + c_2 \times rand() \times$$
$$(gBest[] - present[])$$

```
        Update position using equation
```

$$present[] = present[] + v[]$$

```
    End
While termination criteria not achieved
```

FIGURE 14.8
The pseudo code of the PSO.

14.7 Comparison: Genetic Algorithm, Genetic Programming and Particle Swarm Optimization

The above discussion can be better understood with the summary of the advantages and disadvantages of each algorithm given in Table 14.1 below. The tabulated summary of the EAs and Swarm Intelligence (SI) based algorithms will help in understanding their applicability in specific problems of optimization.

TABLE 14.1

Comparison of GA, GP and PSO

Algorithm	Advantages	Disadvantages
Genetic Algorithm (GA)	• Easy to implement with faster and efficient solutions. • Parallel execution, which addresses the problem of local maxima efficiently. • Requirement for information on derivatives is nil. • Provides better solutions rather than just one single solution. • With the help of size of population, decoding time and number of generations, we can predict solution time. • Complex computational problems can be easily solved with simple operators. • Works well with multi-objective problems, and single as well as discrete functions.	• No standard method to derive fitness function; it totally depends on the user. • Approximation of control parameters such as size of population and crossover rate is difficult. • No single termination criterion is defined. • Scalability issues when the number of variables is high results in larger chromosomes and thus time consumption is also high. • The quality of the solution cannot be guaranteed.
Genetic Programming (GP)	• Output is a program which can be expressed as a mathematical expression which makes it easy to understand. • Tree based representation gives it an edge over GA. • There is flexibility of fitness function (designed on the basis of the problem specified). • Efficient results can be derived when the problem space is not clearly understood. • There is no fixed length of solution (depends on hardware limits).	• It has a high computational cost due to the fitness evaluation of each individual after every generation. • It requires a large dataset to derive an optimal solution. • It does not guarantee an exact solution.
Particle Swarm Optimization (PSO)	• Implementation is easy in terms of coding compared to GA and GP. • PSO implementation is easier with the requirement for few parameters for adjustment. • It provides efficient solutions with a shorter calculation time. • It does not work on evolution operators like mutation and crossover.	• It does not have a strong mathematical foundation for analysis. • The continuous nature of PSO makes it unsuitable for discrete problems. • Compared with classical approaches, it has slow convergence.

14.8 Conclusion

This chapter presents bio inspired algorithms, namely EAs and swarm intelligence based algorithms, as efficient optimization solutions. All EAs, namely GA and GP, share some common features, such as population based algorithms based on best survival criteria; iterative evolution for a best solution; great complexity in fitness function fixation; and natural selection operators—mutation and crossover—with differences in chromosome representation and length. On the other hand, swarm intelligence based algorithms, namely PSO, aim to explore the search space by intimating the optimal particles (swarm). PSO is comparatively easy to implement with fewer parameters and does not involve evolution operators like crossover and mutation. Lastly, the chapter presents a tabulated summary of the bio inspired algorithms with their respective advantages and limitations so that their applicability can be understood.

References

Alba, E. and Tomassini, M., 2002. Parallelism and evolutionary algorithms. *IEEE Trans. Evol. Comput.*, 6(5), 443–462.

Coello, C. A. C. and Lamont, G. B., 2004. *Applications of Multi-Objective Evolutionary Algorithms* (Vol. 1). World Scientific, Singapore.

Dasgupta, D. and Michalewicz, Z. (Eds.), 2013. *Evolutionary Algorithms in Engineering Applications*. Springer Science & Business Media, Berlin.

Goldberg, D. E. and Holland, J. H., 1988. Genetic algorithms and machine learning, *Mach. Learn.*, 3(2/3), 95–99, https://doi.org/10.1023/A:1022602019183.

Kachitvichyanukul, V., 2012. Comparison of three evolutionary algorithms: GA, PSO, and DE, *Ind. Eng. Manag. Syst.*, 11(3), 215–223.

Krink, T. and Løvbjerg, M., 2002. Improving particle swarm optimization by hybridization of stochastic search heuristics and self-organized criticality, University of Aarhus, Aarhus.

Lobo, F. J., Lima, C. F., and Michalewicz, Z. (Eds.), 2007. *Parameter Setting in Evolutionary Algorithms* (Vol. 54). Springer Science & Business Media, Berlin.

Løvbjerg, M.: Improving particle swarm optimization by hybridization of stochastic search heuristics and self-organized criticality. Master's thesis, Department of Computer Science, University of Aarhus (2002)

Macaš, M., Lhotská, L. 2008. Social Impact and Optimization. *International Journal of Computational Intelligence Research* 4(2), 129–136

Nowak, A., Szamrej, J., and Latan, B., 1990. From private attitude to public opinion: A dynamic theory of social impact, *Psychol. Rev.*, 97(3), 362–376.

Pytela, J., 2012. *Implementation and Testing of Social Optimization Algorithms*, Czech Technical University, Prague.

Ursem, R. K., 2002, September. Diversity-guided evolutionary algorithms. In *International Conference on Parallel Problem Solving from Nature* (pp. 462–471). Springer, Berlin, Heidelberg.

Wolfgang, J., Peter, N., Robert, E. K., and Frank, D. F., 2009. *Genetic Programming: An Introduction on the Automatic Evolution of Computer Programs and Its Applications*. Morgan Kaufmann Publishers/Dpunkt-Verlag, San Francisco, CA/Heidelberg.

Zhang, Y. and Cheng, H., 2009. Improved genetic programming algorithm applied to symbolic regression and software reliability modeling, *Software Eng. Appl.* 2(5), 354–360.

Appendix: Policy Template

Name: *Name of The Policy*

Version: *Current Version Number*

Classification: *What is the classification of this document? Published policies are usually "PUBLIC," while company procedures maybe "INTERNAL."*

Published Date: *Date of Publishing*

Table of Document History: *Insert table of Document History, could include information such as Version Nos, Published Date, Description or Major Changes, Approver Name*

Legal Mandate: *The Legal Mandate is necessary for documents issued by government or regulators. Corporates may replace it with Background, where they may provide information about why the particular policy has been issued or how it relates to an existing approved policy etc.*

Introduction: *Provide a brief introduction of the document. It provides a brief needs and justification for having the document.*

Scope and Application: *Clearly define the scope and application of the document. Who would be covered in terms of persons, business, systems etc.?*

Audience: *Clearly identify who is the intended audience for the document. Who should read the document?*

Policy Statements: *Articulate your policy statements here, if it is a standard policy, or articulate your control statements and the control objectives.*

Governance (Roles and Responsibilities): *Identify how the policy will be governed. Who will have what roles and responsibilities to play?*

Enforcement: *This is mandatory for a policy document. The disciplinary action in case of non-compliance to the policy should be clearly stated.*

Exceptions: *This is mandatory for a policy document. Specify how the exceptions to a policy should be managed.*

Issuing Authority: *For a policy, it is important to state who is the issuing authority. Who will sign the policy statement?*

Appendix

Definitions: *Supporting information. List out definitions of critical terms used in the policy.*

Acronyms: *Supporting information. List out the acronyms/abbreviations used in the document and what each stands for.*

Supporting Documents: *Provide a link to associated procedures/guidelines/forms that will support this document.*

Index